CUMBRIA HERITAGE SERVICES
LIBRARIES

COUNTY COUNCIL

This book is due to be returned on or before the last date above. It
may be renewed by personal application, post or telephone, if not in
demand.

C.L.18

D1437405

Sin City

London in pursuit of pleasure

Sin City

London in pursuit of pleasure

Giles Emerson

Foreword by
Bettany Hughes

GRANADA

First published in Great Britain 2002

André Deutsch, an imprint of André Deutsch
Carlton Publishing Group
20 Mortimer Street
London
W1T 3JW

In association with Granada Media Group

Plate section
Corbis/Bettmann: 8, /Burstein Collection:10 top, /Hulton: 9 top; **Hulton
Archive**: 5 top; **Mary Evans Picture Library** : 2 bottom, 2 top, 3 bottom, 3
top, 4 bottom, 5 bottom, 6 bottom, 6 top, 7 bottom, 7 top, 10 bottom, 11 top,
12 bottom, 13 bottom, 13 top, 14 top, 16 top; **Topham Picturepoint**: 1, 3
top, 9 bottom, 11 bottom, 12 top, 14 bottom, 15 bottom, 15 top, 16 bottom,
Every effort has been made to acknowledge correctly and contact the source
and/or copyright holder of each picture, and Carlton Books Limited apologises
for any unintentional errors or omissions which will be corrected in future
editions of this book.

MUSEUM OF LONDON

The publishers, author and Granada would also like to
thank The Museum of London for their invaluable help and
support with this project.

Typeset by E-Type, Liverpool
Printed and bound in Great Britain

2 4 6 8 10 9 7 5 3 1

CONTENTS

ACKNOWLEDGEMENTS

I was given only a short time in which to write this book but it was possible because of the amount of research that had been assembled when I started, or was put in hand as the project got underway. I am extremely grateful for that research and to those who so assiduously compiled it. Substantial material was provided by Paul Larsman and his hard-working team from London News Network, who devised and produced the London Weekend Television series, *Sin City*, which this book accompanies. Bettany Hughes, the presenter of the series, was responsible with Paul for the concept of the project and for preparing and giving shape to the initial bank of research. I wish to thank Bettany for this, and for her encouragement and valuable comments on the typescript.

I should also like to thank Kate Bomford for her considerable research which has fed and underpinned the section on gluttony; and sports historian, Peter Radford, for his equally detailed research which provided the direction, and much of the content, for the section on sport and gambling. I have frequently pestered various curators at the Museum of London and want to thank them for the generous way in which they fielded my stupid questions and illuminated my notions about London in Roman and later periods. Curators at the British Museum also deserve thanks for their readiness and knowledge.

Given the scope of the book, and the time available to prepare it, I have relied heavily on secondary sources, all of whom are noted in the bibliography as well as in the narrative, where I have quoted them. I am grateful to all these scholars and biographers, their fine minds and pens.

I wish to thank my agent, Araminta Whitley, for delivering me from the closet I have occupied as a professional and mostly ghost writer; also for her astute red pen and assistance with the typescript. My warm thanks go to Gillian Holmes, Roland Hall and the editorial team at Carlton Books. And I am very grateful to my wife, Susanna, for her accomplished editorial support, sufferance and skill, as she balanced her own busy work schedule and the needs of our young children, having precious little help from me.

Finally, I thank London itself for being such a den of sinful pleasures.

FOREWORD

A few years ago I stood on the banks of the Thames with ten thousand others, watching as two men crossed the river by tightrope. No safety net, no safety wires. Without a doubt a fall into the river 130 feet below would have killed them. It was a heart-stopping spectacle; even in the centre of town you could have heard a pin drop. A blinding explosion of fireworks celebrated the wire-walkers' safe arrival.

Flicking through a book on circuses recently I saw what I thought was an illustration of the event. Then I realized I was looking at a drawing from 150 years before. A cloudy afternoon, when Victorian London had turned out in force to watch 'The Female Blondin' attempting the same feat. The press of people and the expressions on the faces of the crowd were identical to those I remembered. World-weary, techno-savvy 20th century Londoners were seeking their pleasures in *exactly* the same way as their Victorian ancestors.

Trying to get under the skin of men and women from the past is a difficult, but addictive exercise. People want to remember the good times, and the history of Londoners' pleasures offers up a fantastic ragbag of evidence to rummage through. Paintings, invitations, court edicts, parliamentary bills, prostitutes' chits – all play a part in attempting to recreate a sense of how it was to live in London's past and an understanding of why men and women did what they did (and do what they do) to enjoy themselves.

Add to that London's detritus – the unexpected archaeological finds such as a Roman leather bikini, a medieval silk purse, an erotic Victorian pipe – and you are embarking, satisfyingly, on the journey Pope recommended in *An Essay on Man 1* … 'The proper study of mankind is man'. It was this wealth of sources – many on display in the Museum of London or stored within its extensive archives – that made this project a possibility. *Sin City* has been lucky enough to undertake some original research, but also owes a huge debt to those historians and archaeologists who have spent, between them, centuries immersed in London's written and physical past.

The aim of the author and of the producers of the TV series has been to pull together a 'pageant of pleasure'. When the idea was first dreamt up, appropriately enough in a watering hole on the South Bank, it was the thought that the themes of pleasure and excess would be contiguous with the present that attracted us. Sex, extravaganzas, sport, drink and drugs, and feasts have never stopped diverting Londoners. But, more importantly, they have constituted a constant and central part of the landscape of the city over the centuries.

Some periods are better sourced than others and therefore this is a history that will occasionally hop, skip and jump through the years. London's history has been so catastrophic that in some ways we're lucky to have any records relating to the capital at all. Evidence and sources have had to make their way down to us through a fiery past. In 43 AD, the Divine Emperor Claudius' men, according to Dio Cassius, 'spread fire and destruction all the way to the Trinovantan capital, Camulodunum' (Colchester in Essex); Boudica in AD 61 – vengeful against the procurator Decius Catus who had seized land and property from her people, the Iceni, flogged Boudica herself and raped her daughters in front of her – burned the city to the ground; in 1212, on St Benet's day, starting in Southwark, 'London brigge and the mooste parte of London was brent'; and then, of course, the Great Fire of London in 1666 and the Blitz of the Second World War swept even more of the past away.

Fortunately, a melange of evidence of early London pleasures remains. The creators of *Sin City* were keen to concentrate on subjects that, in their time, captured the popular imagination of Londoners. As a result, many of the events in the book and the series are not only the most extreme examples of fun and abandonment of their day, but also represent the *Zeitgeist* of a historical moment – and of course tell us something about the needs and desires of their protagonists.

The pursuit of pleasure (dictionary definition, the gratification of the senses or of the mind) is without a doubt a universal that stretches back to pre-history. *Sin City* deals with the period spanned by the Roman and Victorian empires. It was the Romans who founded Londinium, and who made the city an international cross-roads. A money-making machine where you worked hard and played hard. The Romans planted notions of civic pleasure and excess into the consciousness of London. And therefore Roman London, Londinium, is where the book picks up the trail. Unfortunately, although there are some prize pieces, relatively little hard evidence survives for the Roman period (a little more for the Anglo-Saxons, even less for the Dark Ages). On the advice of academics, *Sin City* has envisaged some of Roman Londoners' pleasures, using the evidence we have and taking as our model other similar outposts of the Roman Empire, and the mores of the imperial capital, Rome.

The Romans founded a number of urban centres throughout Britain, so what makes London special? Looking at the sources for the whole country, what is clear is that London has supported excess and pleasure-seeking on a quite massive and often unique scale. The simplest explanation is that, from its inception, London has been dedicated primarily to the creation of wealth. Londoners have there-fore spent a great deal of their time either enjoying the fruits of their labour or escaping from the miasma of misery that a massive, capitalist metropolis can generate.

But in researching this project it has become clear there is a lot more to it than can be explained with a simple reference to money. There is a medieval German phrase *Stadtluft macht frei*, 'city air makes men free'. With this in mind it is clear to see that London has provided a kind of experimental laboratory for experiences and social relationships. What is more there have always been willing lab assistants to take part in the trials – as well as plenty of spectators to watch the results.

London's cosmopolitan character also encouraged a pretty constant through-flow of new ideas. From the Roman foundation onwards, with only the exception of the Dark Ages before Anglo-Saxon Lundenwic was established when the place was essentially a ghost town, London has heaved with people. Men and women from all over the world brought their ideas, experiences and appetites to the capital. London's rulers, first Roman, then Icelandic/Scandinavian, then French, Dutch and finally Germanic, all had one problem on their hands: How to contain and please the London tribes they'd brought with them.

Because of its diverse, ever-fluctuating population, the city had the advantage of being able to draw on the three kinds of talent needed to sustain the shows, spectacles and sensations that would mark London out as a centre for pleasure and excess; dreamers and impresarios who have the great idea; promoters, producers and pimps who make it all happen; and the performers, prostitutes and athletes who have the gumption or driving need to earn their living keeping other people amused.

As a result, London has always attracted sensation-seekers, tourists and long-term visitors – keen to exploit what London has to offer. Whether it be a Tudor Essex farmer's trip to St Bartholomew's Fair to trade a few fleeces, enjoy a 'Bartholomew babe' and catch some unfortunate political prisoner being boiled in oil; a Victorian theatrephile's chance to see the notorious Boulton and Park, two middle-class boys who enjoyed dressing up in women's clothes and strutting their stuff at The Strand Theatre; or even today's bi-sexual tourism to places like Soho and Clerkenwell – for centuries London has been the place to see and be seen.

Catch any pleasure boat on the Thames today, and a voice down the crackly tannoy system will fill you in on what heady times those grey riverbanks have seen over the centuries. If you're unfortunate enough to be cruising on one of those flat, freezing October afternoons it is hard to imagine, but the river – the very reason for London's existence – has been a constant in the Londoner's experience of pleasure. From its earliest use as a ritual site for religious ceremonies people came here to celebrate life. Over the centuries, millions from the city made their way over to the South Bank, to indulge in the 'suburbs of sin'. The international port brought in all kinds of pleasure-giving substances from gin and tobacco to bhang and opium – as well as new ideas, new models for pleasure-seeking.

The river encouraged socializing and has also done a good job in preserving London's social past. Up until the nineteenth century all of London's rubbish stayed in the capital – much of it tossed away into the Thames, used to infill London's extinct rivers, the Fleet and the Walbrook, or packed into the refuse tips that lined the bank. Curious things have survived. For instance, as 14th century traders and hedonists travelled forwards and backwards over the river, their shoes would sometimes be sucked off by the Thames mud. Fabulously preserved, their outsize winkle-picker toes (check them out at the Museum of London, some are four inches long) look as ludicrous now as they must have done then. Even though Wat Tyler's Peasants' Revolt threatened the capital, and the country was at war with France, some Londoners felt jaunty enough to wear extremely un-sensible shoes.

Take a walk through London and you are treading on tons of human history. Finds are constantly emerging from the earth and the river. Just recently the Museum of London excavated an exquisite Anglo-Saxon brooch, surprisingly luxurious, studded with jewels from as far away as India. Who knows, in ten years enough data might exist to write a full and detailed description of the pleasures of two of the scantest periods, Dark Age and Anglo-Saxon Britain.

The great and the good generally leave the best paper trails, and historical evidence for their lives is always easier to find. The well-to-do have their place in this book – but so do less familiar characters, the faceless, nameless poor, who've enjoyed themselves with as much gusto and imagination as their wealthier co-habitants.

The heart of *Sin City* therefore is really on the London streets which are, and have always been, an electric place to be. Experiencing London today can be a lot about keeping abreast of what is considered to be the latest and the greatest the capital has to offer. Tourists and residents alike pride themselves on knowing where to find the hottest ticket or the coolest café. In London, both the culture that bubbles up through street-life and the word on the street, carry real weight.

The energy of the capital's street-life has become one of the city's most defining cultural characteristics. Throughout the centuries, the streets were where London's population mingled freely. You have to imagine, along all the major highways of the capital and down its darkest alleys, Londoners of all sexes, ages and economic resources, constantly hustling and jostling together – eyeing each other up, checking each other out, fleecing each other. Everyone had a pretty good idea of how everyone else was enjoying him- or herself and, on some occasions, the most powerful and the most poverty-stricken were inspired by each other to experiment with new kinds of pleasure and excess.

Even after the crises of rebellion, fire, plague and war, Londoners have still managed to maintain a party spirit in their streets. In fact, London's catastrophic history seems to have given it more, rather than less spirit. The energy of the place can sometimes be overwhelming. There are still cries of protest today from all over the country that the nation's political and cultural life is too focused on the capital. People have felt the same throughout its history. James I opined that 'England will onely be London'.

I am a Londoner born and bred. Maybe it's because I'm a Londoner – and I have a bias even my most stringent historical neutrality can't shake off – but when it comes to a combination of excess and pleasure, London seems to have done it bigger and better than anyone else. The imagination of London's pleasure merchants has inspired the nation and the rest of the world. From the thrills and spills of the circus ring and fish and chips to the nineteenth century erotic-dancers, 'The British Blondes', London exports have come to influence pleasure-seeking all over the globe.

It would be a treat if this book encouraged today's pleasure-seekers to view their capital with different eyes. When you visit the Guildhall Library or Gallery, spare a thought for the victims of pleasure, the gladiatorial condemned, waiting for certain death in Londonium's amphitheatre. Scurry to work at Old Street or to the coffee bars of Clerkenwell, and imagine the men and women of the Enlightenment doing their laps in a swimming pool at Peerless Street – itself converted from the appropriately named Perilous Pond where duck-hunts had always been a fixture. Sniff the garlic wafting out of cafes and restaurants in Soho and thank the seventeenth century Huguenots and the eighteenth century refugees fleeing the French Revolution, aristocrats who set up shop here and gave the place a name for good, continental food and ripe smells.

Aristotle wrote that there was, 'In life itself a certain well-being and a natural sweetness.' Despite the nits, the agues, the hunger-pangs, ordinary Londoners still managed to enjoy themselves. Dressed in the hand-me-downs from one of the capital's many second-hand clothes markets, they fluffed their neckties and cocked their hats and set off for a great night out. I'd like to think the *Sin City* project has been created in the memory of inspirational men and courageous women, both past and present, who have spent many hours in London in pursuit of pleasure – and made the city a better place.

Oh, and a quick aside. Human history on the geographical site of London is a long one. Next time you pass through Piccadilly Circus spare a thought for an apish looking man, homo erectus – homo sapiens wasn't yet on the scene – lumbering around Piccadilly Circus, discarding a blunt flint axe which has now ended up in the Museum of London. Who knows what his pleasure was (apart from the obvious), but we've got him and his colleagues to thank for recognizing what a perfect site for human habitation London was set to be.

INTIMATE PLEASURES

✍ ROMAN LONDON: POTENT AND INFLAMED ✍

Early one May morning in AD 124, a young half-naked woman hurries along a gravelled street near the newly built Basilica. She stops at the statue of a pagan deity on the street corner. Pulling a garland from around her neck she decorates the large erect penis – the foreskin painted bright red – with flowers. After this first devotion of the day she moves on to meet the group of girls and women at the end of the street. Her mission is to help carry an enormous wooden phallus in the parade that will initiate the Floralia, the Feast of Flowers. The festival celebrates the earth's rebirth at springtime, a time when many of the earth's large population of Roman inhabitants articulate their joy through unfettered sexual freedom, indulged particularly by society's 'beautiful people' – high class prostitutes and entertainers.

This is an imaginary snapshot of Roman London, or Londinium, in its heyday. It is a year before the town suffered its second major fire, comparable in devastation to the Great Fire of 1666, which disrupted the course of London's early history and buried the scant evidence of such festivals. The scene described would have taken place at a level which is some 30 to 40 feet below the City of London today. For most of over 1,500 years since the Romans left Britannia, London has been one of the busiest trading ports in Europe. It has been built and rebuilt, usually on top of the rubble of former dwellings, shops and municipal buildings. This is 40 feet of life, death and survival with sex at its core.

Londinium was established in AD 50, seven years after Emperor Claudius' highly successful military campaign which made Britannia another province of the urgently expanding Roman Empire. A few straggling inhabitants were initially displaced by the Romans who built their far more carefully planned town on a marshy site with two low hills where the River Walbrook run into the Thames. The few mud huts of any former British inhabitants were quickly swept aside to make room for a proper city befitting the Roman's lifestyle; a city that was civilized beyond compare with anything the early Britons would have known or enjoyed. The 'new' Roman lifestyle was based on centuries of practice of Roman republicanism followed by empire building, and much of this was borrowed from yet earlier Etruscan and Greek civilizations. By comparison with almost any other period in its history, Roman Londinium in its blossoming was a place of almost continuous excitement, carefully contained by a securely structured government.

In common with the other thriving provincial trading places of the period, citizens in Londinium were well looked after. Even the poorest members of society were pampered – in many ways – for the good practical reason that this prevented civil disobedience. For example, in Roman thinking, one of several well-proven ways of ensuring civic ease and providing an outlet for the potentially dangerous energies of the mob, was to provide large-scale public entertainments. These mostly involved gladiatorial contests where men fought with men, women with women, men with beasts – often to the death. Public executions involving naked victims being thrown to savage dogs, and sometimes to panthers or lions, took place during the quieter periods of a gladiatorial show and were probably considered rather boring.

Even the poorest Londoners would probably have had access to brothels that were plentiful and well-kept; some of them offering great choice, as detailed below. Roman Londoners also enjoyed bath-houses of a degree of sophistication that has never been seen since. These were places for real relaxation and indulgence, for manicures, skin-scraping, massages with sweet-smelling oils; also places for exercise or afternoon leisure. Sex would most probably have been available, as required. The entrance fee to these baths was usually the lowest denomination coin in circulation at the time. It would be like paying just a penny to make use of all the facilities of a top London sports and leisure club, although the Roman penny offered still more.

The self-enforcing strength of the Roman state enabled it to embrace a reasonable degree of religious freedom. Citizens and those aspiring to citizenship could pick and choose from among the worship of hundreds of gods and goddesses from the Greco-Roman pantheon. This worship involved many different rites and observances, often including plenty of wine drinking, and culminating in orgiastic sex. Where cult rites were concerned the Empire allowed great freedom although Roman principle drew the line at human sacrifice, so British druidical practices were not acceptable. But, within reason, the Romans would not have been generally concerned about the way some Mediterranean pagan practices were adapted to suit native tastes or needs.

So, in AD 60, the new town of Londinium, positioned tidily on the banks of the Thames, was already thriving. The chronicler Tacitus records that it was a town teeming with merchants working as importers and exporters on a large scale. These merchants were there most probably to invest in the new province and make loans towards the costs of Romanization and exploitation; they traded in people and goods from across the huge Roman Empire.

British palates would have quickly become used to Roman foodstuffs, plentiful red wine and new delicacies. These came from an Empire that stretched as far as Asia and took in the Middle East and North Africa. In those early days the myriad influences on the fast-growing town would have amazed native Britons. It was not just Roman military skill, administrative know-how and Mediterranean passion that arrived, it was multi-culture personified. Soon London was populated by Greeks, Syrians, Germans, Africans and Gauls. The burgeoning town quickly turned into a honeycomb, buzzing with activity in service of the Empire. Previously ousted British tribes people and those from surrounding areas joined the throng as workers and traders. Londinium was a cosmopolitan, money-driven town that attracted cosmopolitan, money-driven people.

But there were setbacks to the steady growth of the young trading port. In this same year the city suffered its first major disaster: Boudicca. Avenging her own whipping at Roman hands, the rape of her daughters and the plundering of some of her chief Iceni tribesmen after the death of her husband, Queen Boudicca swept into the new town, having already laid waste to Verulanium and the previous Roman headquarter town at Colchester. Joined by the Trinovantes tribe, the Iceni razed the small port to the ground. A thin red layer of oxidized iron in the clay, evidence of the fire deep in City of London soil, is one testimony to Boudicca's visit. Another is Tacitus' report that the avenging queen and her followers massacred some 70,000 Roman British inhabitants. His account is almost certainly an exaggeration, given that Londinium in AD 60 probably had fewer than 30,000 inhabitants. But he makes his point. By the time the Iceni and supporting Trinovanti tribesmen arrived at the Thames, their bloodlust was insatiable. No one who remained in Londinium was spared. The timber and mud houses with thatched roofs were systematically torched. People suffered death by sword, gibbet and cross, regardless of their sex or age. Another chronicler, Dio, records that the women died most painfully by obscene torture. The embedding cycle of human life – growth, depletion, regrowth and the occasional reaping on a large scale – is a leitmotif in the history of London up to the Blitz.

But it was not long before the town was rebuilt and the Roman pageant continued unstoppably. As more soldiers and administrators, traders and religious men and women arrived, they continued to assert the three traits in which the Romans excelled. The first, as mentioned, was expertise at masterminding large-scale events – when the Romans put on a show, you could be sure it would run pretty much like clockwork. The second was an enthusiasm for letting their hair down in public with fellow citizens. And the third was a code of morality that placed sex at the heart of their religious and secular celebrations.

The Floralia, with its large phallus and general nudity, was by no means unique as an event in the Roman calendar. The Romans in the western provinces, which included Londinium as the capital of one of four provinces in Britannia, introduced myriad rites and observances which promoted fertility both through the use of sexual symbols and copulation. Sex as part of pagan worship was uninhibited and natural as a result of centuries of practice.

For example, the Lupercalia, the feast of the wolf goddess, was a major Roman festival. Because of its importance, it is most probable that it existed in some form in London. The wolf goddess was the mythical mother of Romulus and Remus, founders of Rome. Contemporary writing reports that, in Rome, the feast began with the sacrifice of goats and a dog by superintending priests, called Luperci. After the sacrifice, two young Luperci were led to the altar, their foreheads were touched by a bloody knife and the blood was wiped off with wool dipped in milk. The ritual then required that the two young men laugh. The sacrificial feast followed, after which the Luperci cut thongs of skin from the sacrificed animals and ran in two bands round the Palatine Hill. At this point young women, usually naked, entered the spectacle. They were chased by the Luperci who would attempt to whip them with their thongs of goat hide. A blow from the thong was supposed to render a woman fertile. Other versions of the Lupercalia indicate a more sexual climax than this in that the chasers and the chased would work themselves into a lather, exchange small phallic statuettes and then have sex with each other. The Lupercalia was celebrated on 15 February, how the Italian version of the festivities was adapted to suit the chilly winter of Londonium has to be left to the imagination.

Religious rites such as these were adapted and changed over time. The Catholic Church under Pope Gelasius I appropriated the form of the Lupercalian rite – if not the full monty – as the Feast of Purification in AD 494.

More important to the Christian calendar was the way another major Roman festival, the Saturnalia, celebrated between 17 and 24 December, became transposed. The Saturnalia was a feast of wild merry-making and domestic celebrations when businesses schools and law courts were closed so that the populace could feast, dance, gamble and generally enjoy themselves. The 25 December was the birthday of Mithra, the Persian god of light and a day devoted to the invincible sun. Cannily, the early Christian church adopted this day as a celebration of the nativity of Christ to counteract the more libidinous aspects of the Roman ways of enjoying themselves. But the libidinous aspects held sway for a long time.

Bacchus, the Roman equivalent of Dionysos, is one of the most important gods of the Graeco-Roman pantheon. He is thought of mainly as the wine god, partly because the orgiastic and ecstatic rites of his worship did involve drinking wine, often in large quantities. The word orgy now refers to sexual depravity but at the time it was just the corruption of the word 'mystery' as part of a religious cult. We can presume that during festivals such as the Bacchanalia any woman was fair game for copulation if she ventured outside her home.

Bacchus was also a major deity concerned with the fertility of plants and, to a lesser extent, of animals, and with the cycle of birth and death mirrored in the seasons. The early cult of Bacchus/Dionysos was widespread and lasted from early Hellenistic Greece to Christian Imperial Rome in the fourth century. Pan/Faunus and his satyrs or fauns were among the associates of this powerful deity. Bacchus also had troops of ecstatic women in his wake, known as bacchantes or maenads. In myth, these women had the power to tear limb from limb any creature, human or animal, which crossed their path.

With many people gathered together, fuelled by a great deal of alcohol, some of these cults did get out of hand. In the early days of the Roman Empire, the authorities stamped down on some Bacchanalian excesses and a number of people were exiled or executed for performing unnatural acts. These included bestiality and sexual perversions that exceeded even the Roman's generally permissive ideas about what was tasteful. But it is clear that they continued in Roman London and elsewhere for several more centuries.

In 1954, the excavation of the Temple of Mithras in the City of London offered conclusive evidence of the existence of Bacchic and other cults. Archaeologists and Roman scholars have unfolded a story of worship that started with Mithraism, the worship of the bull-slaying god Mithras, a cult originating in Persia, which spread throughout the Roman Empire. In the late third century, the temple was taken over by followers of Bacchus, who were probably still using it when much of the Roman Empire was being Christianized by Emperor Constantine [in the fourth century]. Erotic celebrations would have been common in the precincts of this temple, around the area of modern Gracechurch Street and Leadenhall Street.

In the old Roman calendar there is evidence to suggest that 108 days were used for religious rather than commercial purposes, and by the fourth century AD as many as 177 days may have been put aside for festivals. Many were explicitly sexual. For example, huge phallic – and sometimes vulvic – figures would be erected to preside over the festival of Bona Dea (Good Goddess), a fertility celebration in honour of the daughter of the satyr god Faunus. Group sex typically ended the ritual. The cult of Isis – originally from Egypt and known to have been popular with Cleopatra and then with women of all ranks in the Roman Empire – allowed any kind of sexual excess in the streets on her feast day.

How much of this kind of activity existed in Londinium is hard to say. We know that Roman Londoners followed the old Roman calendar. We know that they adopted Roman ways and lived in a cosmopolitan society. The findings at the Temple of Mithras confirm the existence of Mithraic, Bacchic and other cults, as do other Roman London artefacts. There may not be hard evidence of Thames-side festivities involving orgiastic revelries but there is a great deal of evidence of this form of worship generally in the period. Some of the best is offered by the many exquisite examples of Graeco-Roman pottery, sculpture and other remains, Samian ware from central Gaul, and the plentiful supply of paintings and decorative imagery from continental, Middle Eastern, Asian and North African sources.

Throughout this imagery and in these artefacts the phallus is a dominant and potent symbol. In the worship of Bacchus or of powerful nature gods such as Pan/Faunus, revelries feature prominent penises swinging in pursuit of girls, boys, men, goats or untargeted ecstasies. Priapus, son of Dionysos, had the most prominent phallus of them all. He was another early fertility god, often depicted bearing fruit in his arms with his toga lifted to reveal a phallus of staggering proportions. A wall painting from the House of Vetti in Pompey portrays Priapus with an organ of such enormous size that he appears to be having difficulty supporting it on weighing scales. The story goes that Priapus used his phallus to club a donkey.

More urbane and sophisticated Romano-British inhabitants in Londinium and elsewhere would probably have regarded such exaggerations with a certain amount of ribaldry, but when these deities and their organs were central to a festive rite, they were all part of the day. There would have been little sniggering.

Public models of phalluses, or organ-shaped amulets and charms were not merely promoters of fertility. According to Dr Catherine Johns, in her definitive work on sexual symbology in Graeco-Roman art, *Sex or Symbol*: 'Use of the male sex organ alone as a symbol has a specific meaning connected not with any individual deity, but with the apotropaic power of the phallus itself, that is, its power to overt and overcome evil influences.' In effect, phallic symbols warded off evil spirits and were used as a means of protection. They protected the boundaries of properties and specific areas. Amulets in the shape of male sex organs were plentiful throughout Roman Londinium and there are a number of examples on show in the Museum of London. We know that in other Roman towns of the period, phalluses also marked areas of danger such as street corners. Phallic designs decorated even the tiny gold rings produced for the children of wealthy households. Mosaic constructions of phallic symbols were built into the dining room walls of the more sophisticated town villas; phalluses were portrayed even on the Roman mosaic equivalent of the doormat, as a sign of welcome, perhaps into a brothel, but possibly into a large family villa.

It is probable that there are many more examples of models of phalluses than of female vulva because this was a male-dominated society and also because male genitalia is easier to shape either in repose, or in 'ithyphallic' form – that is, erect. The British Museum and the Museum of London have some examples of depictions of the vulva, particularly on oil lamps, but these are rare. Portrayal of the vulva may have been more threatening in this society; the vulva is also less easy to represent in detached form.

Of course the newly arrived Romans did not hold the monopoly on heady, sexually-driven rituals and potent symbols. Pre-Roman inhabitants also worshipped sexual potency. But two things made the Romans different. Firstly, as aliens in Britain they had an invader's psychology. They had a subconscious drive to outpopulate the natives in the land they had decided to call their own. There was a very pragmatic compulsion to participate in fertility rites; and sexual activity, although subject to its own codes, was an uncomplicated and constant part of Roman society's day-to-day life. The idea that any of this alfresco eroticism was sinful would have been laughable – these were intense and sacred rituals. Roman Londoners were worshipping their gods through the ecstasy and pleasure of their own bodies.

Secondly, and perhaps more importantly, the Romans had the economic resources to realise their festive ambitions on a grand scale. The wealth of an empire was circulating in the new town. London cannot have known what hit it.

Roman Londoners also enjoyed sex for its own sake, within and outside their marriages. And where sexual freedom and choice are concerned, Londoners had never had it so good. As long as the family was held firm and the 'paterfamilias' was the production of more good and loyal Romans, he in particular would have had reasonable licence to indulge as he pleased. Homosexuality at this time had a long pedigree in the Roman and earlier Hellenic civilizations and was tolerated, if not actively promoted. More deviant sexual activity such as bestiality was probably not condoned, although there is evidence to suggest that the occasional public rape by or of animals may have been used to add spice to mass entertainments in the amphitheatre. Incest, however, was forbidden and taboo. The Romans were well aware that this led to poor breeding and caused great ructions in the family, which was a central part of the social structure.

But it would be wrong to suggest that it was only the men who held sway. The writings of Juvenal set the tone for sexual excess at the time of Roman London, particularly when describing Messalina, Emperor Claudius' third wife. As the Empire grew, the imperial capital began setting an increasingly colourful example for the moneyed upper classes in its satellite provinces. Messalina was well known both for her licentious tastes and her murderous capabilities. She even disguised herself as a prostitute to compete with her professional counterparts in Rome. Juvenal takes up the story of her sorties in his *Sixth Satire*:

So soon as his consort (Messalina) saw him sleep she lightly remembered
In the self-same hour the harlot's mat and the emperor's couch
With nocturnal hood abandoned and a single serving-maid.
O most illustrious of strumpets, dark-haired but golden-wigged,
Off to the steamy-curtained brothel's chamber long reserved,
Imperial gold at bosom but all else naked flesh for sale!
There, Britannicus noble, the womb is shown that once bore thee.

Smiling she welcomes her clients and claims the chinking
coinage . . .

'When at length the keeper dismissed his girls, ah, how
sorrowful
She then departed, yet still whenever she could as the last,
Closing the door behind her, still all agog with her lusts
On homeward way, for the men had wearied but never appeased
them.

Prostitution was condoned and certainly legal by the time of
Claudius' reign; many brothels throughout the Empire would have
been fine establishments, even palatial. The chastity laws that
Augustus, the first Roman Emperor following the republican period,
had attempted to impose were swept aside by the time early
Londinium was getting into swing as a busy, cosmopolitan trading
port in the western provinces. Ports have always attracted prostitutes. Many of the teeming number of merchants and traders in
Roman London at the end of the first century were a long way from
their families and homes. Walk today along the site of the wharves
outside the Fishmongers Guild and you can imagine the babble of
languages as cargo was unloaded. Oysters and hunting dogs were
being packed into ferries for export. Delicately decorated slip-ware
from France, fish paste from Antibes, figs and grape juice from the
mother country, spices imported from the Middle East – all these
were taken into the storehouses behind the quayside. Along with
them came fresh shipments of slaves, the youngest and prettiest
destined to provide others with pleasure.

A Roman prostitute could have the rank of either freedwoman or
slave and the most exotic were likely to be booty, the human spoils
of war and imperial expansion. While British natives were shipped
out to boost the enthusiasms of war-weary generals and jaded
administrators all over the Empire, dark-eyed beauties flooded into
Roman London. Syrian girls were particularly popular. The London
brothels were probably colourful and ethnically diverse places –
small reminders of Rome's own dens of pleasure. Even so, one
wonders whether the Romans missed the variety of women that
would have been on offer back in their home town. In Rome itself,

you could select from '5.00 tea-time part-timers' or '*meretrices*'; or perhaps you might choose the self-explanatory '*delicatae*', or even the 'Dorides', beautiful young girls whose trademark was to stand naked and nymph-like in their doorways. But perhaps this was a less viable prospect on a British November afternoon.

In Rome the best 'lupanars' – whore-houses – were attractive villas with gardens and fountains. The erotic and explicit wall-paintings at Pompeii give an idea of the kind of interior decoration in which you might have enjoyed your sex session. But London had its refinements too. In the Museum of London there is a sun-set golden Roman wall-painting. Originally a decoration in one of Southwark's bathhouses, it lay undisturbed, face down in a back garden, until 1983. Cupid stands nonchalantly in the doorway. Perhaps he is inviting you into a world of literally steamy sex. There is no current evidence that the Roman London brothels were situated close to the bathhouses, but it is reasonable to assume that sex services were provided to clients alongside manicures and massages.

Roman prostitutes catered for most tastes: girls for men, men for men, boys for noblewomen, children for whoever wanted to pay. You can imagine twisting and turning through the narrow Roman lanes, walking along the main thoroughfare called the Via Decumana, past bakers and wine-stores, to pick out your chosen form of carnal delight.

Brothels in Rome were legal and generated useful taxes for the city. The Leonium Vectigal de Meretricium et Exsoletorum (Tax on Whorehouses, Prostitutes and Mercenary Catamites) was used to repair the circuses, amphitheatres and other public buildings where prostitutes worked; any money left over went to the treasury. It is reasonable to assume that Londinium's brothels would have been well-kept and may also have contributed to municipal finances.

Of course sex would have come cheaply too. In Rome, unlicensed prostitutes operated from '*fornices*'. Originally these were the arches of colonnaded public buildings, but they could end up being shacks or simply pallets by the roadside. Quick, casual copulation in such places was 'fornication'. The quaysides of London would probably have presented the same opportunities for quick gratification.

Even the Roman foundation myth may have had a connection with sex-sellers. In some early versions of the Romulus and Remus myth, the children were nurtured by a 'she-wolf', a colloquial term for a prostitute, called Larentia. Larentia earned so much money through her work that she was able to leave her property to the two foundlings. Thus, in mythic terms at least, it was from these small beginnings that the city mushroomed; Rome itself was founded on the profits of sex.

There is still today the erroneous belief that it was the hedonistic Roman lifestyle, involving excesses in drinking, eating and unfettered sexual freedom, that brought about the downfall of the Roman Empire. By comparison with today's behaviour it is true that the Romans were given to unbelievable excesses in many aspects of their lives, particularly in the freedom to enjoy themselves, often in ways that we see as barbaric. But the Romans did not believe in half measures in anything they did. They were brilliant at organizing, building, beautifying and controlling. They could integrate mixed populations in cities far flung from the imperial capital and although their tactics were often brutal they probably knew more about ensuring 'social inclusion', in the sense of joining everyone in the values of the society, than we can boast today, despite our best hopes and worthiest efforts. The deviant and brutal tastes of some later Roman emperors are well documented, but the headiest excesses were indulged in by a minority. For the most part the people of Londinium and other towns in the western provinces would have led relatively ordered lives, enjoying their pleasures in a more restrained way. In comparison with the ructions of Anglo-Saxon and medieval London, they lived in a period, lasting some 360 years, of relative stability; a time when the mechanics of Empire worked for the most part like clockwork.

The reasons for the fall of Rome in the west and in other parts of this vast and hugely successful domain have far more to do with the effects of internecine wars and power struggles. Rome fought itself to death, and London was too much of an outpost not to have lost its relevance in time. After the second major fire in AD 125, the town was never quite the same. There were still large beautiful villas, trade and commerce continued, but evidence suggests that, despite attempts, affairs never reached the peaks of the early years. Nor was Londinium exempt from the political upheavals of the later Roman Empire.

The Romans had trumpeted their imperial power for over 600 years; at its zenith the Empire embraced 100 million people and two million square miles. Eventually, they bowed from the international stage in a quiet, rather sad fashion. The soldiers were re-called from Londinium to the imperial capital in AD 407 and following the army train went the last of the dancers and prostitutes. What the legionnaires also took with them was living memory of a time when the concept of 'sin' simply did not exist. Roman London spent a short time as an independent state and then gradually collapsed in on itself. What the Romans left behind was a ghost town.

ᴖ SEX AS A SIN: A NEW MINDSET ᴖ

Even a journalist from the most popular national newspaper would find it hard to conjure up a convincing account of sexual activity in Dark Age London. But any account whatsoever is difficult following the 450s, when Angles, Saxons and Jutes started to invade, take land and overpower the numbed and insular local populations of post-Roman Britain. We can be sure that sex happened in the fifth and sixth centuries but most probably it took place in domestic confines – that is, when it did not form part of the cycle involving pillage, rape and bloodshed. Moreover, among the settling communities, it took place within the confines of a carefully codified Anglo-Saxon society – a society of warrior-peasants that was based on kinship, obligation to warlords, complex protocols of land ownership, agriculture and barter. In what becomes Anglo-Saxon Lundenwic considerably later, towards the end of the sixth century, we may even assume that the brothels that were well documented in medieval Southwark were in existence – in some form – even at this time. It is likely that any trading port of the geographical importance of London would have continued to provide a population of itinerant traders with these and other services.

But archaeology allows us only a small glimpse of life after the Romans. The city, if it could be called this, was largely in ruin, perhaps occupied by a few goats and some opportunistic squatters. There was at least one large Roman house with a sophisticated underground heating system and private bath-suite that was still lived in, probably well into the late fifth century. The occupants used, or hoarded, Roman coins from previous decades and imported large amphora, jars from the eastern Mediterranean. So we may conclude that some form of commercial activity was still going on. It has been suggested that, during these troubled times when the scattered British population was subjected to invasions by the Germanic tribes, the return imports from this remnant trading post would have been slaves.

For this particularly dark period of the Dark Ages, the town appears to have been known by the late Celtic name of 'Caer-Lundein' and it may have been the centre of a small kingdom also encompassing St Albans. None of which supposition throws much light on the way London's early inhabitants enjoyed themselves, coitally or otherwise.

What is interesting about the sexual mores of the people of London in post-Roman Britain involves the establishment of a fundamentally new mindset about sex – a mindset that has lasted largely intact right through to the present day. Christianity was slow in arriving in London but once it arrived, in the 7th century, it started to become embedded in the physical and emotional framework of the city, framing sex in its stride.

From the first generation of the Apostolic Church, the early Christian evangelists, although greatly and savagely persecuted and known to be fodder for public entertainments in the amphitheatres of the Roman Empire, were steadily successful in promoting the Christian message. It was a unique message centred on the unifying power of one God and the salvation, redemption and eternal life offered to followers of Jesus Christ. There is, however, little evidence of Christianity in Londinium until the end of the third century at least, although by this time the gospel had spread far and wide on the continent, where Christians were becoming a thorn in the side of the Roman state. But then came Emperor Constantine. To this day, some Christians still believe that the conversion of Constantine in 312, before he became Roman Emperor in 316, was a matter of divine intervention. It can be argued that Constantine's espousal of Christianity did change the course of history dramatically. It certainly led to the Christianization of the Roman Empire; and the developments of the fourth century contributed fundamentally to the nature of later Byzantine and western medieval culture. Although the upper classes of this period maintained the tradition of a classical education which was still deeply integrated with paganism, a specifically Christian, biblical culture was soon established.

However, Londinium and its closely positioned later neighbour, Lundenwic, seem to have had only sparse Christian influence before the arrival of Augustine at the end of the sixth century. He was the papal emissary, sent by Pope Gregory I to convert the British heathens – a population overlorded by the relative recently-arrived Germanic tribes.

When Anglo-Saxon invaders and settlers first moved into Britain in the 450s they began to divide up the country into many small kingdoms. Initially, the Saxon settlement of Lundenwic fell within the kingdom of the East Saxons, but its geographical and trading importance was obviously recognised by the newcomers and the town was often taken under direct control of the Essex overlords; these were variously the kings of Kent, Mercia or Wessex. Then, in 597, Augustine, later the first Archbishop of Canterbury, converted King Aethelred of Kent to Christianity.

The first St Paul's Church was built on Ludgate Hill in 604 and several other churches were built in the following 150 years. Soon the concept of sin had become firmly embedded in Sin City. From this point on, sex becomes the forbidden fruit, a necessary evil; something that in much later 'respectable' society in the suburbs of Victorian Islington should never be discussed in front of the children and seldom even mentioned between married couples. In marriage, sex was taken into the personal and private domain and largely buried. The motif, of lust and sin continue unabated in the many records of the chroniclers of London society, a society that becomes coloured by what was considered to be a pagan darkness; a society living in a place where one's lust could readily and cheaply be assuaged by prostitutes including men, women and children. And lust was associated with dirt, disease, poverty and death because in a city driven by commerce, the poor had nothing to sell but their bodies.

In the Christian subversion of a former pagan culture, the depiction of the horned devil is a crudely reconstructed version of the deity Pan/Faunus, originally so much more innocent. With the advent of

Christianity the worship and encouragement of eroticism was no longer a means of promoting fertility; they were the slippery slope into the jaws of hell. But were the Lundenwic folk of the seventh century slipping in that direction? Unfortunately, the Anglo-Saxon chronicles avoid mention of bad behaviour except of the killing and bone-breaking kind. And when religious writers step in, their views are often biased towards doctrinal conditioning, if not manacled by it. The Venerable Bede, one of the most famous of the Christian chroniclers writing in the seventh and eighth centuries, castigates the prosperous *emporium* of Lundenwic ('a mart for many peoples coming by land and sea') for its 'sinfulness'. He was one of the first of a very long line of the appalled writing about the appalling. And it all started with St Augustine. Even the most extravagant sexual indulgences and orgiastic abandon of 18th century London are framed within the morality of the founding fathers of the Church, introduced in the seventh century.

There is some confusion about the Church's guidance in this area during the second half of the first millennium. While the Church was expected to preach against the sin of lust, it is also recorded that it was the Church's role to weave spells of erotic magic. The earliest collection of ecclesiastical law in England – the seventh century Penitential of St Theodore – forbade the making of love potions or 'philtres': 'It is unlawful for any, cleric or layman, to exercise the craft of seer or charmer, or to make philtres, and all such as practise such arts or use them we order to be expelled from the church.' The church is not only trying to assert its authority here. It is also trying to move out of the dynamic in which the role of holy man in the 'new' religion involved the adoption of practices that actually belonged to former pagan and Druid religions.

As the church gained influence in the ninth and 10th centuries, such Anglo-Saxon practices as buying and selling of women were no longer allowed. Such activity belonged to a former, heathen Germanic era. The penitentials were developed by the Church Fathers in Europe to become the foundation stones of a new, sacralized social order, one that had a profound effect on the lives of the people of later Anglo-Saxon and Middle Ages London.

The penitentials provided the laws and codes that enabled the church gradually to take dominion over most former Anglo-Saxon institutions. Of particular importance, the church adopted a central role in marriage and in the teaching about sex, both within and outside marriage. According to this teaching, sex was for procreation only and anything else was a sin to be punished by penances. Even at a time when supposedly celibate priests were often the prime clients of prostitutes and openly indulged in lechery, it was down to the same priests to teach the married about when and how they could perform sex.

The early penitentials of the Catholic Church were very detailed about what was allowed and what was sinful, particularly when it came to intercourse. The only permitted form was what is now known as the 'missionary position', face to face with the man on top. There were penalties for all other versions. Anal intercourse incurred seven years' penance. There was three years' penance for dorsal intercourse, with the woman on top – because this was contrary to the natural hierarchy. Oral intercourse required three years' penance, as did heterosexual intercourse from behind, which reduced the man to a mere copulating dog or horse. The penitentials encouraged sex only at night and only when partially unclothed.

These restrictions may appear bad enough, but the church also forbad sex on all feast days and fast days. There were 273 of these each year in the seventh century, although they shrunk to 140 days by the 16th century. Sex was also forbidden on Sundays and on days when the woman was deemed to be unclean – during menstruation, pregnancy, breast-feeding and for 40 days after childbirth. Mutual consent was essential to the married partners, although there is an inherent contradiction in this teaching in that the woman's role was always subordinate. If a woman somehow indicated that she required sexual intercourse, it was up to the man to oblige but he must always take the lead.

In the Middle Ages the woman was universally held to be inferior and this was a belief developed by the Church Fathers. Woman was the daughter and heiress of Eve, who was the source of Original Sin and the instrument of the Devil. Eve's inferiority was proven by her birth from a rib of Adam, and her evildoing owed to the fact that she had introduced Adam to carnal delight, succumbed to the serpent and then tempted Adam to eat the apple that led to man's downfall and expulsion from the Garden of Eden. The view of women's inferiority was widely propagated in theological, medical and scientific treatises and it became an unquestioned basis of the social order.

Because of these notions, women were believed to have far stronger sexual appetites than men and were invariably to blame in the case of adultery or fornication. Men received penances for fornication and adultery outside marriage, but they were only minor ones if the sin had occurred between a master and a servant girl, who was eminently inferior. Because of their inferiority, women needed disciplining and Canon Law allowed wife-beating, which took place at every level of society. Women were not allowed to hold public office or serve as a military commander, lawyer or judge. The promotion of the cult of the Virgin Mary in the 11th and 12th centuries offered women the two role models of virginity, to resist the sin of Eve, or motherhood, for those not suited to the life of religious celibacy.

These precepts took gradual hold in Anglo-Saxon society and became standard beliefs by the medieval period. But in the London before the Norman invasion, it is hard to say just how strongly the church's teaching controlled the thinking or behaviour of inhabitants. It is attractive to think that the Anglo-Saxons still retained less doctrinally correct attitudes towards sex and sexual activities.

For the purposes of the development of London – its teeming markets, thoroughfares, festivities and holy days – the Anglo-Saxon period was an immensely formative time. Many of the traditions that underpin today's City of London – aldermen as city elders and magistrates, the formation of city wards – owe to the late Anglo-Saxon period. So too does the geography of a significant number of London streets. Wooden quays were built along much of the riverfront at Queenhithe, Billingsgate and Dowgate and near the mouth of the River Walbrook by modern Cannon Street Station. There was an extensive network of small gravelled streets especially near the Thames and in the western half of the modern city: Milk Street, Bow Lane, and Ironmonger Lane, all off Cheapside are surviving examples. Cheapside (Westcheap), itself and Eastcheap became the main market streets (*ceap* is the Anglo-Saxon word for market).

Some of London's street names date from the medieval period, but employ a language that is clearly Old English or Anglo-Saxon in origin. For example, there was Gropecuntelane in the late 13th century in the two parishes of St Pancras and St Mary de Colechurch (later tastefully renamed Groping Lane). Conhop ('cunnies' or 'cunt') Street is another self-explanatory reference and probable testimony to the libido of earlier Saxon inhabitants and visiting traders, many of whom would have surely enjoyed the temptations of the 'horhus'. Another street located in Cheap Ward in the parish of St Mary de Colechurch, where prostitutes were strictly forbidden in the medieval period, carried the name of Bordhawelane. Some historians believe that this derives from the word 'bordello'.

We can be sure that carnal pleasures did not stop with the arrival of the Anglo-Saxons and their Viking successors, but we know more about them following the rude arrival of the Normans.

∽ NORMANS AND MEDIEVAL STEWS ∾

The Norman invasion in 1066 provided a new thrust to Londoners' sexual experience. The Normans had distinct characteristics and traits that must have accounted for their success in building a significant empire. Over the period of the 11th and 12th centuries this empire included the former Frankish kingdom of northern France, part of which remains as Normandy; and later colonies in southern Italy, Sicily, England, Wales, Scotland and Ireland. In a process akin to natural selection, this Viking family group from Denmark, Norway and Iceland was notably energetic and enterprising in the way it took over new territories and then absorbed and adapted the institutions in each culture.

In post-1066 England, even by the end of Henry 1's reign in 1135, the whole structure of royal government remained fundamentally Anglo-Saxon – monarchy, king's council, royal seal and writing office, the shire system and the sheriffs and the twofold revenue system consisting of cash from royal estates and a direct tax levied on landowners. All this was pre-Norman. But the Normans added innovations such as the exchequer, the itinerant justices, and the sworn inquest. They built castles and arranged secure defences. Ironically, England under the Normans became safe from foreign invasion for the first time in its much invaded history.

Meanwhile, although Winchester was in fact the official administrative and spiritual capital of the country, London remained its trading heart. This was also the city most constantly exposed to overseas influence. The often reckless and adventuring spirit of the Normans caught on quickly, together with the carefully fostered Norman cult of knighthood. Normans knights were fierce and brutal; their conduct on and off the field of battle left little room for mercy or chivalry – the more romantic ideas of knighthood propounded in Thomas Malory's *Morte d'Arthur*, filter in the post-crusade period, saturated in Christian morality. But only 30 years after the Norman invasion, crusade-fever gripped the aristocratic and knightly ranks of Londoners. Soon influence on the morals and culture of the city would come not only from a western tradition, but from the world of Islam.

Tangentially, the 11th century notion of courtly love stems in part from crusaders and knight orders of this period. There is no real precedent for courtly love. It seems to have evolved from various influences and arrived in London society via the French court, a concept confused also with worship of the Virgin Mary, and with certain Arab influences on the first crusaders. The courtly lover, celebrated by the troubadour poets, existed to serve his lady. His love was almost always adulterous, mainly because most real marriages were the result of business interests or the seal of power alliances. There is a certain pagan tang to courtly loving because, ultimately, the lover saw himself as serving the all-powerful god of love and worshipping his lady-saint. Based therefore on religious, social and erotic influences, this notion of lady-worshiping love was essentially a male-thing, a means by which poets could celebrate physical passion outside the typically unsexy constraints of marriage. Courtly love did achieve high poetic status, particularly in the court of 12th century Elaine of Acquitaine, married first to Louis VII of France and then to Henry II of England. But it can be seen as a poetic and codified means of elevating the natural sexual instincts of men too often holed up with their chums.

Crusaders also brought a more tangible refinement of love-making back to London from the Middle East – the Turkish hot bath. No evidence substantiates the general use of the reasonably rare hot-tubs of medieval London as places for abandoned sex, but it is a worthy idea and one that is suggested by the notable London historian, EJ Burford. In his thesis, steam-rooms had gone with the

Romans, but Londoners were very quick to embrace the return of the hot bath. The combination of wet bodies, heat and steam clearly has tremendous sex-appeal. In London today there are clubs and societies devoted exclusively to steamy sex. But in the 12th century the popularity of hot baths might have been buttressed by the commonly-held belief that sweating was a good cure for venereal disease. However, it is quite probable that a hot-tub session passed infection from one person to another even more speedily.

A 'Company of Bath Men' was established in the 12th century and their premises became known as the Turk's Head, acknowledging the inspiration for the craze. Most baths could fit in about half a dozen people standing up; some were designed to accommodate a couple reclining horizontally. In his book *Synfulle City*, Burford conjures up a vivid picture of 'small boys sent running through the streets announcing when the water was hot'. These baths must have provided a rare, sensual pleasure for grimy, ague-ridden, bone-chilled Londoners.

Contemporary European woodcuts indicate that sex was very much on the agenda at some bathing places. One medieval example shows men and women bathing together. There are couples bumping and grinding in the gardens round about. There is accompanying mood music – as ever the 'food of love'. In the woodcut an ambiguous figure hovers in the background – a papal representative – demonstrating that there is very rarely a public display of sexual appetite that goes unmonitored by the moral arbiters of society.

Even if there was no sex involved, the popularity of the hot bath endured and gradually adopted far more illustrious associations. Following his coronation in 1399, Henry IV is traditionally associated with the founding of the 'Order of Knights of the Bath', although The Honourable Order of the Bath, which remains in place today, was formally created by King George I in 1725.

↬ THE OLDEST PROFESSION ↫

Sexual desire itself was not denied by the Christian church but, while adultery was prohibited, other forms of extra-marital activity posed a theological dilemma. St. Augustine had written 'suppress prostitution, and capricious lusts will overthrow society'. In the 13th century Thomas Aquinas, canonized for his leadership as a protector of Christian orthodoxy, states that 'Prostitution in towns is like the cesspool in the palace; take away the cesspool and the palace will become an unclean and evil-smelling place.' Women were known to be more driven by lust than men, and prostitutes, rather than the clients who paid for their services, were viewed as the fount of sin. As is ever the case in London, which has always been atheistic in its habits if not its aspirations, prostitutes were nevertheless plentiful and widely enjoyed.

So, risking eternal damnation and with only sporadic official sanction, prostitutes occupied a kind of no-man's land in Medieval Christendom. In London and other English towns, they were mostly banned along with bawds (procuresses) and brothel keepers, or were made to operate outside the town walls. But, ironically, some medieval London brothels were licensed, run and taxed by the churches themselves. Given the barbarity of some contemporary punishments, penalties for prostitution outside 'licensed' areas were not especially harsh. There are records of prostitutes being driven away from what were the western suburbs, around modern day Fleet Street and Holborn; and there were intermittent attempts at fining and banning pimps and women of doubtful virtue. But through much of the 12th-to-late-14th century period, many areas of London at certain times of the day would have presented the chance for business. So, much did not change.

In 1383-84 the city aldermen resolved to crack down on what they considered to be a problem of public order by ordaining harsher punishments. They decided that laymen offenders taken in the wards were to have their heads shaved and women were to have their hair cropped; then they would be paraded through the streets attended by a minstrel band to draw public attention. A second offence would receive the same treatment plus ten days in prison; a third would result in banishment from the city for ever. Considering that children could be hanged for stealing an apple several hundred years later, they were getting off lightly. London's biographer, Peter Ackroyd, has it coined when he says 'Londoners are characteristically lenient in matters of sexual impropriety.'

A few years later, in 1393, another city ordnance had to acknowledge the impossibility of banning or punishing everyone involved in the oldest trade. Instead the proclamation forbade prostitutes to 'go about or lodge' in the city and determined that they should 'keep themselves to the places thereunto assigned, that is to say, the Stews on the other side of the Thames, and Cokkeslane'. This was the area of Bankside in the separate burgh of Southwark and Cock Lane in Smithfield.

At this very period, in 1395, prostitutes were busy in some other, quite respectable parts of the City. One such called Eleanor was found *in flagrante delicto* beneath the stalls of the lace-makers of Soper Lane, just off Cheapside. Eleanor's case is poignant and notable because Eleanor was a transvestite male prostitute and this is the earliest record of a prostitute of this kind. Eleanor's real name was John Rykener and he frankly disclosed the nature of his services to the Mayor, John Fressh, and the assembled aldermen in the City court. Rykener explained to the court that, passing himself as a woman, he had been 'accosted' by his co-defendant, John Britby from York, who suggested they took part in a libidinous act to which he agreed provided he was paid. They crawled under the nearby stall and were then caught 'committing that detestable, unmentionable and ignominious vice'. On further questioning, Rykener told the court that he had learned to dress as a woman, and to provide this particular service, from a woman called Elizabeth Bronderer, who 'also brought her daughter Alice to diverse men for the sake of lust'. He also explained how he serviced both men and women and that his primary customers were members of the church, including monks, rectors and other priests, because they paid the most.

What Rykener's punishment was is not known, but as there was no law against this unusual crime at the time, it is possible he got off lightly. He may have been tried for sodomy by a church court, but there are no records surviving from this period.

The incident is interesting not only because of the evidence of a medieval cross-dressing homosexual but also because it is a prime example of the Victorian and post-Victorian attitude to sexuality. Rykener's story was brought to light by scholars David Boyd and Ruth Karras in 1995 when they were examining the *Calendar of Select Pleas and Memoranda of the City of London AD 1381–1412*, prepared by AH Thomas in 1924–32. Thomas would have read the entire account but merely mentions the 'examination of two men charged with immorality'. Like many 19th century scholars before him, Thomas preferred to suppress this kind of information, finding it distasteful.

✌ WINCHESTER GEESE ✌

The area known as Bankside was the eastern part of today's South Bank. It was a riverside thoroughfare on the south side of the Thames that stretched roughly from what is now Blackfriars Bridge towards London Bridge. From the 12th to the 14th century it formed the northern boundary of Paris Gardens and the Liberty of the Clink (an area free of royal jurisdiction, and later the location of Clink Prison, whence the term 'clink'). The sexual history of this area is remarkably well documented. *The Domesday Book* – which manages to miss out London, even though it accounts for almost every last pig and goat elsewhere in the land – describes 16 brothels in *messuages* (plots of land) on Bankside. Later, in 1161, an *Ordinance for the Government of the Stews under the Bishop of Winchester's Liberty of the Clink on the Bankside in Southwark* was issued by Henry II's Parliament and endorsed by Thomas à Becket, the Archbishop of Canterbury.

This remarkable document formally started the regulation of the Bankside brothels by the bishops of Winchester in Southwark. It also became the basis of later ordinance documents – 'customaries' – that provided a surprising degree of protection for prostitutes. A surviving customary shows that brothel-keepers could not charge more than 14d (a little over a shilling) per room, nor could they employ nuns, married women or servants, nor force prostitutes into service or hold them there against their will. Servants in the household could include no more than one male ostler and one female laundress, whose business was strictly the linen. Bailiffs working for the Winchester bishops were supposed to check that these stews were empty of their whores during daytime – except between 11a.m. and 1p.m. – and also during all holy days. The 'stewholders' themselves were supposed to be married men and they were not allowed to sell food, drink, fuel or candles on the premises. Nor were they or

their wives allowed to hinder the comings and goings of the prostitutes who stayed in their houses. Rules even covered the way
prostitutes could solicit custom. Prostitutes 'might not spin or card
with any stewholder, or cast any stone or make any *contenance* to
any man or cause any disturbance'.

Most sympathetically, men were supposed to 'lye stille' with women
for a whole night (most likely to prevent the offence of 'night-walking'
whereby women stalked their customers in the streets). Woe betide you
if you formed an attachment for an individual after a long night together.
Prostitutes could not marry or attach themselves to any one lover – they
were 'common women' and belonged to the community. Even their
dress was regulated in that they were not allowed to wear aprons
because this was the mark of a respectable woman. But some degree of
comfort and protection on earth was perhaps a small consolation for
the Bankside whores, or 'Winchester geese', when their career-choice
meant they would be buried outside consecrated Christian soil – usually
in ground called the Crossbones – and be denied eternal salvation.

The word 'stew' may come from either the old French *estuve*,
meaning stewhouse, a kind of bathhouse; or from the old French
estui, meaning case, sheath and a tub for keeping fish in a boat.
Archaeological digs in modern Bankside have uncovered a number
of fishponds, all located in areas where prostitutes would work, close
to the river where there was good access to trade. There was certainly
at least one bathhouse recorded in this period, owned by one Joan
Hunt and her paramour Bernard, but this was not part of the
Bankside regime. John Stow, one of the most accurate and busi-
nesslike of 16th-century historians, says that Stew Lane, near
Queenhithe, derived its name from a 'stew or hothouse there kept'.
Bankside was also known as Stews' Bank by Henry VIII's time.

Bankside with its licensed stews remained in service until the
Puritans under Oliver Cromwell abolished it in 1641. It is famous
during this period because of the wonderful records that have been
kept by the ecclesiastical licensors, but it represented only a small
part of the sex industry of medieval London. In the 14th century
there appear to be only seven licensed stews in total, a number which
grew to 18 by 1506. A great many unlicensed, 'self-employed' prostitutes existed in Southwark and elsewhere, many using the alehouses,
taverns and brewhouses in quayside areas to seek out clients. There

were frequently complaints from upright citizens that non-licensed public brothels were being set up and causing a nuisance in manors outside Bankside.

In 1381, petitioners to the king's council complained that five brothels were in operation in the parish of St Olave in the king's own guildable manor. They alleged that these places were patronized by 'all manner of persons of religion, namely monks, canons, friars, parsons, vicars, priests', also married and unmarried men; and that prostitutes, married women and servants were taken there against their will. The five alleged brothel-keepers were sent before the king's council immediately. This time, two of the accused brothel-keepers were taken to the Tower and kept there for two weeks.

London, with its ever-changing anonymous population was a magnet for women from all over the country ready to eke out a living in the sex trade. There are records from the mid-1300s that list women from, for instance, Lincoln, St Albans, Staunton and Houndsmoor. They came to seek their sexual fortune in London and escape who knows what at home; this was a time when incest was still rife and where famines and the Black Death were devastating rural populations.

⁓ HENRY'S REFORMS: FROM TRICKLE TO FLOOD ⁓

Throughout the medieval and early Tudor period, there was a steady trickle of these proto-prostitutes into London. It took the actions of Henry VIII, the most powerful of all British kings, and his passion for one woman, Anne Boleyn, to turn the trickle into a flood.

By isolating the Church of England from the Roman Church, Henry forced a break with almost every Catholic tradition. The Reformation shook up the entire country. The monasteries were dissolved, the great Church estates broken up, and many ordinary people were forced to change masters, occupations and homes.

Henry's reforms, which were on the face of it ecclesiastic, were, in consequence, also economic. Dislocated women poured into London. For many there were only two options: offer your services as a wet-nurse or become a seller of sex. Most simply ended up on the streets. The authorities recognized the problem pretty smartly. From 1546 onwards, Henry VIII overturned the system whereby brothels were allowed to be licensed by certain civil authorities. In essence he drove yet more of London's prostitutes underground. Many who were caught would be whipped or would suffer a period in the stocks. And if these penalties did not teach them the error of their ways, there was a third approach. In 1553, the Bridewell received its charter 'for to be a work-house for the poor and idle persons of the city'. It was one of four institutions set up to try to cope with the flood of social misfits that buzzed through London: the sick, children of the poor, orphans, crim-inals, prostitutes. Inmates of the Bridewell were frequently destitute women. Under Queen Mary, a few years later, they could be asked to work on the treadmill – a large, human-powered grinding system for corn. Women would also beat out hemp with heavy wooden mallets. Sometimes the Bridewell proved too effective in reducing the avail-ability of prostitutes in Elizabethan London. 'Serving-men' – fornicators – would on occasions raid Bridewell to free women, known as 'Bridewell baggage', to return to their former occupation.

It is typical that men who took part in illicit sex were called 'serving-men' or just 'men' while women who provided this much-needed service were branded and ridiculed with many illustrative names over the centuries: 'punks, madams, fireships, jilts, doxies, drabs, smuts, cracks, mawkes, trulls, trugmoldies, bunters, does, punchable nuns, molls, mother midnights, blowses, buttered buns, squirrels, mackerels, cats, ladybirds, blowzabellas, and others' (*London the Biography*) – not to mention 'strumpets'. However, men selling sex to other men did give rise to some linguistic inventiveness: today's 'bum-burglar' or 'rent boy' carried the cheeky soubriquet of 'apple squire' in Elizabethan times.

Prohibition of any kind has never stopped Londoners from having their pleasure, and there's nothing as tempting as forbidden fruit. However, the growing phalanx of sex-workers needed a safer haven to entertain their clients, who increased in number as London's popu-lation doubled, from 100,000 to 200,000, in just the second half of the 16th century. Without other 'official' outlet, the sex industry went back to the protected areas of Bankside.

Free from the constraints of the city at this time, Bankside became internationally recognized as a suburb of sin. And just as Henry VIII's reforms had speeded up brothel development on Bankside, his daughter Elizabeth I's heady reign consolidated it.

⊸ ELIZABETHAN PROSTITUTES ↤

The world and wiles of Elizabethan prostitutes are vividly described by contemporary pamphleteers. The playwright Thomas Dekker, who was oddly at home in the bawdy theatre scene that started in the Elizabethan era, heartily disapproves of strumpetry in his pamphlet, *Lanthorn and Candlelight* (1608). In this, the suburbs are a first stop off for a visitor from hell: 'And what saw he there? . . . He saw the doors of notorious carted bawds like Hell gates stand night and day wide open, with a pair of harlots in taffeta gowns, like two painted posts, garnishing out those doors, being better to the house than a double sign.' By 'suburbs' he would have been referring to no further south than Borough Road or the Elephant & Castle, rather than the suburbs of modern-day London, such as Streatham. (Even 20 years after the heyday of notorious sex therapist Cynthia Payne, Streatham still attracts kerb-crawlers.)

The whore-houses, or 'trugging-houses' as they were sometimes known by contemporaries, (although whore-offices would be a better description, since the women were no longer allowed to live in their place of work), were always whitewashed. Their signs – for instance, The Crane, The Cardinal's Hat, The Bell, The Swan – were painted on to the buildings, rather than dangling at right angles as was the case with most inns.

By Shakespeare's day, Bankside was a strip of taverns, fishmongers and mercers, quayside sellers, stews, bear-pits and theatres, backed by fields, orchards and market gardens. It drew actors, bawds and whores, cut-purses and cut-throats – all servicing or preying on the men who came over the river in search of forbidden pleasures. Picking your way across the trampled timber pavements and muddy fields in search of an afternoon or evening of pleasure, you would run the gamut of competitive innkeepers. The notion of selling goods with the promise of 'freebies' thrown in is by no means a modern one. Clients in search of sex would find themselves assailed by Elizabethan landlords bellowing out offers of free wine to go with a roast. In fine weather the atmosphere there would have been pleasantly bucolic. Maps of the time show how green spaces dominated the landscape. It must have made a pleasant change from the city where new building and development of old sites was escalating at such a rate that in 1580, at the Mayor's request, Queen Elizabeth made a proclamation prohibiting new building on any vacant site within three miles of the city.

In Southwark you found women, and occasionally men, sitting in the doorways of their stews to advertize their wares, although some of the former edicts remained. They were not allowed to solicit actively, or 'chide or throw stones' at passers-by. The notion of throwing things to get attention has a long tradition. In the dainty literature of the early 19th century, the discreet throw of a small stone is replaced by a bout of hanky dropping, usually followed by a fit of fainting to gain attention. In Thomas Hardy's *Jude The Obscure*, comely Arabella throws a pig's fizzle over a hedge to land on the studious young Jude as he passes by. Lusty Arabella gets her man and thereby hangs a tale.

Just as they do today, virgins, or girls passed off as virgins, fetched the best price in Elizabethan times. But, as the records of grumbling contemporaries reveal, the hit could be substantial whatever the quality of the goods on offer. In 1584 one broadsheet, *A Mirror for Magistrates*, describes how 'forty shillings or better' would buy 'a pottle or two of wine, the embracement of a painted strumpet and the French Welcome' (Elizabethan slang for a sexually transmitted disease). In the middle and upper strands of this complex market, the money was generally good and 'keeping' was a lucrative profession. According to Alan Haynes in *Sex in Elizabethan England*, Mistress Blunt – one of the madams of the day – 'took a minimum of six pounds per week in rent and this ignores possible tips' from her six bawdy houses. Many artisans did not earn more than sixpence a day at this time and would have shifted themselves to the poorest quarters to make do with 'a threepeny stondinge'. Half a day's wages or less might buy the same goods today at King's Cross.

Many brothels had gardens so alfresco sex was common. Holland Gardens and Paris Gardens (today, dismal and littered and more like a bombsite) were particularly notorious. We have the Puritan Philip Stubbes' disapproving zeal to thank for some of the most detailed descriptions of Elizabethan whore-houses. In his *Anatomy of Abuses* (1583), he writes 'there is no greater sin before the face of God than whoredom'.

He goes on to describe how:

in the fields and suburbs of the cities they have gardens, either paled or walled round about very high, with their arbours and bowers fit for the purpose. And lest they might be espied in these open places, they have their banqueting-houses with galleries, turrets and what not else therein sumptuously erected; wherein they may (and doubtless do) many of them play filthy persons. And for that their gardens are locked, some of them have three or four keys apiece, whereof one they keep for themselves, the other their paramours have to go in before them, lest happily they should be perceived, for then were all their sport dashed. Then to these gardens they repair when they list, with a basket and a boy, where they, meeting their sweethearts, receive their wished desires. These gardens are excellent places, and for the purpose; for if they can speak with their darlings nowhere else, yet there they may be sure to meet them, and to receive the guerdon of their pains; they know best what I mean.

Philip Stubbes' disgust with the profession was such that he advocated execution as a punishment for prostitutes. But his was a squeaky voice in the crowd, particularly a crowd that loved the theatre. There was a strong connection between theatres and brothels – Henslowe, Alleyn and Longley, who were leading Elizabethan and Jacobean impresarios, were owners of both.

Another pamphleteer and playwright, Robert Greene, gives us an idea in *Disputation* of what 'all in a day's work' meant to a working whore like 'Nan' – and shows that the Elizabethan sex industry was just as happy as Soho's is today to make considerable money through exceptionally overpriced 'value-added' commodities. Greene's fictitious Nan reports:

But if he (the client) come into a house, then let our trade alone to verse upon him, for first we feign ourselves hungry, for the benefit of the house, although our bellies were never so full, and no doubt the good pander or bawd she comes forth like a sober matron, and sets stores of cakes on the table, and then I shall fall aboard them, and though I can eat little, yet I make havoc of all. And let him be sure every dish is well sauced, for he shall pay for a pippin-pie that cost in the market fourpence, at one of the trugging houses eighteenpence.

In the company of a Soho escort today you may well find yourself responsible for a bill for quite ordinary Champagne, the 'pippin-pie's equivalent', priced at £125 a bottle and more.

The whores depicted by Robert Greene were artful and enter-prising and could turn a trick easily to milk their clients. Like many of the companions that surrounded them they were good actors, and this enabled them to roll a client's money without exchange. As Alan Haynes in his book *Sex in Elizabethan England* writes: 'Money/coin is of course sexualized by the Elizabethans; to "coin" a child was to engender one or create one as one mints a coin.'

A great deal else was sexualized by the Elizabethans. The plays of the period – and right up to the abolition of the London theatre under the frosty rule of Cromwell – indulged the theme of sex, toting the mastery of women, the comedy of passion and the slavish imbecility of lust. Shakespeare is a rich source of new coinage, in words and imagery, that would have fetched hoots of laughter from the packed audiences at the Globe. Even the most tragic of his tragedies offer various short breaks of on-stage intermission; low comedy buttered with sexual innuendo. *Hamlet, King Lear, Othello* and *Macbeth* all have their *Viz* comic moments, but with far greater shelf-life and depth. Curiously powerful, strangely reviled, the Elizabethan prosti-tute also owes her most pertinent epitaph to Shakespeare's King Lear who shouts out:

> Thou rascal beadle, hold thy bloody hand!
> Why dost though lash that whore? Strip thine own back;
> Thou hotly lust'st to use her in that kind
> For which thou whip'st her.

By the end of the 16th century, the explosion of London's population ensured that 'public' brothels were to be found in many more loca-tions. They were outside the east city walls in Petticoat Lane, Hog Lane and St Katherine's; in Smithfield; in Shoreditch; Westminster; in Clerkenwell (Turnbull Street) and in the Liberties of Whitefriars, St Martin-le-Grand and Coldharbour. Others were within the city's own jurisdiction at Billingsgate and Queenhithe. All-comers could find a service to suit them in Ave Maria Alley by St Paul's.

Many London prostitutes would have been easy to identify. Henry VIII had at one point decreed that whores be branded, but not many were. By James I's reign, the monarch would ask for them to be branded on the forehead with an 'R' for rogue. Oliver Cromwell continued the trend, introducing an Act in 1650 that proposed that prostitutes should be 'cauterised and seared with a hot iron on the cheek, forehead or some other part of their body that might be seen, to the end [that] the honest and chaste Christians might be discerned from the adulterous children of Satan'. In other towns, such as Bristol, whores were supposed to wear red and yellow striped hoods or capes. Since medieval times, stripes and contrasting patterns were deemed to represent the cloth of the devil.

In another pamphlet, *A Notable Discovery of Cozenage* (1592), Greene makes reference to 'apple-squires', but it is clear that this was largely an industry where girls were on top. The picture Greene paints is of highly motivated businesswomen working well outside the proscripted areas. Some had even joined the households of the aristocracy. For example, there was an establishment run by a Mrs Higgins in the Earl of Pembroke's Thames-side mansion, Worcester House. Gradually we see that some women in the Elizabethan sex industry took control of their own lives and were certainly not worse off than many of their female counterparts. Having a woman as powerful and controlling as Elizabeth I on the throne may have helped women to increase their potential for independence, however achieved.

But even before Elizabeth's reign, satirist Charles Bansley showed in his *Pryde and Abuse of Women* (1550) that 'Strumpettes' could often be role models:

. . . the Citie of London
For therein dwell prowde wicked ones
The Poyson of all this Region.
For a stewed Strumpette can not so soone set up
In Lyght lewde Fasyon
But every wanton Jelot [young impressionable girl] wyll lyke
    ytt well
And catch it upp anon.

Prostitutes, then as now, offered a double-edged sword: a moment of pleasure with the potential for a lifetime of pain from a sexually transmitted disease. The playwright Thomas Middleton expresses the spectre that sexual diseases represented to the times in the words of Leantio in the play, *Women Beware Women*:

> When I behold a glorious dangerous strumpet,
> Sparkling in beauty and destruction too,
> Both at a twinkling, I do liken straight
> Her beautified body to a goodly temple
> That's built on vaults where carcasses lie rotting;
> And so, by little and little, I shrink back again,
> And quench desire with a cool meditation.

Syphilis or 'the French Pox' was already in vigorous circulation in London. It probably came from the Far East and was present in the skeletons of medieval victims dug up around London. Edward II – the king who was infamously murdered by gaolers at Berkeley Castle by having a red-hot poker thrust up his anus – had opened one hospital for women in Southwark for the treatment of syphilis ('*morbis indecens ae cunniensis*'), and another in Kingsland for men with gonorrhoea ('*morbis turpis*'). The chain of disease meant its effects stretched far and wide – even Queen Mary is reputed to have stunk of rhinitis, an inflammation of the mucus membrane of the nose, and a legacy of her father's syphilis. Some brothels had a reputation for being cleaner than others. From the early 14th century the 'froes' or 'frowes' of Flanders ran famously clean 'bordels' in their homelands, and then emigrated to practise their art in Bankside brothels.

The risk of venereal disease may have had a curious silver lining. During the Black Death, which ravaged much of London and the rest of the country in the mid-1300s, an urban myth circulated that having sex with whores and contracting a sexually-transmitted disease would protect you from the plague. Three hundred years later in Restoration London, during the Great Plague, an apothecary called William Baghurst noted: 'While fresh young bodies of men and girls suffered from the Plague, the common prostitutes in the back streets and alleys, foul as they were with the Itch Scabbe and Sores, were scarcely even struck.' Possibly some of these women had God on their side rather than the devil; or perhaps their resistance had something to do with immunity resulting from wide experience of 'fishing in that most peculiar streame'.

Largely because of their reputation as promulgators of disease, the old London brothels always got into trouble. They were the scape-goats, blamed in numerous proclamations for destabilizing society. We should not overlook the virginal enthusiasm of the boy-king Edward V, when he introduced a famous ordinance in 1483 which made the monarch's feelings clear:

For to Eschewe the stynkynge and horrible Synne of lecherie . . . he means of Strumpettes, mysguyded and idyll Women dayly vagraunt and walkynge abowte the streetes and Lanes . . . repairinge to Tavernes . . . provokynge manie other Persons to the sayd Synne to the grete displesure of ALMYGHTIE GOD and the brekynge of the Kynge's . . . Peace . . .

London brothels were also subject to attack throughout medieval, Tudor and later history by the real breakers 'of the king's peace' during times of civil disturbance. As rioters flooded into London from Kent during Wat Tyler's 'Peasant's Revolt' in 1381, they set about 'despoylinge the brothels on bankside'. When the charismatic Irish malcontent Jack Cade marched on London in 1449, his followers burned down all the Bankside whore-houses and 'reviled the women'. There are also records showing that apprentices attacked brothels on Shrove Tuesdays. Their motive could have been resentment of the moneyed folk who patronized the premises. In the far more libertine age of Restoration London, a petition of whores was given in 1668 to Charles II's mistress, Barbara Villiers, protesting against the bullish vandalism carried out, again by apprentices, against the London brothels.

But we would be very wrong to think of all women in 16th and 17th-century London as sexual victims. Women had fun at the expense of men too. In the early 17th century on the Thames shore-line three miles east of St Paul's stood a very pagan-looking pole topped with animal horns. Nicholas Breton in his pamphlet *Cornucopiae* (1612) describes how the pole was erected in honour of Lady Fortune – the subversive spirit of marriage and cuckoldry – 'to which horns of all kinds and descriptions are fixed, in honour of all the English cuckolds or horn carriers . . . and the English have much fun and amusement with each other, as they pass by and doff their hats to each other and to all around.'

Peter Ackroyd in his book *London the Biography* quotes one visitor to London who wrote of:

a woman carrying a figure of straw representing a man, crowned with very ample horns, preceded by a drum and followed by a mob, making a most grating noise with tongs, grid-irons, frying pans and saucepans. I asked what the meaning of all this was; they told me, that a woman had given her husband a sound beating, for accusing her of making him a cuckold.

The tourist concludes that female Londoners 'are the most dangerous women in the world'.

✍ LIBERTY RESTORED ᔐ

Dangerous maybe, desirable certainly. Selling sex in London to make money was a sure fire winner in the 16th century; but selling yourself as an erotic icon became an art in the 17th-century capital thanks to the restoration of King Charles II.

In 1660, with Cromwell and his puritan Commonwealth out of the way, Charles II returned to Dover. On 29 May, on the eve of his 30th birthday, he entered London in Roman style. Diarist John Evelyn describes:

. . . a Triumph of above 20000 horse & foote, brandishing their swords and shouting with inexpressible joy: The wayes straw'd with flowers, the bells ringing, the streets hung with Tapissry, fountains running with wine: The Mayor, aldermen, all the Companies in their liveries, Chaines of Gold, banners; Lords & nobles, Cloth of Silver, gold and velvett everybody clad in, the windos & balconies all set with Ladys, Trumpets, Music & myriads of people flocking the streets . . .

Restoration London was springtime after a long winter. Despite the ignominy of losing naval battles against the Dutch, despite his inability to withstand petitioners and keep his finances in order, Charles II was a liberator who gave hedonism a quasi-divine status. Called the 'merry monarch', he revelled in the good things of life and his courtiers and members of London's social elite were quick to copy him. High living and indulgence rippled throughout the capital.

Although Charles was still the upholder of a religion-based morality, sexual immorality became fashionable. It was even a sign of loyalty to the king; an indication that you were not upholding the standards of the hated former puritans. In drama, verse, prose and general conduct the standards of what became acceptable widened in deference to his majesty's example. But after 18 repressive years, not everyone was immediately adept at fashionable behaviour. There remained many in parliament and elsewhere whose attempts at the libertine were cosmetic; yet others frowned and grumbled privately.

Nevertheless London's example spread throughout the kingdom. The Scottish royalist William Drummond (son of the famous poet) appears to have been the first man ever to record the act of 'tossing the caber' in his diary. While London's great diarist of the period, Samuel Pepys, started to report his sexual activities in extraordinary detail, a habit of diary-keeping that was taken up by many others following this extraordinary period. Unlike Drummond, Pepys never recorded masturbation but it was close: on one occasion he writes of a spontaneous orgasm caused by reading a French pornographic work; on another he reports a similar moment happening in church, as he looked at and lusted after Charles II's delightful mistress, Lady Castlemaine. (Samuel Pepys in the 1660s sounds a bit like James Boswell in the 1760s. One entry in this inveterate self-recorder's journal reads: 'What a curious, inconsistent thing is the mind of man! In the midst of divine service I was laying plans for having women, and yet had the most sincere feelings of religion.' As a meeting place, the church may well have been a precursor of today's supermarket.)

The restoration of the theatre to London was one of the most popular moves that Charles made. In 1660, the women were allowed to act on stage for the first time and soon this became the custom. On 21 August 1660, the Royal Warrant that granted two entrepre-

neurs the rights to set up theatres in London included the remarkable injunction that '. . . thenceforth only women should play
women's parts . . .'

Having been kept very firmly in their place as child-bearers and
servants of their husbands, ordinary women suddenly had the
chance to join the charmed circle of court and high society. Not only
were they wives and whores, but the newly restored theatre enabled
some of them to become much-publicized sex symbols. On stage or
in front of a camera on a film-set certain people somehow become
more alluring. It certainly worked for the 'pretty, witty' Nell Gwynn,
the most famous, most loyal and most cherished of the king's
mistresses. An anonymous contemporary bears witness to Nell's rise
to stardom at the tender age of 15 in *A Panegyric upon Nelly*:

> Fate now for her did its whole force engage
> And from the pit she mounted to the stage;
> There in full luster did her glories shine,
> And long eclips'd spread forth their light divine.

Pepys records that Nell Gwynn, born the daughter of an alcoholic
bawd in Covent Garden (at least in one of three versions of her biography), was brought up 'to fill strong waters [brandy] to the guests'.
At 14, with a heart-shaped face, hazel eyes and chestnut-brown hair,
she was spotted selling oranges in Covent Garden by Charles Hart, a
leading actor of the London theatre.

By 1666, Nell was the leading comedienne of the King's Company
at the first of the buildings of the Theatre Royal on Drury Lane. She
became Hart's mistress, and then Lord Buckhurst's, who became 6th
Earl of Dorset. By the age of 20, in 1670, she was the mistress of
Charles and bore him a son. Established in a fine house and
admitted to the inner circles, Nell spent the rest of her life entertaining the king and his friends, living extravagantly and intriguing
against her rivals.

This was a time when the in-crowd wore exotic fashions –
including patches of velvet or silk on their faces. The actresses' days
would have been easy to trace. A call at ten o'clock for rehearsal, a
three o'clock performance (making the best possible use of natural

light), then private shows or liaisons to fill up the evening. The dramatist Charles Gildon complained that actresses would turn up at rehearsals, 'too often scarce recovered from their last night's debauch'. For trips to court, actresses from the King's Players (the founding company that occupied the first of many buildings of the Theatre Royal in Drury Lane) were marked out by their scarlet cloaks and crimson capes, trimmed with velvet.

Nell and her fellow actresses were buttressed by the extravagant work of the stage designers and set-painters. Evelyn for instance described a production of Dryden's *The Indian Queen*, 'so beautified with rich scenes as the like had never been seen here as happily in a mercenary theatre'. As had always been the custom for actors in play-houses, particular roles were written for actresses. Suddenly women were given full-bloodied, passionate roles – and if they were good movers, a few energetic dances would be added for good measure.

And the entertainment industry was beginning to garner the characteristics that still mark it out today. Costumes for the women were titillating; dresses scooped to nipple level or breeches ('rhine-graves') slashed to the top of the thigh. Cross-dressing was popular for women as well as men. As Derek Parker points out in his biography of Nell Gwynn, lovers like Nell and her leading man Charles Hart were an early 'gay couple' of the Restoration Theatre. These were without a doubt the 'Hello' magazine couples of their day, just as Nell and the Merry Monarch became the Posh and Becks of the late 17th century.

So Restoration London was the London of prototype celebrity sex goddesses such as Nell. And most of these women were courtesans as well as actresses. The word prostitute conjures up a rather grubby and sad image; replace it with 'courtesan' and you immediately hear the rustle of silks and smell the perfume. Other women, such as guitar-playing Mary 'Moll' Davis, were depicted by the royal painters in court and at their leisure. Mary moved in the same circles as women such as Lady Elizabeth Felton, painted by Bennedetto Gennari as Cleopatra. These were strong, seductive women who exploited the sex appeal they knew they had and who were part of a golden circle which provided vicarious and actual pleasures of all kinds; sirens whom Pepys records as being attractive to women as well as to men.

These courtesans could earn serious money. Charles was not just paying for Nell's sexual favours or emotional support; he was paying her dearly for her status as a sex goddess. A few years after becoming his lover she could afford to gamble away a lord's annual income in one night (about £1,200), while her own earnings for one year outstripped that of a baronet by about fifty times. Bishop Burnet wrote of Nell Gwynn: 'The Duke of Buckingham told me, that when she was first brought to the king, she asked only five hundred pounds a year: and the king refused it. But when he told me this, about four years after, he said she had got of the king above sixty thousand pounds.'

Riches aside, in the eyes of their adoring public the actresses of the day were infinitely more accessible than modern-day sex symbols such as Kylie or Madonna. Not only were they present in the streets of London but they traded in sex, the most democratic of pleasures. The London these women inhabited was typically the same as that of their old muckers: orange-sellers, street whores and bar-maids. Charles and Nell drank together in alehouses and the courtiers followed suit. Evelyn wrote that some great ladies were to be found in taverns, where they 'drink their cups roundly, strain healths through their smocks, dance after the fiddle, [and] kiss freely'.

The theatres themselves were heavy with sexual overtones. Dramatist and poet John Dryden describes the role of the sex-sellers and the audiences, who were seldom there to improve their minds:

> The play-house is their place of traffic, where
> Nightly they sit to sell their rotten ware . . .
> For while he nibbles at her amorous trap
> She gets the money, but he gets the clap.
> Entrenched in vizor mask the giggling sit
> And throw designing looks about the pit,
> Neglecting wholly what the actors say.
> 'Tis their least business there to see the play.

The theatres were described as being frequented by 'sparkish gentlemen' and libertines who enjoyed 'buzzing' around the actresses' 'honey-pot'. The inflated price of oranges that girls like Nell Gwynn sold (the equivalent of a £15 packet of crisps in today's theatre) more than suggests the potential for other services to be thrown in. If not sex itself, there was at least pimping, or message-carrying between amorous theatregoers.

The contrast of the activities of this circle with the realities of London at the time must have been acute. As the beautiful celebrity actresses learned their lines by day and spent the evenings in the company of the king's favoured companions and sycophants – 'the Wits' – the city struggled through the double devastation of plague and fire. Rotting alleys such as Turnmill Street, packed with brothels and bawd-houses, provided the less well-laundered majority of Restoration London with their experience of commercial sex.

Returning to the capital after the outbreak of the plague, the king and his courtiers found many sites vandalised and grass growing in the streets. As Nell Gwynn was winning new admirers on the Drury Lane stage in 1666, the Great Fire of London was devastating a large part of the city. The fire destroyed most of the civic buildings, old St Paul's Cathedral, 87 parish churches and about 13,000 houses. Smoke blotted out the sun as far away as Oxford.

In 1660, the court's libertarian behaviour had been a form of constitutional public relations demonstrating that the monarchy was back in business after the puritan interregnum. After the Great Fire, the vibrant, sensual actresses and their entourage were proof positive that Londoners had the spirit to rise again from the city's ashes.

Nell and fellow courtesans lived the life of Riley right up to the moment of Charles' death. Again, we have John Evelyn to thank for a description of the atmosphere enjoyed by those in the king's company on the last night of his life:

I shall never forget the inexpressible luxury and profaneness, gaming and all dissoluteness ... to which I was witness; the King sitting toying with his concubines, Portsmouth, Cleveland, Mazarin etc. A French boy singing love songs in that glorious gallery whilst about twenty of the great courtiers and other dissolute persons were at basset round a large table, a bank of at least £2000 in gold before them, upon which two gentlemen who were with me made reflections with astonishment.

The gossip surrounding Nell Gwynn tells us as much about the role that Londoners wanted her to adopt as it does about the real facts of her life. She certainly ended up with houses all over the city, including Pall Mall, and a splendid residence in Windsor. Whether she had a silver bed encrusted with delicate engravings is another matter – one source suggests that mirrors embellished the walls and ceilings of her bedroom. Fact or fiction, the point was that her life represented for both men and women a kind of ideal sexual fantasy. The ghost of this idealization has never been laid to rest. You would be hard pressed to find a Londoner today who has not heard of Nell Gwynn.

We should add that Charles loved her dearly. 'Let not poor Nelly starve' was his deathbed request to his brother in 1685. James II obeyed Charles' wish and settled a pension of £1,500 a year on Nell. Sadly though, this charismatic figure, best loved by the public among the king's women, died in November 1687, after being stricken by apoplexy and paralysis. She is buried in St Martins-in-the-Field, Covent Garden.

London's 17th-century entertainment industry and the proximity of its female stars to the influence of a man's world gave real clout to the notion of sex-appeal. It has been central to the allure of stage, film and television ever since. More than this, the official sanction of sexual promiscuity uncorked the libido of the nation. The diehards of the Church – pamphleteers, preachers and leaders of the low Church – joined with philosophers of the Age of Enlightenment in their condemnation of the visceral excess of the capital. But no one wanted to return to the deep frost of the Commonwealth.

৩ 18TH-CENTURY ABANDON ৶

No age in London has been more closely associated with unbridled libido than London in the 18th century. The late historian Roy Porter, who was interviewed for the LWT series that this book accompanies, provided a marvellous account of the period, both in detail and abstract impression:

> 18th-century London was a great time for sex-lovers, and that was partially because everything was just on tap. You didn't have to look very far for your sexual pleasures. Let's say if you're a

man with some money in your pocket, out for a bit of fun, it was said that there were something like twenty to thirty thousand streetwalkers around London . . . The many writers and novelists of the age conveyed to us that this was a sexy time, an entertaining time, a great fun time. And it was very easy to publish almost anything . . . You could easily get extremely lewd prints depicting intercourse, sodomy, buggery, rape . . . and in the 18th century one of the favourite forms of perverse sex was the lash, the whip. It was called 'Le Vice Anglais'.

The exploration of sex went hand in hand with the Age of Enlightenment. The impetus among leading thinkers of the day towards collecting, observing and quantifying the things of this world led to a freedom in evaluating what was permissible in human behaviour. As David Stevenson writes in *The Beggar's Benison*:

One conclusion emerging from such rethinking was that the enjoyment of earthly pleasures was not simply a sadly necessary concession to human weakness and depravity, but valid in its own right. If the universe which God had created made pleasures available, then they were legitimate. A libertine would stop the argument there.

In London, libertarian exploration involved new experiences as well as the excessive celebration and pursuit of old but 'forbidden' habits. There were novel methods of prolonging potency, achieving and sustaining orgasm and curing sexually transmitted diseases. These were promoted by serious physicians and academics as well as by charlatans who were very much at home in an era in which a fool and his money were easily parted.

The breadth of the human condition in 18th-century London, its variety and its extremes must have seemed as unbelievable to visitors from overseas as they were seductive to the gentlemen and their families who came from the shires for the winter season. For this was a place of infinite pleasures and one where fortunes exchanged hands rapidly; a place in which the denizens lived by the seat of their pants. Sexual freedoms were among many pleasures enjoyed by the wealthy, supplied by the poor and aspiring classes alike and mediated by a multitude of traders: bawds, publishers, illustrators, pimps, hawkers, quacks, gypsies – even bogus priests. Fashion in dress was outrageously flamboyant and the tumble of life included feasting, great drunkenness, extraordinary gambling, animal fights, the Hell-Fire and other sex clubs – and every kind of sexual perversion.

Come to London and you could have whatever you wanted – for a price, or in the protection of the right fraternity. Just as nowadays out-of-towners come to the West End for the best choice of, say, shoe shops in the South East, in the 18th century you could also be guaranteed, for example, the largest variety of establishments featuring foot-fetishes.

The English Vice was generally well-catered for. Ned Ward, a journalist and tavern-owner, wrote a monthly magazine called the *London Spy* between 1698 and 1709. In this he set out to expose the 'Vice and Villainy' as well as the 'Follies of Mankind' and according to Roy Porter, 'He did this with gusto and an eye to his readership figures, regaling his public in one paper with a lively account of a brothel wherein the proprietor ensures her girls have an adequate supply of rods with which to whip elderly clients who come to her establishment for that pleasure.'

Some thought of flagellation, perhaps topped up by semi-strangulation, as a means of assisting male potency – an early form of Viagra. Others just enjoyed being punished for their sinfulness by half-naked women or playful catamites.

Exponents of promiscuity sometimes justified their excesses by drawing on misconceived notions of pre-Christian cult practices. Sir Francis Dashwood, briefly Chancellor of the Exchequer, was also the founder of the 'Medenham Monks', one of the best known Hell-Fire clubs of the period. Banned from London, the club met in the ruins of St Mary's Abbey, near High Wycombe. Club members indulged in flagellation, debauchery and orgiastic behaviour. They brought mistresses and prostitutes and openly reviled the Christian religion with parodies of the Mass and devotion to Venus replacing Christ on the Cross.

The English Vice was a favoured perversion throughout the entire 18th century and the far more ostensibly prudish one that followed. By the 1770s and 1780s, flagellation was advertized in the language of the circus. Mary Wilson in Tonbridge Place backed up her live trade with a publication, *The Exhibition of Female Flagellants*, promoting her women as the best whippers in town. The Prince Regent patronized Mrs Collett's establishment in Covent Garden and then gave her the means to move to a better address in Bloomsbury. In Soho Square, Theresa Berkeley ran the White House. Clients could choose from the Gold, Silver or Bronze rooms, the Painted Chamber, the Grotto, the Coal-Hole or even the Skeleton Room. The eponymous Skeleton would pop out now and then, presumably adding a certain frisson to the proceedings.

Londoners appeared to take their perversions seriously. As Paul Langford points out in his book *Englishness Identified*, 'foreigners found the English attitude to sex puzzling and hypocritical. Sexual excess and abnormality seemed endlessly fascinating but not admissible as cause for innocent mirth.' However, some of Ned Ward's readers would have chuckled openly at the excesses of their fellow-Londoners, although they may have had a more mixed response to homosexuality.

Despite the activities of certain courtiers in the Tudor and Stuart periods and the availability of the 'apple-squires' and other boys, homosexuality was not openly practised before this period. No one would have wished to oppose the 1533 Buggery Act which decreed that sodomites should be hanged. But in a city with a population of 700,000 which was so libertarian in its values and conduct, coteries of homosexuals formed and grew more confident. Until the end of the 17th century, as E J Burford states: 'such men were mythologized as monsters, akin to werewolves and basilisks, outside a divinely appointed natural order of things'. He explains that those who indulged in homosexual practices did not think of themselves as non-human or even as sodomites at all. Rather they 'created a more acceptable picture of themselves as men in whom an active libido led them to make love to both sexes equally, as the occasion arose'.

Homosexuals in London had many cruising grounds from Wapping to Westminster and declared themselves by signs, such as using handkerchiefs or patting the back of the other's hand. Known as 'mollies' – a term which reflected their effeminacy – London's homosexuals took to gathering in 'molly houses', places where they would meet, party and make love. Like modern-day transvestites, they called themselves by girls' names and dressed in women's clothes, but unlike modern transvestites they loved to do ludicrous imitations of women and women's primary roles. They played birthing games and carried out mock weddings among other amateur theatricals. Ned Ward writes of mollies who met in one tavern in the city reporting that they had 'so far degenerated from all Masculine Department that they fancy themselves female, affecting to speak, walk, tattle, curtsy, cry, scold & mimick all Manner of Effeminacy'. He adds that they imitated 'all the little Vanities . . . of the female sex . . . not omitting the indecencies of lewd women . . . to commit these Odious Bestialities that ought forever to be without a name.'

Mother Clap's (this was her real name) house in Field Lane near the Old Bailey, now the subject of a West End play, was one of the best known in London. The contemporary London crime lord, Jonathan Wild provides a vivid account of the arrest of a number of what he calls 'he-whores' dressed extraordinarily, as they emerged from what was probably Clap's house. 'Some were dressed like Shepherdesses, others like Milk-maids with fine green hatts, Waistcoats and Petticoats, and others had their faces patched and painted, and wore very extensive Hoop-petticoats, which were then very lately introduced.' Mother Clap's establishment was closed in 1726 following a severe clamp down on sodomy.

Paedophilia was rife. In poverty-stricken areas, parents would sell their daughters into prostitution as young as nine years old, or younger. The Haymarket was a known venue for the selling of young flesh. Men taking streetwalkers into the courts and alleyways of London for an 'evacuation' costing sixpence or a shilling may not necessarily have been seeking the youngest girls, but they may have considered that these were less likely to carry disease. In James Boswell's incredibly candid accounts of his adventures in London in the early 1760s, any notion of paedophilia as something unusual or wrong is entirely absent. An outing recorded on 13 April 1763 reflects the easy wantonness of a gentleman in search of sport:

I should have mentioned last night that I met with a monstrous big whore in the Strand, whom I had a great curiosity to lubricate, as the saying is. I went into a tavern with her, where she displayed to me all the parts of her enormous carcass; but I found that her avarice was as large as her arse, for she would by no means take what I offered her. I therefore with all coolness pulled the bell and discharged the reckoning, to her no small surprise and mortification, who would fain have provoked me to talk harshly to her and so make a disturbance. But I walked off with the gravity of a Barcelonian bishop. I had an opportunity tonight of observing the rascality of the waiters in these infamous sort of taverns. They connive with the whores, and do what they can to fleece the gentlemen. I was on my guard, and got off pretty well. I was so much in the lewd humour that I felt myself restless and took a little girl into a court; but wanted vigour. So I went home resolved against low street debauchery.

As with many of Boswell's resolutions, this one came to nothing. He became adept at dipping 'his machine in the canal', as he puts it on one occasion. Despite the use of 'armour', a form of condom made of animal intestines, to protect the man against infection, Boswell contracted venereal disease about 20 times during his busy and exceptionally well-recorded life. Men like Boswell and another contemporary diarist and sex adventurer, William Hickey, sported through London as they pleased. The problem of venereal disease did not appear to stop them even though they were mostly the means of spreading it.

A woman called Mother Whybourn was well acquainted with venereal disease. According to Maureen Waller in *1700 Scenes from London Life*, it 'cost her her beauty and a fortune to cure'. When she died, she left the following benefit in her will: 'To His Grace the D— — of —— a gross of right Dutch c——ms, newly imported from Holland by M—-ez the Jew.' But at least Mother Whybourn's health problems were an occupational hazard of broadly her own choosing. Many wives and mistresses of men who indulged in the ladies of Covent Garden and elsewhere contracted the pox too. One quoted by Maureen Waller lived in Clerkenwell: 'Thomas Ashworth had often had the carnall knowledge of the said Joanna's body and . . . had given her the pox to which she was reduced to so very great weakness that she could not go without crutches.'

The term 'sensibility', denoting the nicety of intellectual and rational thinking, came of age in the 18th century but, by modern standards at least, it appears not to have included much sensibility to the plight of the very poor. It is heartening that on one occasion, Doctor Johnson, Boswell's own closest friend and greatest mentor, records his profound sadness at being offered sex by a pitifully young, poorly dressed girl. Earlier, in 1746, the Lock Hospital was beneficently established for venereal disease just behind St George's Hospital for the Sick and Lame at Hyde Park Corner. Inmates included young children and even babies who suffered as a result of the commonly held belief that you could get rid of syphilis, or 'sad distemper', by having sex with a healthy person. The younger the person, the more likely they were to be healthy. One commentator wrote that 'it requires the most extensive publication in order to prevent such horrid acts of barbarity and cruelty'. It is perhaps not surprising that members of the Church likened London to 'a great wen', or carbuncle, that affected the very body politic with its sinfulness. But little changed. In 1784, a certain Mother Kelly of Duke Street in St James's mounted an 'Auction of several Orphan Virgins'.

There is plenty of evidence from the records that women enjoyed romantic encounters with each other as much as with the opposite sex. Romantic friendships were fashionable in the upper circles of English society as early as the 17th century. Certainly in the literature of the time, chic, passionate and sometimes erotic relationships between women were accepted without demur.

John Cleland's *Fanny Hill* famously starts with a lesbian encounter when the young innocent comes to the capital. It is clear that Fanny makes the assumption that in London 'anything goes':

> She . . . turned to me, embraced and kiss'd me with great eagerness. This was new, this was odd; but imputing it to nothing but pure kindness, which, for aught I knew, it might be the London way to express in that manner, I was determin'd not to be behind-hand with her, and returned her the kiss and embrace, with all the fervour that perfect innocence knew.

Novels such as William Hayley's *The Young Widow* (1789) and Charlotte Lennox's *Euphemia* (1790) give clues as to why passionate relationships between women were possible. As long as sex was not perceived to be genital, it was acceptable. Talking about a young

Italian woman, the character Lucy insists: 'If one of our family had been tempted to sleep with her it would have been your humble servant Lucy, and not innocent Edward [Lucy's brother]', but she adds, 'as I am absolutely in love with her myself, and have not also the power of metamorphosing myself into a husband, I should most vehemently wish for Edward's success.'

This female homoeroticism or homosexuality did not belong only to the realms of fantasy. Women could caress and even spend the night with each other – and few eyebrows would be raised. More importantly, these same-sex romances were actually considered to be 'rehearsals in girlhood' for conventional marriages with the opposite sex. Maria Harley pines for the eponymous Euphemia. Her uncle suggests that her fiancé 'has reason to be jealous of a friendship that leaves him but second place in [Maria's] affection', but the fiancé replies, 'Miss Harley's sensibility on this occasion is the foundation of all my hopes. From a heart so capable of a sincere attachment, the man who is so happy as to be her choice, may expect all the refinements of a delicate passion.'

As Liza Picard records in *Dr Johnson's London*, the 18th century was also the golden age for patenting medicines both to increase sexual performance and to cure the diseases that resulted. In 1748, the *Gentleman's Magazine* published a list of more than 200 'nostrums' that were then sold over the counter, including a 'confect for impotency' at five shillings a pot. Dr Marten's Chymical Drops were the Viagra of the time. Take one teaspoonful night and morning and men 'have been so fit for the marriage bed that their effects that way have been wondered at . . . as thousands of people, many of them of the first rank, can testify.' Among many potions for countering venereal disease were Walter Leake's Restorative Pills which contained calomel, antimony and steel. To fight the 'King's Evil' and 'all scrophulous distempers' a Frenchman introduced his Royal Military Drops, containing mercury and 'acqua pluvialis'. Thomas Jackson promised an immediate cure with his Venereal Lotion, made up of sublimate of mercury and 'sal vitrioli', or hydrochloric acid. Then there was the renowned Dr Rock, who sold his pills and potions from a cart in Covent Garden and also advertised in the press. His Cathartic Electuary would cure 'the most inveterate degree . . . without impairing the constitution'.

In an age when flagellation and the swallowing of potions containing poisonous elements such as mercury were believed by some to enhance potency, it is scarcely surprising that the seriously wealthy of London also submitted to the astonishing ministrations of a Scottish doctor called James Graham. A man of great invention and pseudo-scientific dabbling, Graham had settled in Bristol where he advertized wonderful cures of all kinds. Then, after a period in the genteel and elegant resort of Bath where his cures involved electricity, milk baths and 'friction', he came to London. Here he set up his Temple of Health in the Adelphi just off the Strand. In this sumptuous building, newly built by the Adam brothers, Graham installed a gigantic four-poster known as the celestial bed, which had a mattress stuffed with stallion hair. This was linked by a system of electromagnets that were supposed to vivify the surroundings. Soft music was piped in from outside. Having paid the fifty guinea fee, those seeking improvement in their sexual performance, were led into the chamber by a bevy of scantily clad 'goddesses of health'. If you, your wife or your mistress were infertile, sex on the celestial bed would cure the problem – satisfaction guaranteed. Such was the price that punters could scarcely admit it did not work. One of the first batches of health goddesses was Emma Lyon, later Lady Emma Hamilton, mistress of Lord Nelson and mother of his daughter, Horatia.

The creative doctor also offered rejuvenating help to flagging Londoners by setting up a mud bath establishment in a small theatre in Panton Street, off Leicester Square. The idea was that by covering yourself in mud you became energized and reinvigorated by natural forces. Graham would strip off in front of his audience, immerse himself in a massive tub of mud and then lecture his audience on the subject of sex; he called it 'generation'. Such was the power of this method, he said, that it would enable customers not only to protect and promote their erections and their pleasure, but also to live for 200 years. Graham was clearly energized by the mud that surrounded him: sometimes he lectured for two or three days at a time. But he did not live much longer than the normal span and his last days were spent in a lunatic asylum in Edinburgh.

Wherever there is hedonism there is a Turkish bath and London offered a number of exciting bagnios. These tended to be at the top end of the market, an area with which Giacomo Casanova was familiar. But even this hard-loving Italian adventurer was impressed by London's bagnios and amazed by the riches of the courtesans in some of them:

> I visited the bagnios where a rich man can sup, bathe and sleep with a fashionable courtesan, of which there are many in London. It makes a magnificent debauch and only costs six guineas . . . We went to see the well-known procuress Mrs Wells and saw the celebrated courtesan Kitty Fisher who was waiting for the Duke of —— to take her to a ball . . . she had on diamonds worth 5,000 francs . . . she had eaten a banknote for 1,000 guineas on a slice of bread and butter that very day'.

Further downmarket, for those who enjoyed titillation or needed fuel to pursue the 'secret vice' there was plenty of what would later be called pornographic literature and prints available. Before the age of the photograph, famous illustrators such as William Hogarth, Thomas Rowlandson and James Gilray, all of whom were formidable satiricists, fed an avid marketplace with direct and erotic drawings and prints. For handy hints, *Aristotle's Masterpiece* was the most common sex manual. In 1749, *Fanny Hill* or *Memoirs of a Woman of Pleasure* was published. This scandalized the authorities who ordered the destruction of all copies; but somehow Arthur Wellesley (the future Duke of Wellington) was able to pack nine copies when he left for India. The Bishop of London fervently denounced these kinds of publication and, in 1750, attributed an earthquake in London to the wrath of God: 'Have not all the abomination of the public stews been opened to view by lewd pictures exposed to sale at noonday?'

Despite such denouncements, publications of all kinds remained easy to buy and were explicit in their contents. By the close of the century there were even comprehensive guidebooks available for punters. One of the most intriguing is *Harris' List of Covent Garden Ladies or Men of Pleasure's Kalendar 1793*. This carries the addresses, prices and proclivities of some 70 women. It is written with a jaded affection for the 'pretty fillies' it describes, combined with the critically detached eye of the horse-trader. If 'Harris' likes the product, he is fulsome in his praise. Of 'Mrs G—frey' at No. 6 Newman Street, he writes: 'every part about the frame is blessed . . . neither has too frequent use of the most bewitching spot rendered it the least callous to the joys of love; she still feels all that torrent of rapture, the mutual dissolution of two souls in liquid bliss can possibly afford . . . her price is one pound tho' ten shillings and sixpence will do.'

If the object of scrutiny does not appeal, Harris can be brutal:

Miss W——n is about twenty-four, light hair, rather above the common size. How such a piece of goods first came to our market we are at a loss to guess: we have indeed heard that she lived some time servant in Wapping; and as the tars [sailors] are good-natured, free-hearted fellows, and, after long voyages, are not very nice in their choice, they may perhaps have done her a good-natured action; this is the only way we can account for it, every other seems absurd to us. Her hands and arms, her limbs indeed, in general, are more calculated for the milk-carrier, than the soft delights of love; however, if she finds herself but in small estimation with our sex, she repays them the compliment, and frequently declares that a female bed-fellow can give more real joys than ever she experienced with the male part of the sex . . .

But Harris at this time was perhaps already part of the old school. In the last two decades of the 18th century we start to witness an almost abrupt reversal of behaviour and attitude that appears to stem from the aspirations of middle-class Londoners – a strange yearning for respectability. Many of the younger generation of this well-to-do class in the early 1780s would have been critical of their parents' lewd behaviour and commonplace speech which was often peppered with oaths and profanities. In a reversal of what we might consider to be normal teenage behaviour, they tried to set new and better standards. Recapturing the moral high ground they set about the revival of 'sensibility' and learned to express their deep and private feelings in ornate prose. Libertarian behaviour was seen by this emerging class as base and godless. At its root, sex itself started its journey to the carpet, to be pushed firmly underneath.

✍ VICTORIAN REPRESSION AND PORNOGRAPHY ✍

Of course, the tanker of immoral behaviour was very slow to turn and, although hidden from view, its cargo remained in place. Georgian London continued to be a place of excess and pleasure right to the end of the Hanoverian dynasty with the death of George IV in 1830. Nevertheless, in the middle and upper reaches of society at least, London was a place of increasing nicety in its manners and elegance in its aspirations, as reflected in Regent Street, built between 1811 and 1825. Broadly though, it remained a London full of anomalies and one that reflected the gamut of human existence. Wealthy dandies and rakes could still lose themselves in low dives or in fashionable whoring, drinking and gaming houses.

In the human and physical geography of 19th-century London, the gulf between exceptional wealth and extreme poverty was a narrow one. Just as the wealthy and well dressed emerge replete with culture from today's Covent Garden Opera House to confront street beggars, so the wealthy of the early Victorian period would walk proud and proprietorial among wretched urchins, shoeless beggars and hawkers. Some of the worst tenements of the early Victorian period in the mid-century were a stone's throw from the prosperous Strand, where vendors of high-quality goods would pander to the needs of customers stepping from their hansom cabs, broughams and chaises. The degree of wretchedness of the tenements is hard to imagine. Some housed up to 30 people in one room with no cooking facilities or running water and barely a mattress and chair for furniture. In the cellar-homes mothers had to be vigilant that rats did not gnaw at the faces and fingers of their infants in the dark, foetid environment. The whole metropolis was patched together by hideous slums that were sometimes acres wide and sometimes mere nooks between better houses. Like certain infamous tenement estates in London today, these were no-go areas. Despite the fact that the metropolitan government was desperately concerned to 'improve' and modernize London, there were certain areas of the city that seemed to be sliding in the opposite direction – slipping backwards to the Elizabethan era where much of the architecture still belonged.

Nevertheless, mid-century Victorian government strove hard to redress poverty and impose a new order of moral rectitude on its citizens. The early Victorians were driven by the idea of continuous, necessary moral and material advance. Where intimate pleasures were concerned, Victorians demonstrated a smothering zeal that brought repressiveness to new heights. New recruits – spawned within the framework of a family dominated unquestioningly by the 'paterfamilias' – were needed to provide for the march of Empire, but in respectable society that was about the upper level of expression where sex was concerned. Exposing the least smidgeon of female flesh was an impropriety. A bare ankle would draw a frown from a Victorian matron; a nape of neck could induce poetic ecstasy in an insipid admirer; chokers were more the vogue than necklaces because they could still be seen above well-covered bosoms. It has been conventionally suggested that even the sinuous cabriole table legs – firm and shiny remnants of the unmentionable Queen Anne period of furniture design – were *de trop*. The legs of pianos, tables and other furniture would all be covered with cloth. The makers pandered to this morally fervent taste by designing tables that were lumpen in the extreme. As a counter argument, we should admit Matthew Sweet's cogently argued view that there were other reasons for covering furniture legs than sexual repression; namely the Victorian's love for hanging and draping material all over the house. But there can be no doubt that Victorian sexual nature was heavily dressed and that the growing middle class in particular went out of its way to avoid reference to sex in the demonstration of their respectability.

Within the sacred bounds of marriage itself, women were no longer deemed capable of enjoying the pleasure of sex. Their role was to receive semen for the purpose of reproduction, with minimum fuss. In the most fervently Catholic homes, the missionary position was adopted and occasionally the act was carried out with participants arranged either side of a sheet, appropriately cut. It was quite typical for husbands and wives to have separate bedrooms; a discreet euphemism in her ear would forewarn of a tryst for the purposes of sexual relations.

In such an atmosphere it was hardly surprising that most sex was enjoyed furtively – often vigorously and even with complete abandon in some quarters of the city. *Le Vice Anglais* continued to be provided for and perhaps the lashings were less playfully administered now that the whipped had so much to be sorry about. Men of means took mistresses and some of them even had understandings with servant girls in their own households. One of the less abashed of these men is known to have had sex with his servant in every room of his considerable house in Berkeley Square.

For the average Londoner, man or woman, who felt that something was missing as a result of the moral manacles of the age, the outlets were the same as ever. The same bargains were made; the same hierarchy existed among the doers and the done. At the very hub of upper-class London, between the end of the Strand and the Regent Street Quadrant, close to Whitehall and the clubs of St James's, there was a flourishing quarter openly dedicated to prostitution. By the time the gaslights were lit, the byways would be filling with women and children to suit most tastes and the poorest of pockets.

Theatre land remained, as ever, a place where men could find what they wanted at the night houses, casinos and dancing palaces, all places that were seldom acquainted by women who were not expensive prostitutes or courtesans of a sort. The dancing palaces or casinos were a prominent and relatively new feature of mid-Victorian night life in London. They were large buildings occupying significant space and were scattered across the area of central London as a result. There was Laurent's Dancing Academy in Windmill Street where it was considered rather low to dance. According to Kellow Chesney in *The Victorian Underworld*, 'the more stylish clients loitered in the gallery above, overlooking the languid and mildly unsavoury scene below.' Near Laurent's was the Argyll Rooms, once a modern tavern, now a famous Haymarket resort with a racy atmosphere. A regular feature in the entertainment was an acrobatic black man called Kangaroo who would twist and turn for clients. Lord Hastings, a well known sportsman, put some spark into the dancing at another casino called Argyll's by emptying a sack of rats on the dance floor. But the main purpose of a visit to Argyll's or to the Portland Rooms better known as Motts, and to supper places such as Evans's in Covent Garden, or the various snug and private supper rooms at The Garrick's Head off Bow Street, was to meet women. At The Garrick's Head there was the additional bonus of a comfortable bedroom and complete indiscretion. This is where gentlemen could see the night through and enjoy a lady's company for breakfast.

But the picture is so much seedier than this too. There are records of a few 'closed-houses' during the period; these were brothels which virtually enslaved the women in their keeping and hid behind the façade of a respectable business or residence. They were maintained by landladies or their husbands and sometimes just by men alone, often those with a sporting inclination as members of the underworld's prize-fighting or dog-fighting fraternity. Some landlords would be ex-bruisers capable of intimidation and worse. More numerous than these places – from the West End to the Ratcliffe Highway – it was the roaming prostitute who drew the vested interests of London's many pimps. Many of these prostitutes were scarcely in their teens. In *The Victorian Underworld*, Kellow Chesney explains how the depravity of people's circumstance led to a Babylonian style of sexual depravity well documented in court reports of the period. In these, we learn of a man convicted 'of outraging a small child begotten by himself on his own daughter.' Born in such an environment, brought up to fight for existence by every means to hand, children were ready to exploit their one readily cashable asset.

London then, like Bangkok today, was a global centre for sex tourism and, as Chesney puts it: 'Where women were often almost hags at thirty, and underdeveloped girls were ready to prostitute themselves, it was inevitable that even men who were not particularly drawn to very young girls should have sometimes taken the chance to misuse them.' In one report to a Lords Committee, a police superintendent describes a visit to a house in Windmill Street:

> I went in with my Chief Inspector, and in each of the rooms in that house I found an elderly gentleman in bed with two of these children. They knew perfectly well that I could not touch them in the house; and they laughed and joked me . . . It was four shillings if there was only one girl, but six shillings if there were two girls for the room.

You may have got away with sex with a nine year-old, but intercourse between consenting males was a serious criminal offence during the Victorian age. With the Amendment Act in 1885, any impropriety at all between males, even in private, became a serious criminal offence. Long gone are the bashful freedoms of the 18th century. The pressure of Victorian morality and the ostracism that was accorded to perceived deviators meant that most homosexual men – and women – would appear in society to conform to 'normal' tastes and behaviour. But, as ever in London, there were always enough so-called 'she-shirts' to cater for those who required some form of servicing, particularly if they wandered in the area between Windmill Street and Covent Garden and had the right air or manner in their walk. Catching homosexuals *in flagrante delicto* was difficult and often dangerous so policemen reported relatively few offenders.

It is small wonder that, in this city of subverted or covert sex where you could satisfy any type of desire if you knew where to go, photographic and textual pornography came of age. In some of London's streets the windows steamed up with the press of viewers and prospective purchasers.

Imagine yourself, a young Victorian woman of any class, out for a stroll in the capital, perhaps around Westminster, along the Strand or in the City, in the second half of the 19th century. Your domestic background is one of fidelity, purity and self-denial, but here you confront a cityscape which is overtly sexualized. Either by chance, or following a slightly sneaky detour, you find yourself walking past shop-front after shop-front displaying erotic illustrations and photographic prints that loosen your jaw.

Some of the images being touted were hard-core, some would seem totally innocent, some very beautiful to us today. There were, according to the memoirs of one compositor, 'guinea books of erotic engravings, imported from Paris'. Alongside such fine pieces, there were the cheaply produced pennyworths of 'smut'.

But it was the new art of photography that really developed the potential for porn (although some influential thinkers such as John Ruskin refused to classify photography as an art). Daguerreotypes by Linley Sambourne, the *Punch* illustrator, reveal very sexy and very modern shots of young actresses in the Camera Club in the Charing Cross Road. *The Daily Telegraph* warned that: 'Any one who takes his walks abroad through our streets must be aware that in almost every shop window devoted to the sale of photographic prints there are exhibited . . . a swarm of cartes-de-visite of tenth-rate actresses and fifth-rate ballet girls in an extreme state of picturesque dishabille . . .'

In the 1 July 1868 edition of the *Bookseller*, an analysis of 'Mischievous Literature', meaning illustrated broadsheets, describes how: 'These disgusting pictures of vice in all forms are printed on the outside page of each publication, and every Saturday the windows at which they are exposed are crowded with eager admirers.' Again the *Daily Telegraph* was quick to point out the potential pitfalls:

First-class engravings and handsome lithographs are now almost entirely driven from our print-shop windows; their places are usurped by myriads of stereoscopic slides, showing us interesting duplicates of young ladies trying on crinoline petticoats, exhibiting their ankles to an undue extent while engaged in the arduous occupation of lacing their Balmoral boots, and washing or ironing fine linen.

There was clearly an appetite for this material, and London had the wherewithal to meet the demand. Stamp duty was abolished on newspapers in 1855, and taxes on paper in 1861; the economics of mass-circulation suddenly made sense. There were photographic studios springing up all over the capital; printing presses and distributors aplenty. Via the boat-train, there was also easy access to French erotica – much sought after by novices and connoisseurs alike. Victorian London produced pornography on a massive scale. The porno films of the late 20th century with titles such as *Hot Nurses in the Linen Cupboard* and *My Body Burns with Hot Lust*, had their equivalents in titillating literature accompanying the photographs: 'Intrigues and Confessions of a Ballet Girl', 'The Romance of Chastisement' (1866) or 'The Amatory Experiences of a Surgeon' (1881).

Of course there was censure throughout this period. The Society for the Suppression of Vice was founded as early as 1802. In 1824, the Vagrancy Act made the public exhibition of illustrated prints an offence. The Lord Chief Justice, John Campbell, first registered his concern in 1857 in the House of Lords where he announced that he 'had learned with horror and alarm that a sale of poison more deadly than prussic acid, strychnine, or arsenic – the sale of obscene publications and indecent books – was openly going on'. A decade after Lord Campbell's Obscene Publications Act of 1868, the *Saturday Review* pointed out that: 'It was not for the purpose of punishing obscenity that Lord Campbell's Act was passed, but because the sale of indecent books not only corrupted private morals, but led directly to breaches of public peace and order'.

One of the first pornographers to be charged under Lord Campbell's Act was a Mary Elliott of 14 Holywell Street. She was sentenced to 12 months' imprisonment with hard labour. On 26 September 1857, the *Illustrated London News* approved: 'The *razzia* must be renewed at intervals, until these pests are convinced that they will not be permitted to live by poisoning the minds of the young, and pandering to the tastes of the corrupt old.'

Lynda Nead, in her book *Victorian Babylon*, points out that the new campaign against pornography did in fact reflect some of the imperial ideals of the time. London would be modernized, its Empire purged of all malign influences (the bloody Indian Mutiny had just demonstrated with horrific and tragic consequences what goes wrong when a submissive population still has fire in its belly). Interestingly *'razzia'* was a colonial term meaning a military expedition, and had in its original Arabic described raids against the infidel. Within the conservative establishment it was thought that the British Empire supported dangerous aliens who needed controlling with an iron fist. London, in particular, supported dissipated decadents who needed suppressing.

The objection of the 'outraged of Tunbridge Wells' of the time was not purely a moral knee-jerk. Anyone who had followed political developments earlier in the century might have heard how the Chartist Movement – a hugely popular, radical massing together of workers all over the country – funded its more worthy publications with the profits from erotic prints and narratives. Some of these, for example *Exquisite* (1821–4) aimed to fire up the proletariat and activists by including passages about high-class sexual debauchery. And although the Chartist movement failed in 1848 despite the efforts of its charismatic leader, Fergus O' Connor, the production of pornography by its members continued.

Some big-time pornographers were well known to be critics of the

Establishment. William Dugdale was one such who mass-produced pornography in Holywell Street. One raid on his premises in 1856 yielded 3,000 books. Dugdale was associated with an attempt to blow up Lord Liverpool's Tory Cabinet in 1821. Then there was William Lazenby, who published *The Pearl*, 'a monthly journal of facetiae and voluptuous reading' which frequently used aristocrats in its storyline. *The Pearl* is still in print. Henry Spencer Ashbee was a great collector of some of the most amazingly explicit books, many now stemming from Paris. Under the pseudonym Pisanus Fraxi, this 'erotomaniac' book-lover compiled three beautifully printed and annotated bibliographies of forbidden literature: the *Index Librorum Prohibitorum* (Index of Books Worthy of Being Prohibited, 1877); the *Centuria Librorum Absconditorum* (A Hundred Books Worthy of Being Hidden Away, 1879) and the *Catena Librorum Tacendorum* (String of Books Worthy of Being Silenced, 1885). Ashbee is also purported to have written *Walter – My Secret Life*, a lengthy, anonymous diary containing a bodice-ripping account of the sex life of a man-about-town.

Later pornographers such as Leonard Smithers were huge fans of 'the decadents', aristocratic pleasure-seekers, and the artistic coterie in the later Victorian period. Smithers was a friend and publicist of Aubrey Beardsley and Oscar Wilde and his lucrative business made him the king of the porn publishers. He had a house in Bedford Square, shops in Burlington Arcade and 5 Old Bond Street, and flats in Paris and Brussels, each with a printing press and a mistress. He managed to run this supposedly clandestine business quite openly and even put up a sign in a shop window to cock a snoop at passing policemen: 'Smut is cheap today'. (However, his beautifully produced publications, including translations of the *Karma Sutra* by Richard Burton, would cost between three and five guineas.) Meanwhile, artists such as Beardsley were generating extremely 'decadent' images, classed then, as they are today, as high-art.

Although denigrated and viewed suspiciously by influential Victorian thinkers, pornography did not belong to a distinct underworld, as it does today. It was not top-shelf material in the newsagents, nor did access to it involve joining nefarious illegal or semi-legal clubs. The facilities and shop fronts of London ensured it was still part of the Victorian Londoners' street furniture. In many ways, these streets probably felt closer in spirit to those during the raucous 16th, 17th and 18th centuries, than to our own 21st-century capital, where sex is blunted as a commercial appendage to the sale of anything from cars to ice-cream. When Victorians were exposed to full-frontal nudes in the streets of London, nine times out of ten this offering would have been made to excite the possibility of a sexual experience, pure and simple.

Perhaps because of the social canopy of Victorian morality, the Victorians were greatly interested in sex, particularly when its display was presented in art form and could be read as sensual rather than pornographic. But the overtly erotic lure of nudes of the period is palpable as revealed in the exhibition, *Exposed*, held in 2001 at the Tate Britain. The official promotion of 'the nude' as a favoured form of English figurative painting had Victoria and Albert among its ardent supporters. The Queen and her consort famously hung a number of such nudes in their private apartments.

The reality of Victorian London is a million miles from the sanitized Pears Soap image, promoted in a far more inhibited 20th-century age (even Pear's Soap bought a fully-frontal nude oil painting for one of its campaigns, but bottled out before the time came to distribute the images).

In the age of the railway, sexual adventures were commonly reported. There are accounts of reciprocated or enforced pick-ups, romances and sexual encounters on the trains into Paddington, Waterloo, King's Cross and Victoria. This hardly gives the impression of a sex-shy population. One case that caught the public's imagination involved the appropriately named Colonel Valentine Baker, who was arrested as he disembarked at Waterloo for the attempted rape of a governess, Rebecca Dickinson, in June 1875.

Sexual desires and crimes, refinements and deviances are a constant in any community, but particularly in one as prosperous, fast-moving and cosmopolitan as London. Today's streets of Soho – where sex is a commodity sold with tongue-in-cheek – are a very small part of the story that, in an ideal world, would begin and end with the pursuit of reasonably innocent pleasures. But London is not an ideal world; it is a place where people can be sucked into a maelstrom and can go with the flow, or hurt themselves, often both. It is small wonder that Londoners are so famous for their love of escape through wild and extravagant entertainment.

BREAD AND CIRCUSES

ᴥᴥ 'GIVE THEM BREAD AND THE CIRCUS' ᴥᴥ

There is no better way of cajoling the 'masses' into controllable shape – or of diverting their energies – than by providing truly spectacular entertainment, particularly when it's free of charge. In Londinium and the western provinces and most of all in the imperial capital, these entertainments were plentiful. They were often sumptuous affairs, organized with ritual precision to reflect a culture of martial violence and virtue, to instil fear and awe, to demonstrate power. The big shows came in various forms: triumphal processions of Roman generals returning from conquest, attended by compulsory carnival festivity; hunting extravaganzas; chariot-racing and horsemanship in the circuses; theatrical performances and acrobatics. But there was nothing so enduring in its popularity as the gladiatorial contests.

Londinium's Roman amphitheatre, surely a site of many a gladiatorial contest, was discovered only as recently as 1988. Before this, with about 80 other amphitheatres uncovered or still remaining as ruins in the former trading towns of the western provinces of the Roman Empire, archaeologists had been convinced there was one in Londinium. But everything is so deeply buried here, overlaid by the compressed rubble of the lives of Saxons and Vikings and the detritus of later centuries, that it took the chance excavation under Guildhall Yard to reveal Londinium's own centre of public entertainment. A kink in modern Basinghall Street to the north, and a similar

---

curve in Gresham Street to the south, are the modern boundary markers of the amphitheatre's east–west oval shape. It was here that sometimes as many as 10,000 people, up to a third of the population, would gather to enjoy shows that have no equal today.

In Londinium, the big spectacles, usually sponsored by the leading magistrate of the province, occasionally by wealthier merchants in this thriving port, could last several days. No one was ever coerced to attend them. Tacitus himself describes how the Romano-British population soon became inured to the sophisticated lifestyle introduced by the Romans – and to so much else that gave them a relatively comfortable life if they knew their place in the pecking order. On the days of the *munera* – gladiatorial extravaganzas – Londoners would have turned up in hordes, excited and soon fuelled by alcohol; wine, the 'red infuriator', was plentiful.

The audience took their seats according to their rank in society. An ordinary but respectable merchant would sit above the governing elite who took the ringside seats, but below the freed slaves, who in turn sat below the common slaves and the women. They were the lowest in status, occupying the 'gods', near the awning of the solid stone building.

The noise was deafening when the triumphal procession of the gladiators, in chariots at this stage and wearing fine equipment, started across the arena – a name deriving from *harena*, Latin for sand. In the London amphitheatre the arena was an elliptical area roughly three cricket pitches in length across, therefore about 64 metres by 44 metres over all. This was nothing like the size of the big amphitheatres, such as the Coliseum in Rome, which could seat upwards of 50,000 spectators. The amphitheatre that was built for the epic film *Gladiator* (1999) gives some idea of scale. It appears to be enormous but would seat only a mere 30,000 spectators.

People came to the amphitheatre for three forms of entertainment. First and most popular was the gladiatorial combat, fights between men mostly but occasionally between women too. They were always bloody and often involved maiming or fatalities but, according to Professor Roger Dunkle, classicist and expert on Roman amphitheatres, they were rarely billed as *sine missione* ('without release' or 'to the death'). Secondly, the arena was where men fought with wild animals; the panthers and lions imported from India and Persia and

North Africa would probably have come to London on rare but special occasions. Londinium probably used large wild dogs, trained for the purpose and known to have been exported to other provinces on the continent and Mediterranean seaboard. Occasionally, there may have been a bear or two. Thirdly, the amphitheatre was a place for elaborate public executions, sometimes involving the barbaric penalty of being thrown to the beasts stark naked, an agonizing death that was deemed as bad as or worse than crucifixion. In a one-day or longer event, all these functions were staged to keep the audience in a high state of tension and excitement.

Once in the arena the gladiators would pick up wooden or blunt weapons and warm up – a mock-fight prelude during which the quietening audience could admire the physiques and agility of some very finely built fighters. Although most of the gladiators were conscripted criminals or slaves, organized into travelling schools run by men called *lanistas*, many were professionals. As former slaves or criminals they would have been freed and offered the chance to leave the *munera* because they had sufficiently impressed audiences with their ability and prowess over a number of fights. Nevertheless, the fix of adulation, the money and kudos earned from successful combat – some had many kills to their credit – led them back to the arena on their own terms. Both the professionals and the enslaved gladiators were fine specimens. It was customary for punters and curious onlookers to visit a designated area close to the amphitheatre on the eve of the fight where the 'last supper' could be witnessed. This offered the chance for both men and women to assess the apparent readiness of their heroes before deciding who to bet on. It was like visiting the paddock to check out the horses before making a bet at a modern racecourse.

According to Mark Corby, historian of Roman London: 'Some of the professional gladiators were superheroes; the equivalent of pop stars and football stars and American presidents all rolled into one and then glitzed on top of that.'

Following or alongside the mock-fights and displays of men and weaponry, there were sometimes animals performing tricks before the crowd in true circus style. Occasionally, the animals, including quite exotic creatures such as tigers and their cubs, were used in an elaborately staged re-enactment of a hunt, one of the Romans' favourite pastimes. To spice up the morning's entertainments there might be some bloodshed in the form of men fighting wild animals. Another day there were acrobatic performances. On display in the Museum of London is a leather bikini, one of four found in London's depths, which was probably the costume worn by a young acrobat performing in Londinium in or around the second century AD.

By noon the attention of the audience might be waning and this was always the appointed time to start the execution of the worst criminals: murderers, thieves, deserters, arsonists and Christians. Christians were deemed utterly treasonous because they refused to worship the gods of the state or to recognize the divinity of the emperor. Their execution in Londinium would have been a rare event, however, because of the predominantly pagan make-up of the early town.

The executions were only partly intended as entertainment; they were also meant as a warning and were therefore another form of Roman control. As a penalty, the lowest ranks of the criminal classes – criminal slaves and Christians – were sometimes made to fight wild beasts without armour or weapons. Otherwise they were forced to fight each other to the death, the winner having to fight again and again until he was himself killed. In this way Roman justice was served and the bloodlust of the crowd was stoked in anticipation of the real thing.

Mark Corby takes up the story: 'At this stage the sun is probably getting up quite high. The people have probably been drinking at lunchtime and the awning is pulled over so that those who are in the sun aren't going to suffer too much heat stroke. Every creature comfort is thought about.'

Signalling the start of gladiatorial combat, there was a parade before the sponsor of the games who would check the sharpness of the weapons, just as the Spanish inspect the bull's horns today to ensure they have not been blunted. The gladiators were paired off to fight in various ways and with different styles of dress and weaponry. For example, the 'netman' (*retarius*), evoking a fisherman, carried a strong net and a trident; he wore a high metal shoulder guard and had a *manica* – a protective quilted sleeve – on his left arm. He was pitted against the 'pursuer' (*secutor*) who had a helmet, a curved oblong shield and a dagger. There were about 20 different types of fighter, matched so that a well-armed lumbering giant would be pitted against an agile, smaller fighter, less cumbersomely equipped. 'An awful lot of thought has gone into this,' says Mark Corby. 'The crowd will be full of all the nuances of who wears what and why, and of their track record.'

When a fighter was wounded or at bay, he signalled his submission by raising the forefinger of his left hand. The crowd then yelled, '*Habet, hoc habet*' (he's had it) and they gestured or screamed out their wishes as to the fate of the wounded man. The decision was made by the game sponsor, the 'editor'. Sometimes he would decide that the man had fought feebly, in which case he would be forced to fight again, prompted to his feet with hot irons. Otherwise, the *editor* would make the life-or-death decision, usually following the will of the crowd, with a 'thumbs up' or 'thumbs down' gesture. The thumbs up – indicating a sword in the neck – meant death to the vanquished gladiator. The killing was ritual in its manner and it was to the honour of the defeated gladiator if he took his execution bravely and nobly. Ideally, he would kneel in front of the victor whose thigh he would clasp with both hands. The victor took hold of the doomed man's helmet or head to keep him steady as he thrust a sword through his neck. The ensuing silence of the crowd was then broken by trumpets heralding the arrival in the arena of a mysterious figure, with his face painted black. Carrying a large hammer, he was known as the Charon – a demon of the underworld associated by the ancient Greeks with the man you paid to transport you after death across the River Styx. His role was to check that the dispatched man really was dead. If the Charon found him still alive he would use his hammer to finish the job. Again from Mark Corby: 'At this stage fish hooks would be inserted under the dead man's ribcage and he would be dragged like a bull today across the arena to a gateway named after Libertina, the goddess of funerals.'

Although they were bloody beyond belief, the gladiatorial contests were deeply embedded in Roman culture. In times of peace they were a form of artificial battlefield; in times of war they were a means of encouraging preparedness or celebrating triumph. In Rome itself, they could be on a massive scale; the largest recorded contest lasted 100 days and involved 5,000 pairs of gladiators in an entertainment celebrating the triumph of Emperor Titus in AD 107. Such was their popularity that they continued until the sixth century. Even the Christian emperor, Constantine, who removed all evidence of pagan cults and celebrations, did not do away with this particular circus.

The intelligentsia was sometimes squeamish in an un-Roman way about these events. Seneca thought that the public executions were 'pure homicide'; Cassius Dio reports how one emperor, Marcus Aurelius, was disgusted by the bloodshed and thought that the gladiators 'should be like athletes fighting without risk of deadly harm', more like wrestlers – but his point of view was the exception. Cicero reports the scorn that a friend of his had for the contests because they were primarily entertainment for the lower classes. This is a more common theme. It was seldom that the cruelty of the fights jarred with more refined members of the audience at these entertainments. Mostly, the classical writers of the ancient Roman period report how badly behaved the crowd was: drunk, rowdy, smelly, yelling and screaming, sometimes fighting among themselves; they were the scum. Until the end of the Victorian era, the extraordinary level of noise of London's bustling streets could have taken its cue from the cacophony at these events.

It was Juvenal, the mostly poverty-stricken Roman poet from the 1st and 2nd centuries AD, who wrote in his *Satires*, 'two things only they earnestly desire: bread and the games of the circus'. His prescient words would prove to be relevant to the masses in cities for the next 1,900 years. In London, there has long been a slim line between communal party time and loss of control. Managing the crowd has always been a preoccupation of the capital's ruling elite.

Once the Romans had withdrawn from Londinium, leaving the gate open for an entirely different inhabitant, this type of public entertainment was soon lost to living memory. The shifting Anglo-Saxon communities in seventh-century Lundenwic enjoyed far less monumental communal activities. Perhaps some animal fights were scratched together; occasionally a thumbs or hand-amputation inflicted on a thief would draw interest, or a beheading would gather the crowd; chiefs honoured their men with feasts, the chance for drunken revelry. But large-scale communal entertainment was a low priority in the context of survival itself.

There was little official sanction for extravagant or overt partying once the Christian ethos, with its stark choice between salvation and eternal damnation, had become embedded in Anglo-Saxon culture. But London – complex, vibrant and cosmopolitan – always had an inclination towards excessive or unruly behaviour: Londoners have converted holy days into riots, Church 'entertainments' into bawdy and subversive theatre. They have capered, sung, gambled, danced, drunk, revelled, whored, fought, stolen, murdered and coveted each other's chattels, wives and husbands irrepressibly right through to the 21st century. In the absence of state-sanctioned extravaganzas in the Roman style, most of this activity took place on the streets.

⨾ STREETS, CARNIVALS AND MAY TIME ⨿

The streets of London have always allowed a passionate display of public feeling. From Roman times to the present day, Londoners have occupied them to parade in rituals, to protest and to introduce an element of anarchy into urban life, a life so often manacled by clerical or secular controls and poverty. Built around the weaving layout of Lundenwic (some of our city streets today still follow the original slightly haphazard grid of this time), the streets of London have provided myriad opportunities for merry-makers or evil-doers – sometimes one and the same – to enjoy themselves extravagantly and then disappear into the wings.

A character in the *Chronicle* written by Richard of Devizes, a monk from Winchester, may have been overly sour in his feelings about the people on these streets (Winchester was still a rival to London at this time), but he offers a vivid picture at the close of the 12th century:

> I do not like that city. All sorts of men crowd together there from every country under the heavens. Each race brings its own vices and its own customs to the city. No one lives in it without falling into some sort of crimes. Every quarter of it abounds in grave obscenities . . . Whatever evil or malicious thing that can be found in any part of the world, you will find in that one city. Do not associate with the crowds of pimps; do not mingle with the throngs in the eating houses; avoid dice and gambling, the theatre and the tavern. You will meet with more braggarts there

than in all France; the number of parasites is infinite. Acots, jesters, smooth-skinned lads, Moors, flatterers, pretty boys, effeminates, pederasts, singing and dancing girls, quacks, belly-dancers, sorceresses, extortioners, night-wanderers, magicians, mimes, beggars, buffoons: all this tribe fill all the houses. Therefore if you do not want to dwell with evil-doers, do not live in London.

There are moments here of today's Camden Market or Covent Garden on a Saturday afternoon; reminders of the Notting Hill Carnival; flashes of Oxford Street during most shopping days; and a sense of Leicester Square, Old Compton Street, Shaftesbury Avenue and Piccadilly Circus on a summer night.

At night time in medieval London, the dilemma of controlling the streets was most acute. London's rulers were only too aware that if they let people roam about the streets at night they were playing with fire. Roamers congregated; congregators grumbled and shared the stomach-driven energy of the mob. Following the Conquest, one of William I's early actions was to institute an eight o'clock curfew to keep his newly conquered population off the streets. Edward I followed suit on his accession in 1272. Little changes. In 1997, an evening curfew and enforced bedtime were among the initiatives mooted by New Labour policymakers in an attempt to keep vandals and troublemaking youths off the streets in the evening – also to make sure everyone was fresh for school in the morning. Of course, the idea was never implemented because sensible officials realized that healthy, full-blooded 16-year-olds in the UK's inner-city estates were even less likely to take notice of Wee Willy Winky than the citizens of London in the medieval period, when attempts at regulation were commonplace and frequently ignored.

In 1409, there was considerable outrage among the aldermen of the Corporation of London at the 'disgraceful sport' whereby groups of men and women would 'capture' one another on the streets of London. The kidnappers held each other hostage until friends paid for their release. Another record for the same year shows that the authorities clamped down on other street-based activities, including unruly football gatherings and 'throwing at cocks'. 'John Kelsey, William Bonauntre, Ralph Spayne, Thomas Wade, Robert Hebbe and

William Bullock, tapissers, and John Port and Philip Tayllour, parishioners of St Dionis Backchurch', were in bond 'for their good behaviour towards the mistery of Cordwainers, and that none of them would in future collect money for a football, or money called cock-silver for a cock, hen, capon, pullet or other bird or for any other use, and that they would not thrash any hen or capon or any other bird in the streets and lanes of the city, under penalty of £20'.

Londoners who occupied the night streets were particularly intim-idating if they went masked. Not only did anonymity encourage people to act in ways they would not dare bare-faced, but disguises made it very difficult for criminals to be caught and brought to justice. Small surprise then that, in 1418, we find that men are forbidden to walk out at night with painted faces and other disguises because 'pepul fell to letcherie, songs and dances, with harping and singing, and also to glotony and sinne; and so turned the holiness to cursydness'.

The urban authorities could not solve the dilemma easily. Should they allow a certain amount of unrestrained dissipation, so that there was a kind of built-in fuse for society; or should they try to regulate pleasure so tightly that all pursuits of indulgence of the mind and senses had to be state-approved? Medieval Britain came to a compromise which still informs to some extent the way we enjoy ourselves today. For certain periods of the year, the church – with the full compliance of the secular authorities – made vice a virtue by instituting the carnival.

In medieval Europe, carnival was a time when the world was turned upside down. This was the chance for the underdog to have some status and for religious proprieties and secular authority to be ridiculed, if only for a short time. The Church sanctioned the heady, excessive, even perverse, activities that took place. In continental Europe lepers would serve bread to customers, prostitutes dress up as queens, fools be crowned and briefly rule as kings, and ultra-real-istic pictures of bottoms be painted on a diptych (an artistic device traditionally used to display religious icons). In 1495, the Theological Faculty of Paris summed up the state that the Church had come to during the carnival period: 'Priests and clerks may be seen wearing masks and monstrous visages at the hours of office. They dance in the choir dressed as women . . . They eat black puddings at the altar while the celebrant is saying mass ... they cense with stinking smoke from the soles of old shoes. They run and leap through the church.'

London had its own 'Lords of Misrule'. Employed by the Court, the Lord Mayor, the Inns of Court and the sheriffs of London, these men had the role of putting a rocket under the status quo – just for the duration. Elizabethan commentator John Stow writes that these extraordinary events provided 'the rarest pastimes to delight the beholders'. But it seems likely that subversion was the commonest thread of these entertainments. In the Inns of Court – where various kings, including a 'King over Cockneys' were voted in throughout the Christmas period – the atmosphere must have been much like that of rag week today. At one Christmas carnival, in 1516, things went too far. A certain 'Jack Straw', who was named after an infamous leader in the Peasants' Revolt in 1381, broke down the doors of the Inns of Court with his followers. He was fined and banned from any future appearances.

Writing in the 1500s, Polydor Vergil describes how the 'mock kings' were appointed from the ranks of underlings but, at Christmas time at least, activities often took place in the households of major and minor nobility. On one occasion at the Temple, lawyers invited none other than Queen Elizabeth's favourite, Lord Robert Dudley, to be their Lord of Misrule: the 'Prince Palaphilos'. On St Stephen's Night, the dashing courtier was joined by the Lieutenant of the Tower of London. Both were dressed immaculately in white armour. As had been the case throughout his period of 'rule' a fabulous feast was planned to last the whole night. But before the company sat down to eat they were entertained by the gory sight of a cat and a fox being hunted by a score of hounds within the hall. Needless to say the notion of the underdog becoming all-powerful did not apply to the animal kingdom at these festivities.

May and Whitsun were times when Londoners had the greatest chance to indulge in carnivalesque excess. Although May ales and games are more commonly associated with the countryside, Londoners loved them too and the May fairs were often events that recalled the pagan celebrations and springtime excesses of the pre-Christian period. We should remember that London, throughout its extraordinary history, has been a magnet drawing fortune-seekers and people dislocated from rural areas, sometimes in vast numbers, from all over the British Isles. Moreover, London was in itself 'rural' in its suburbs, greener in its central gardens by comparison with today. At the May celebrations contemporary reports show that heavy petting and sex were the order of the day:

> Maidens and matrons are groped and handled with unchaste hands, and kissed and dishonestly embraced; the things, which nature hath hidden, and modestly covered, and oftentimes by means of lasciviousness made naked . . . many maidens have been unmaidened . . . [these festivities were] the storehouse and nursery of bastardy.

Lords of Misrule were also appointed in May when the festivities revolved around the May tree or maypole. Maypole dances and games were nothing like the dainty dances occasionally revived today and usually performed by confused children tangling themselves in streamers. These festivities were far gutsier affairs. People would be sent out at night to gather foliage to decorate the pole, although more than the woodland flowers was apparently plucked. The nocturnal rites are referred to by Philip Stubbes in his pamphlet *Anatomy of Abuses* (1583), which is a fountain of disapproval. He thoroughly disliked the importance given to the maypole: 'Twenty or forty yoke of oxen, every ox having a sweet nosegay of flowers tied on the tip of his horns, and these Oxen draw home this may-pole (this stinking Idol rather).' He describes how the celebrants gad about in the woods, groves and hills, 'where they spend all night in pleasant pastimes'. Apparently plenty of 'bussying' went on; some of the boys returned with handkerchiefs and other trophies from the girls, which they would display the following day. Stubbes confirms one's suspicions: 'I have heard it credibly reported by men of great gravity, credit and reputation, that of forty, three-score, or a hundred maids going to the wood overnight, there have scarcely the third part of them returned home again undefiled.'

During the reign of Henry VIII the custom of bringing in the maypole was accompanied by 'diverse warlike shows . . . and other pastimes all day long and towards the evening they had stage plays and bonfires in the streets'. Morris-men arrived with their faces blackened, imitating the devil, the Turk or the Moor, after whom they were named. Records show that the Lord of Misrule and his followers occasionally invaded churches; Stubbes describes one particular crowd as 'bawdy', 'madmen' and 'like devils incarnate'; the Lord of Misrule himself was 'Satan, prince of hell'. Stubbes was a consistent detractor of anything that had the potential to get out of hand, but the May festivities clearly touched a raw nerve with their pre-Christian implications. With such customs as 'warding off the evil eye' they brought diabolic images and activities right into the heart of society. Stubbes was not alone in thinking that these Maytime festivities threatened to subvert the common order sufficiently to damage the 'body politick' itself, turning the world upside down, bringing about total sexual indulgence and corporal excess.

But, for most Londoners, the return of spring really was a good reason to celebrate. Many would have spent the winter freezing and hungry, surviving on a diet of salted meat and gritty bread.

At this time premarital sex was still an accepted part of most young people's lives. The absence of court cases involving drunkenness and ribaldry around May time indicates that, where possible, both the secular and the Church authorities turned a blind eye to what was going on. Young people, or 'younglings' as they were sometimes called, were even afforded special reverence at springtime and their pleasures were celebrated in the pop(ular) songs of the day:

> Worship ye that lovers bene this May,
> For of your blisse the Kalendis are begonne;
> And sing with us, Away, winter, away!
> Come, summer, come, the suete sesoun and sonne . . .

> The fields breathe sweete, the daisies kisse our feete,
> Young lovers meete, ol wives a sunning sit,
> In every streete these tunes our ears do greete . . .

In 1492, Henry VII gave ten shillings 'to the maidens of Lambeth for a May'. Youthful mock kings and queens were crowned; there are records in the 1540s of the 'king-game' being sent between the two Surrey market towns of Kingston-upon-Thames and Croydon. With the sap rising there must have been plenty of cuckolds around at this time. And true to the licentious spirit of the season, duped husbands were the subject of open mockery. In 1562, some of the city's butchers and fishermen 'made great cheer' around a maypole that they had set and decorated with horns. With this they mocked every unfortunate man who had spent a night alone in a cold bed while his wife enjoyed the attentions of some hot-blooded youth.

The combination of youthful bright sparks, an atmosphere of revelry and anarchy and the consumption of a lot of ale did sometimes prove too much, even for authorities indulging their citizens. An enormous maypole, higher than the steeple of nearby St Andrew's Church, was erected in Cornhill. It was first mentioned in a poem in the 1380s, which indicates that – at that time – it was a permanent feature. According to John Stow, the May Day riots in 1517 sent such shockwaves through London that the maypole was taken down and abandoned in a nearby alley, where it lay for years. The riots were remembered as 'Evil May Day'. In 1547, the Corporation of London encouraged property owners to punish servants who attended May games; two years later the inflammatory Cornhill maypole was itself ceremoniously burnt by a Protestant curate.

In 1554, the Privy Council banned May games because 'lewd practices . . . are appointed to be begun at such assemblies'. Although other forms of mass entertainment were becoming more popular – and frequent – by the end of Elizabeth's reign, there must still have been some May celebrations during the 1570s because the ranks of 'the watch' (the closest the Elizabethans got to a police force) were doubled to deal with any fracas.

A great stickler for sex in the right place, Oliver Cromwell, father of nine, was firm in banning the erection of maypoles. They were a 'heathenish vanity, generally abused to superstition and wickedness'. As a result, the pagan culture surrounding May festivities seems to have been successfully discouraged during the Commonwealth period, though some wealthy Londoners certainly preserved their sensual spirit. At one May celebration it was reported that ladies rode 'round and round, wheeling of their coaches about and about, laying of the naked breast, neck and shoulders over the boot, with lemon and fan-shaking' in order to attract the attention of 'vain roisteres'. Today's May funfair in the suburbs, with the hurley-burley or the 'waltzers', the 'twister', the 'wall of death' and with Britney's latest single blasting through the speakers, has much the same sexual charge.

Ironically it was the Puritan repression of May rituals that probably did much to ensure that they survived well into the 18th century. Celebrating the tide of liberty that swept London's streets as Charles II arrived in triumph on 29th May 1660, maypoles were set up throughout London. The Lord Mayor of London removed one erected by 'the rabble' in Cheapside. And barely one year after Charles's restoration, 12 sailors, supervised by the Duke of York (the future James II), put up the most 'prodigious' maypole of all, around 134 feet tall, in the Strand opposite Somerset House. This area was the focus of Londoners' Restoration celebrations for the next 50 years.

In the 18th century the May festivities in London were taken over by the city's sweeps and milkmaids. A leading figure called Jack-in-Green was still there as a subconscious reminder to the crowds that came to watch of the roots of the celebration in earth-worship. The theme of upturning the social order was still there too. One report tells us that the sweeps had their soot-ingrained faces whitened with meal, wore powdered periwigs and pinned paper lace to their filthy, ragged clothes. The milkmaids piled their heads high with silver – usually borrowed from pawnbrokers. As Peter Ackroyd points out in *London the Biography*, the butchers provided a slightly morbid musical accompaniment, banging their cleavers against gory marrow-bones. But by the early 19th century, May festivities in London were starting to lose their highly coloured, lascivious atmosphere.

London was, however, left with two important legacies: an area still known as Mayfair, and a deep-seated mistrust of street celebrations. A passage in an official document written by Henry Fielding, while he was a Westminster magistrate, shows how the streets were often viewed as malicious and threatening – a real urban jungle. Asked to write 'An Inquiry into the Recent Increase of Robberies in the Metropolis' in 1751, he did so, with palpable nervousness:

Whoever indeed considers the Cities of London and Westminster, with their late vast addition of their Suburbs; the great irregularity of their Buildings, the immense Number of Lanes, Alleys, Courts and Bye-places; must think that, had they been intended for the very Purpose of Concealment, they could scarce have been better contrived. Upon such a View, the whole appears as a vast Wood or Forest, in which a Thief may harbour with as great Security, as wild Beasts do in the Deserts of Africa or Arabia.

In 1770 there was general rejoicing in the streets on the release of the popular London politician, John Wilkes, from a spell in the King's Bench Prison. He was a great carouser and clubman in his day and former member of both the Sublime Society of the Beefsteaks and of Sir Francis Dashwood's Medmenham Monks (see page 57). His stay in the King's Bench would not have taxed him unduly; this was not Newgate but primarily a prison for debtors and it was served by a courtyard full of more than 100 traders. Wealthy prisoners, or those, such as Wilkes, who had wealthy friends, could be comfortable and eat and drink well. Most pleasures could be bought at the King's Bench.

A German visitor, quoted in *London The Biography*, reported on the nature of the crowd's reception of Wilkes witnessed from a coach: 'Now I know what an English mob is . . . half-naked men and women, children, chimney sweeps, tinkers, Moors and men of letters, fish-wives and elegant ladies, each creature intoxicated by his own whims and wild with joy, shouting and laughing.'

Much later, in the Victorian period, the London crowd is viewed in a far more dystopian light. Observers and journalists who aimed to shed light on the horrific conditions of the poor, such as the Calvinist James Grant in his work *Lights and Shadows of London Life* (1841), perceived London's streets as the home of the 'London Underworld' – literally a hell for lost souls. In the poorest areas, the streets were crowded and squalid. David Kerr-Cameron in *London's Pleasures from Restoration to Regency*, writes:

. . . in the teeming, claustrophobic courts and stinking alleys, the capital's poor and huddled masses bickered and sweated and loved and drank to excess, living out their lives without hope or dignity in the common glare in their tinder-box ghettos.'

He paints a vivid picture of the disorder and diversion of the streets:

Girls trailed lethargic asses whose milk (fresh from the teat on the doorstep) was said to be beneficial to babies; oyster-sellers trundled their barrows (selling by weight); young mop-selling maidens touted their merchandise bundled on their heads; fruit sellers made their rounds similarly burdened; and so came tinkers and pot-menders, bellows-repairers and rush-seat menders; hot-food vendors and their 'hot pudding pies' and 'hot codlings' [apples]; sellers of sea-coal and discordant knife-grinders; and chimney sweeps trailing sooty child assistants . . . There was scarcely a single commodity that did not come calling at the citizen's door, or into the shadowed confines of the court it spilled into.

Amid this mêlée, among the throng would be the timeless wandering entertainers: jugglers, acrobats, tumblers, strongmen and stuntmen, the buskers of their day fighting for the best corners to catch a passing penny. In Victorian times, some of this crowd would spill into the more prosperous thoroughfares such as the Strand and Regent Street where the other world conducted its business, trying to remain as blissfully unaware as possible of the lives of the unlaundered poor.

Congregation on the streets remains a headache for the metropolitan authorities. Oxford Street at almost any time is a pulsing mass; moving rapidly, the crowd is worked by pickpockets, street hawkers and sharpers and their stooges playing 'find the lady'. Like London itself, the jostling host is so solid it hardly notices the parasites. Beggars, buskers, shoplifters, militant evangelists move in a peristaltic wave alongside curious day-visitors and tourists, bargain-hunters, office- and shop-workers. But shopping keeps the stream flowing, CCTV cameras watch patiently and the slow-moving traffic works as a kind of unpaid police force, unwittingly separating and watching the crowd. There are more controls here even than when peaceful marches and rallies are organized, blocking streets or thronging Hyde Park. Then there is May Day, which brings the anti-capitalist protestors and the disenfranchised left wing out in force and often in bad humour. More mundane is the watchful cordon on mass movements to and from Highbury or Stamford Bridge and other football grounds for Saturday and mid-week games; or the policing of the permanent bustle of the street markets, the boulevard congress of Covent Garden, the night-time throng in theatreland.

Not least, the Notting Hill Carnival has a long history of mutually polite mistrust between organizers and authorities. Hundreds of thousands of people from all over London and outside flock to this most famous and vibrant of modern-day London carnivals. It is almost compulsory for newspapers to carry a picture of smiling police officers dancing or posing with flamboyant revellers to show how well it went. So great is the nervousness, so great the relief. No one was seriously hurt, blind eyes were turned; we all had a jolly good, culturally-integrated time. Thus the carnival, which some believe started in Catholic Europe and made its way over to the slave colonies where it was given a southern hemisphere tang, has reasserted itself in chilly Northern Europe.

✑ ELIZABETHAN THEATRE ✑

There are periods in history when the pulse of creativity, excitement and change is almost tangible. Elizabethan London was one of them: a time when the population doubled in size and appetite; when the promises of global exploration, bringing gold and spices, wrought a sense of wonder and aspiration; when men and women of few means and some imagination became great entrepreneurs. Most of all it was the time when Londoners' vision was fed and charged by the theatre, a drama of extraordinary richness. This was the new entertainment phenomenon. Just as films would be 350 years later, theatre became the new pleasure of the city, playwrights and actors the darlings of society. The spotlight of the known world was on the Elizabethan and Jacobean stage which was both intensely cerebral and immensely popular.

If the quality of the theatrical experience was exceptional, so was the quantity and range of productions. By the time of Shakespeare's death in 1616 around a dozen new theatres had been established and at least 800 new plays had been written and remain as testimony. Hundreds more plays have been lost, some perhaps destroyed by passionate poets dissatisfied with their work; many others swallowed in the even less forgiving conflagration of the Great Fire in 1666. This prodigious fountain of ideas and talent was unparalleled throughout Europe. As a foreign visitor, Fynes Moryson noted in 1617, 'there be, in my opinion, more Playes in London than in all the partes of the worlde I have seene, so doe these players or Comedians excel all other in the worlde'. In the second act of Shakespeare's *Hamlet*, there is a tidy summary of the acting ability on offer too: 'The best actors in the world, either for tragedy, comedy, history, pastoral, pastoral-comical, historical-pastoral, tragical-historical, tragical-comical-historical-pastoral, scene individable, or poem unlimited.'

There have been times of dearth but London today, with more than 40 theatres in the West End alone, is still the theatre capital of the world.

Of course, the London in which Elizabeth I was crowned in 1558 and the one in which Shakespeare arrived about 30 years later had always had its pick of entertainers. Centuries of Londoners would have looked forward to the arrival of mummers, tumblers, travelling minstrels, or even over-enthusiastic amateurs such as the fraternity of skinners, who were banned in 1385 from mounting any more nativity plays in London 'because the plays became so noisome'. The entertainment was mostly of street calibre, the acting was unrefined and the material was the same as ever with minor revisions to suit evolving tastes. For example, a typical mummers' play always involved a champion, usually a Christian hero such as St George, fighting an infidel knight. When one of the duo is killed the doctor steps out and with much ado brings the slain man back to life. Thus, the resurrection story is re-enacted with some jokes and posturing; drums are beaten; a tabard is played by a minstrel-cum-penny-collector; a jig is danced; the players fold away their props and move on. These were side shows heralding something far more dynamic.

In early 16th-century London, the precursors of the purpose-built theatres took two forms. One was the home of the small professional group of actors performing in halls, inns or marketplaces. There was the Cross Keyes and the Bell in Gracious Street (today's Gracechurch Street), the Bull in Bishopsgate and the Belle Sauvage (also known as the Bel Savage Inn) on Ludgate Hill. Going to a show at the inn-playhouses was an exciting and anarchic outing. The performers often had to muscle their way through the crowd to reach the performance platform; dressing rooms were in the stables. Both performers and the bulk of the audience risked attack by flying missiles, hurled down by the slightly more affluent who could afford seats in the galleries.

The second type of theatre, peculiar to London, was made up of amateurs, mostly university students, who performed for the royal court and assorted gentry. Audience and actors were educated, acquainted with the classics and probably knew something about other theatre styles in Europe. The stage had painted canvases placed on removable lathes.

But it was the feisty professionals not the courtly amateurs who developed the London theatre. Despite or probably thanks to their rollicking atmosphere, the itinerant professional venues commanded increasing audience loyalty and became successful financial concerns. Around the 1570s there were some regular 'Companies of Players' attached to the inns. They were mistrusted by the Common Council who decreed in 1574: 'That no innkeeper or tavern-keeper . . . within the Liberties of this City shall openly show or play . . . within his house-yard . . . any play.'

Why did these prototype theatres seem such a threat? One of the theatre's perennial strengths has been its ability to lift an emotional lid off an audience. Visit a West End show today and you can tell the difference between a pre-show and an interval audience with your eyes closed. The sense of excitement and sheer volume of debate is palpable after an hour or more of witnessing someone else's version of the world. But add to this emotion a volatile, drunken crowd, and for a state such as Elizabeth I's, with insubstantial policing powers, the threat of the mob perhaps seemed only a step away.

In a grumble of some magnitude and length, the city elders made it clear that the playhouse companies embodied an impressive range of dangers to the good citizens of London. They refer to 'the inordinate haunting of great multitudes of people, especially youth, to plays, interludes and shows . . . the occasion of frays and quarrels, evil practices and incontinency in great inns, having chambers and secret places adjoining to their open stages and galleries'. Here, said the writers of this proclamation, there was 'inveigling and alluring of maids, especially orphans and good Citizen's Children under Age, to privy and unmeete Contracts, the publishing of unchaste, uncomely and unshamefast speeches and doings'. It does not stop there. The inn-playhouses were responsible for the 'withdrawing of the Queen

Majesty's subjects from divine service on Sundays and holy days, at which time such plays were chiefly used, unthrifty waste of the money of the poor and fond persons, sundry robberies by picking and cutting of purses, uttering of popular, base and seditious matters'. In full steam now, the diatribe adds that there were 'many other corruptions of youth, and other enormities'. And not content with the moral perfidy of the theatres, the authorities warn of the physical dangers: 'besides that also sundry slaughters and mayhemings of the Queen's Subjects have happened by ruins of Scaffolds, frames, and Stages, and by engines, weapons, and powder used in plays'. The 'powder' referred to is gunpowder rather than stage make-up. The Elizabethans were keen to introduce all kinds of pyrotechnics into their plays, whether in the form of fireworks, musket fire or momentous explosions to jolt the crowd.

In 1580, the Privy Council levelled further objections when they laid down instructions '. . . to thrust out the players from the City, pull down the playing and dicing-houses within the Liberties' because '. . . the presence of private rooms led to immorality, gambling, intemperance, gathering of Vagrants and masterless Men, Theaves, horse-stealers, Cozeners, practisers of Treason . . . leading to drunken affrays and blood shed and [riots by] . . . Apprentices and Factions'. You will note that apprentices often appear amongst the culprits when it comes to mobbish behaviour in London.

So theatre was banned from the city – but Privy Councillors and City Magistrates alike had no hope of beating back this particular tide. The bright sparks who championed this new movement were not going to be bullied into submission. The actor James Burbage (who later performed with Shakespeare, but started life in the inn-playhouse at the Cross Keys) had a practical solution. In spring 1576, he built the first permanent theatre, simply known as the Theatre in Shoreditch, just outside the city limits. In 1577, Henry Lanman followed suit when he opened the Curtain, about 200 yards away. This venue was later known as The Green Curtain because of its vividly painted front doors.

Suddenly new entertainment zones were taking hold throughout London. The area that included the Theatre and the Curtain became a popular pleasure spot, with Finsbury Fields right next door where gentlemen indulged in bowling and other sports. In January 1587,

Philip Henslowe and a grocer called John Chomley opened the Rose, on the corner of Rose Alley and Maiden Lane on Bankside. The Swan was then built at West Bankside by the wily goldsmith Francis Langley in 1595-96.

Henslowe was the archetypal new age Elizabethan entrepreneur. He married a wealthy widow and with her money came to own good property in Southwark, including inns and lodging houses. He was involved in various wharf-side businesses such as dyeing, starch-making and wood-selling. He also had a hand in pawnbroking and money-lending, bull and bear-baiting as well as turning good money at the theatre. Various professional companies, each sponsored by an Elizabethan noble (thus 'The Admiral's Men', 'Prince Henry's Men', 'The Earl of Leicester's Men'), acted at the Rose under Henslowe's financial management. Many first performances of great plays were shown there: Robert Greene's *Friar Bacon and Friar Bungay*, Thomas Kyde's *The Spanish Tragedy*, Christopher Marlowe's *The Jew of Malta*, and William Shakespeare's *Henry IV, Part I*.

Then in 1598, James Burbage – clearly an impresario with as much courage as conviction – pulled off a fantastic practical feat and publicity stunt rolled into one. He and his sons pulled down the Theatre and resurrected it south of the river, renaming it the Globe. To compete with this theatre, Henslowe and Edward Alleyn, another great Elizabethan actor, set the trend for London's West End by building the Fortune in the western suburbs. Meanwhile, the higher class 'private' theatre at Blackfriars was built on the site of the old priory there.

The social web surrounding the theatre was extensive. The Mermaid Tavern was a favourite spot for a theatrical rendezvous and here the glitterati and literati met on the first Friday of every month: playwrights such as Ben Jonson, Francis Beaumont and John Fletcher; the architect Inigo Jones and the poet John Donne. The Tavern was allegedly founded by Walter Raleigh, and Beaumont describes the discourse there:

What things have we seen
Done at the Mermaid! Heard words that have been
So nimble and so full of subtle flame.

Antique Roman bronze statues. The phallus was a dominant and potent symbol
during Roman times and was central to many festivals celebrating fertility.

Gambling in an Elizabethan brothel. Gambling and sex were
often joined at the hip, as were gambling and sport.

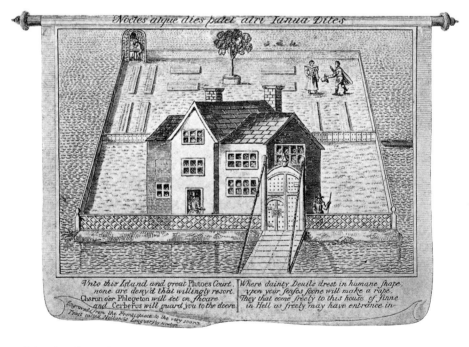

Noctes atque dies patet atri Ianua Ditis

Vnto this Island and great Plutoes Court, | *Where dainty Deuils drest in humane shape,*
none are denyd that willingly resort. | *vpon your senses soone will make a rape,*
Charon oer Phlegeton will set on shoare | *They that come freely to this house of sinne*
and Cerberus will guard you to the doore | *in Hell as freely may have entrance in*

A Southwark 'stew' or brothel on the notorious Bankside. Bankside has a remarkable sexual
history; even the Domesday Book records 16 brothels on Bankside; and arch-puritan Oliver
Cromwell had difficulty repressing them nearly 600 years later.

Victorial sexuality was heavily repressed but thinly veiled. The new art of photography boosted the popularity of pornography during the era.

Transvestite Chevalier d'Eon, also known as Mademoiselle de Beaumont. This engraving was published in *The London Magazine* in September 1777. The first recorded cross-dressing male prostitute was in 1395. Sporting himself as 'Elinour', John Rykener was caught 'committing that detestable, unmentionable and ignominious vice' beneath a lace stall in Soper Lane.

The angelic Nell Gwynn in an engraving by R. Thompson. Nell Gwynn was among the first females allowed on the London stage and quickly became a sex goddess and the adored mistress of the Merry Monarch. Gwynn was reported to have been rich enough, courtesy of King Charles II, to gamble away £1,200 in one night.

La Vice Anglaise was always popular, with specialist flagellant houses catering for London's needs – never more so than during the sexually repressed 19th century. Here police are raiding a house of ill repute.

The interior of the Fortune Theatre. Similar in design and dimension to the Globe Theatre, the Fortune was built in 1600. Londoners' vision of the world was fed and charged by the theatre during the Elizabethan and Jacobean periods.

INDUSTRY AND IDLENESS.

Tyburn offered the handy combination of standing and sitting space for the mob and the gentry, and a suitable build-up to the execution in the slow procession of the condemned from Newgate Prison.

Music and dancing at Vauxhall. The band play for the dancers from a beautifully illuminated bandstand while, away from the lights, there are plenty of venues for illicit liaisons.

VAUXHALL GARDEN.

Life's but a walking shadow a poor player
That struts and frets his hour upon the stage

Drawn & Engraved by Thos. Lan

The most famous of all the great trade fairs was Bartholomew Fair in West Smithfield. By the time it was abolished in the 1850s, there was virtually no trading (of an innocent kind) done at all.

SEPTEMBER

There was no time like show time. Bartholomew Fair gained a reputation for excess of every kind – from freak shows to sex. General cavorting sometimes lasted for a fortnight.

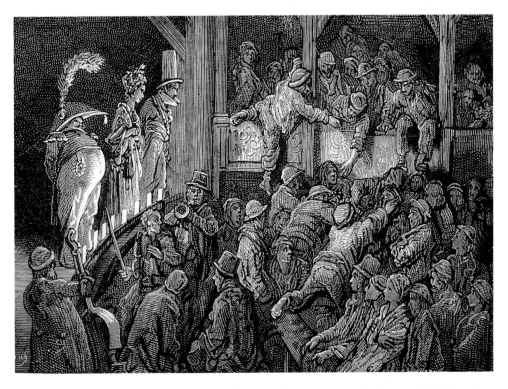

Audience and actors at a 'Penny Gaff'; not only a popular entertainment for impoverished Victorian youngsters, Penny Gaffs were one of the few havens from life in the streets and tenements.

Oliver Cromwell condemned the May Day celebrations as a 'heathenish vanity, generally abused to superstition and wickedness'. By the time of the Commonwealth, May Fairs were starting to be associated with mobbish unrest and even rioting, but mostly they were times for communal celebration and youthful ardour.

Others met to gossip within St. Paul's, which appears to have had the atmosphere of modern-day Paddington Station when you've time to absorb it: delivery boys using it as a short-cut; lawyers discussing cases with clients; publishers setting up shop; it was also a centre for fashion and information and served as an employment exchange. The chattering classes strolled up and down the middle aisle known as 'Duke Humphrey's Walk' or 'Paul's Walk' enjoying, to quote King Lear: 'Talk of Court News . . . Who loses and who wins; who's in, who's out . . .'

The foibles and whims of the court were important to these creative men. Play-acting and animal-baiting (the theatre's very close cousin as explained below) were the means of currying favour at court and with the monarch. Both activities needed royal patronage to legitimize them. The 1572 Act for the Punishment of Vagabonds stipulated that players and 'bearwards' (those who kept or baited bears) who did not belong to a baron or other honourable person were to be deemed vagabonds and would be treated accordingly. During Elizabeth's reign, 150 companies became legitimately patronized. Apart from legitimizing the players, court patronage was also important for the status of companies and individual stars – and for company bank balances.

And it worked both ways. Just as corporations today get kudos for their association with a successful theatre, opera or dance company, or the hippest of visual artists, so the ability to present their own company at court ensured that courtiers could keep their own rating high with the monarch and Privy Council. And beware if you were a courtier who upset the leading lights of the London theatre. Shakespeare's *Hamlet* makes it clear that actors of this time were as powerful in creating or destroying public reputations as television publicity is today. You ignore the power of the playhouse at your peril: 'Good my lord, will you see the players well bestowed? Do you hear, let them be well used; for they are the abstracts and chronicles of the time: after your death you were better have a bad epitaph than their ill report while you live.'

The Master of Revels would choose the best productions on offer to entertain the monarch and the court, for instance at the lavish Christmas entertainments. The monarchs had always enjoyed their entertainers, and court patronage is a constant that stretches back to the Egyptians and earlier. For Queen Elizabeth, patronage had yet another dimension. The monarch was in the enviable position of being able to champion her delightful young men, Leicester included, against their sometime critics, the city and the Church. In 1574 – just when the Common Council were getting uppity about the rising popularity of professional theatre – the queen's support must have felt to her like a show of strength. She issued Letters Patent under the Great Seal of England to James Burbage, John Perkyn, John Laneham, William Johnson and Robert Wilson, all the Earl of Leicester's men:

> . . . to use, exercise and occupy the art and faculty of playing comedies tragedies interludes stage plays and other such like as they have already used and studied or hereafter shall use and study as well for the recreation of our loving subjects as for our solace and pleasure . . . providing the said comedies tragedies interludes and stage plays be by the Master of the Revels (for the time being) be seen and allowed and that the same be not published or shewen in the time of common prayer or in the time of great and common plague in our said City of London.

Plays were put on in a repertory format. It was rare for the same play to be performed on consecutive nights and each drama got a showing about once a month. For instance a company like the Admiral's Men put on 38 plays in the 1594–5 'season', 21 of which were new. The actors tended to live close to the theatres they appeared at most regularly. On the first afternoon of a new show you can imagine them walking to work, desperately reciting Marlowe's tragic drama or one of Shakespeare's monologues, trying to get the words to stick so as not to embarrass themselves in front of the crowd, who often made it their business to get the actors to lose their place.

Players were most popular if they were multi-skilled. Some started off life as tumblers, some as musicians, some as pyrotechnicians. In their earlier days the plays would have involved dramatic stunts and feats of skill. The evening would have finished on a physical high with jigs, acrobatic displays and clowning. The performers had to be athletic, energized and – to cut it in a cut-throat world – clever and charismatic.

Archaeologist digs in 1989 suggest that the Rose Theatre could seat 2,200 in what were probably smelly and cramped conditions. But with the kind of billing that Greene and Kyde had in the 1590s and Shakespeare soon afterwards, the crowd flocked to the performances. Apart from the occasional fair, the only other entertainment for the ordinary punter was bull or bear-baiting, or a visit to the stocks to pillory a thief. On a warm day, the atmosphere would have been sticky and noisome with heavy Thames-side odours of dyers, tanners, starchers and free-flowing sewage adding to the smell of the heckling and hooting audience. In *Jack Drum's Entertainment* Marston gives a good account of the olefactory dangers of the amphitheatres, in contrast to the more refined airs of the private theatres which became increasingly popular among the aristocrats.

> . . . A man shall not be choked
> With the stench of Garlick, nor be pasted
> To the barmy Jacket of a Beer-brewer.'

It was certainly a mixed audience that Shakespeare and his colleagues had to bear in mind when they wrote. Richard Burbage (actor, entrepreneur and son of James Burbage) introduced a ticketing policy of a flat one penny at the Globe. This proved hugely popular. Students from the Inns of Court, soldiers, captains, well-to-do artisans, servants, apprentices, nobles, traders and tourists – all attended. The poorest spent the afternoon closeted with the wealthiest from the city.

But benign equality was not to last. For an extra penny or two, the well-to-do were elevated to the gallery away from the 'groundlings'. Another penny could even get you a cushion. Aristocrats complained about the 'vagrant and lewd persons' who could be found at the theatres. Records show that theatre etiquette was closer to that of our stag nights than a night in today's West End. A slightly later source (1620) describes how:

> sometimes it is fortun'd, that the players were refractory; the benches, the tiles, the laths, the stones, Oranges, Apples, Nuts, flew about most liberally, and as there were Mechanicks of all professions, who fell every one to his owne trade, and dissolved a house in an instant, and made a ruine of a stately Fabrick.

And full of booze, audience members would have relieved themselves or 'pluck'd the rose' in one of London's many Rose Alleys of the time.

Because the work paid relatively well, and there was the kudos of becoming one of a charmed circle, the nefarious theatre trade nevertheless attracted numerous people of good pedigree. Christopher (Kit) Marlowe, tragically murdered in a tavern brawl, was tempted to be involved following his studies at Cambridge (where he was also recruited into the Elizabethan Secret Service). But this was commercial theatre and the great minds rarely lost sight of what their audience wanted. The poets and playwrights (including Shakespeare) often acted in the plays themselves, or directed them. The creators of the work knew immediately if their new show hit the mark – if it did not they would probably spend the most of the early evening picking food and other missiles out of their hair.

To capture the attention of the theatregoers and to charm them, the actors had to be good, the spectacle compelling, the comedy well timed and lewd, the tragedy cathartic without too much sentimentality. Shakespeare's power in this respect was pre-eminent. He caught and lifted the imagination of the crowd in such a way that they begged for more. For 20 years, from the 1590s until he retired to Stratford upon Avon, Shakespeare garlanded his audience with over a million words of poetic drama; more than 30 plays that carried profound insights into humanity, its exploits, grievances and joys. The breadth of Shakespeare's knowledge and imagination stunned the audience, as it continues to do today. As Virginia Woolf once put it in a lecture called *A Room of One's Own*, Shakespeare appeared to have 'consumed the grievances of the world'.

We have to remember that the audiences of the day were not always enjoying the products of Shakespeare's appetite for prose. The fare at the inn playhouses remained far closer to the ground. Thomas Platter, a visitor from Basle, leaves an account of an outing not long after he had watched *Julius Caesar* in the spanking new Globe theatre in 1599:

On another occasion I also saw after dinner a comedy, not far from our inn, in the suburb; if I remember right, in Bishopsgate. Here they represented various nations, with whom on each occasion an Englishman fought for his daughter, and overcame them all except the German, who won the daughter in fight. He then sat down with him and gave him and his servant strong drink, so that they both got drunk, and the servant threw his shoe at his master's head and they both fell asleep. Meanwhile the Englishman went into the tent, robbed the German of his gains, and thus he outwitted the German also. At the end they danced very elegantly both in English and in Irish fashion.'

This is not high art. It is gutsy good fun and revelry described by a foreigner. As is so often the case, it is the commentary of outsiders that offers a mirror on the times.

To some insiders in the Elizabethan theatre marketplace, Shakespeare was considered an outsider himself. In a society when smiles were often veneered and back-stabbing was becoming an art form, it is not surprising that fellow artists showed their teeth at the arrival of the twenty-something school teacher from the provinces. The first mention of Shakespeare in London's literary scene was from Robert Greene in a 1592 pamphlet, his nose distinctly lifted:

There is an upstart crow, beautified with our feathers, that with his *Tygers heart wrapt in a Players hide* supposes he is as well able to bombast out a blank verse as the best of you; and, being an absolute *Johannes Factotum*, is in his own conceit the only Shake-scene in a country.

Whatever this means exactly, it is clear that Greene takes a dim view of the bard.

The smelly and the poor were of course only part of the audience. Shakespeare wrote his hilarious, incisive and sublime verse to be appreciated by the brightest young things in London. Modish young men strutted their stuff in some of the extreme fashions of the time (England's reputation for sartorial restraint developed only in the 19th century). As one contemporary, Thomas Nash, wrote: 'England' was perceived as 'the players' stage of gorgeous attire, the ape of all nations' superfluities, the continual masquer in outlandish habiliments.'

Aristocrats and artisans alike were experiencing the influence of goods, foodstuffs and ideas from countries that their grandfathers never even dreamed existed. They were enjoying and creating the new craze for tobacco – on the evidence of Barnaby Rich's *The Honestie of this Age*, by 1614 there was one tobacco shop for every 30 Londoners. This was a generation determined to enjoy life. As one commentator put it in 1579: 'The realm aboundeth in riches, as may be seen by the general excess of the people in purchasing, in buildings, in meat, drink and feastings, and most notably in apparel.' And the trend continued. It has been estimated that the *beau monde* bought six times more luxury cloth in 1650 than they had done in 1600.

In *Cities in Civilisation*, Peter Hall estimates that, in 1600, London's ports were managing between two-thirds and three-quarters of the nation's trade. Increasingly exotic goods were brought in after voyages of exploration to Persia, Russia and, in Drake's case, a round-the-world trip. Britain's money supply was given a huge boost by the discovery of gold and silver in America. Merchants, traders and financiers were now generating incomes from business which rivalled those that the aristocracy derived from their land. There were new men with new ideas. Robert Herrick's father was a goldsmith, John Donne's an ironmonger. It's no coincidence that Shakespeare, the son of a tradesman, generated some of the most energetic and all-embracing flights of fancy known in the history of British literature. The newly buoyant capital seemed to inspire and stimulate the creative outpourings of its playwrights.

The theatres themselves became accomplished money-making ventures. Investors were keen to play a part. There was a well-oiled publicity machine too with posters or playbills going up early in the morning in the city, advertizing the shows on offer for that day. Considering that at their peak the theatres closed only for a month or so during Lent, the publicity material must have been a virtually permanent part of London's landscape (an Elizabethan would no doubt appreciate the flood of promotional flyers that arrive in our own capital every day). Additional money-spinners included performances on command. The very rich could buy out a venue for a candlelit soirée for favoured friends; or they could host a wedding party where the feasting and celebrations would be followed by a play.

The public appetite for Shakespeare, Jonson, Webster, Marlowe, Kyde, Herrick and others seemed to be insatiable in the first two decades of the 17th century. Peter Hall offers an estimate that around the time of his death in 1616, there were 40,000 watermen, principally catering for the South Bank theatres, and transporting between 3,000 and 4,000 people to the playhouses each afternoon. Plays were staged in mid-afternoon to make the best use of natural light (most theatres faced south for just that reason). On a clear night along the South Bank you must have been able to hear the roar and bellow of other theatre crowds.

Play-acting and animal-baiting of various kinds were close bed-fellows in the Elizabethan and early Jacobean periods. It is hard to imagine similar activities in the foyer of the Theatre Royal or the Aldywch today, but Elizabethan playgoers liked their afternoons to be spiked with blood, gore and savage spectacle. The monarch, courtiers and foreign dignitaries were also entertained by the bear and bull-baiting as much as by the plays, usually promoted by the same entrepreneurs. There has long been a misconception that the playhouses themselves doubled as arenas for bull and bear-baiting. Occasionally they may have done. But it is much more likely that these entertainments were concentrated in older 'bear yards', built similarly to the theatres and probably offering a design template for the more modern Elizabethan theatres.

Recent archaeological excavation at Benbow House on the South Bank appears to confirm that there were two bear-baiting arenas close to the theatres and that the owners or lessors of this land, in the early 17th century, were none other than Philip Henslowe and his close associate Edward Alleyn. These two had fingers in many pies, including the sale of bear meat throughout the South East – a handy spin-off once the bears had been baited beyond usefulness. In 1604, Alleyn and Henslowe were made joint Masters of the Bear, a royal office which put them in prime position to import animals to their bear yards and also to commission their deputy, Christopher Goff, to source fighting mastiffs all over the country.

The bears and bulls suffered relentlessly at the fights, but occasionally they revenged themselves on their tormentors. In one incident, in 1554, a blind bear broke loose and bit a man who later died of his wounds. The sport attracted massive audiences, packed like sardines around the arena at floor and upper gallery levels. On 13 January 1583, the galleries at William Paynes' Bankside bear yard collapsed under the weight of the crowd and seven people were killed and many more injured. One person who witnessed this was a man called John Field, who greatly disapproved of both the theatre and animal-fighting. His words offer a graphic account of the disaster:

> Being thus ungodly assembled, to so unholy a spectacle . . . the yeard, standings, and galleries being ful fraught . . . This gallery that was double, and compassed the yeard round about, was so shaken at the foundation, that it fell (as it were in a moment) flat to the ground, without post or peere, that was left standing, so high as the stake whereunto the bear was tied . . . In the fal of it, there were slaine five men and two women . . . Of all the multitude there, which must needed be farre above a thousande, it is thought by the judgement of most people, that not the third person escaped unhurt . . . For surely it is to be feared, beeside the distruction bothe of bodye and soule, that many are brought unto, by frequenting the Theatre, The Curtin and such like.

'Exit, pursued by a bear' is one of the most famous of all stage directions – occurring in Shakespeare's *The Winter's Tale*. To the modern reader, the image seems laughable and incongruous, but the idea of being chased by a bear had a great deal more meaning to the contemporary audience. They would have laughed loudly and nervously at this joke.

Many people today still believe that life in the past ran very slowly – long day stretching out after long day. This was certainly not the case in the capital. Here fashions and favours changed as fast as the plays themselves; the daily round of life in court and on the streets was rapid and exciting. There were dark times, of course. For a short period in 1583 and again in 1592 all theatres were closed because of the plague; the second closure was the longest. There were 11,000 plague deaths in the capital (about 6 per cent of the total population, the equivalent of losing about 400,000 of today's Londoners). Although food markets were scattered throughout the city, a bad harvest could still mean food shortages. Sometimes both actors and audience would go to the theatre not sure where their next meal would come from. But hardship focused the mind and in the capital there was a pragmatic bias to 'seize the day', along the lines suggested by the Roman poet Horace: 'While we chat, time runs meanly on; seize the day, not relying on the future in the slightest.'

Today we still enjoy the results of those Elizabethan Londoners' energy, imagination and determination to seize the day. Perhaps most of all though we enjoy Shakespeare who is the greatest playwright in history. After his death in 1616 the theatre rampaged on in London until Cromwell banned it summarily; far too much smut and sin was attached to allow this sort of thing to continue. The very welcome rebirth of the theatre in 1661, offered Londoners a great deal of bumptious material; the kind that permitted the fops and dandies in the audience not to hang on every word. The Restoration comedies were for belly laughs as Thomas Brown records in his satirical pamphlet, *Amusements Serious and Comical* (1700):

> When the humour takes in London, they ride it to death 'ere they leave it. The primitive Christians were not persecuted with half the variety that the poor unthinking beaux are tormented with upon the theatre; character is supplied with a smutty song, humour with a dance, and argument with lightning and thunder, and this has often reprieved many a scurvy play from damning. A huge great muff and a gaudy ribbon hanging at a bully's backside is an excellent jest.

Despite Shakespeare's temporary success at moving drama from the gut to the brain, it rapidly returned to the place where the people of London have nourished it most.

✆ BARTHOLOMEW FAIR ✆

London fairs were originally supposed to be for trade, not unlike the purpose of Olympia and Earl's Court today. But for ordinary Londoners the fairs meant pleasure time, a day or three to enjoy some real dissipation; to holler and laugh, drink excessively and take part in or just marvel at a truly bizarre range of entertainments.

The most famous of all fairs was Bartholomew Fair in West Smithfield. By the time it was abolished, there was virtually no trading (of an innocent kind) done at all, except for the odd stall selling 'Bartholomew babies' – gingerbread men – a standard souvenir. But the whimper of the fair's demise does little justice to its tumultuous history, and one that captures the essence of London at play.

Bartholomew Fair was started in 1133 by a monk called Rayer, who had founded the church and priory of St Bartholomew at West Smithfield. Appropriately, Rayer – who was regarded as almost a saint himself by his brethren – received his royal charter to set up the fair from Henry I for whom he had been a beloved court jester.

Rayer had a 'hands-on' approach to ministering to the salvation of the local population and visiting sailors. He knew how to attract the crowd and earned good money for the priory by juggling in the streets. The fair was a means of drawing the crowd and popularizing his priory and hospital. The early Bartholomew Fairs, lasting three days from 24 August each year, were usually opened with some artful wrestling followed by a more raucous wild rabbit hunt across the fields. At the same time scholars from the different London schools would gather to wrangle and dispute on grammar and logic. The Prior and his successors introduced Miracle Plays, Mystery Plays and Morality Plays as a means of edifying and entertaining the crowds. Over the years these were transformed to suit rougher tastes.

Gradually the fair became *the* place to trade in London. It drew merchants from all over Britain and from Europe, particularly businesses that involved clothes, leather goods, pewter and cattle. Alongside the ornate tents of the drapers and clothiers there were wooden trestles offering mousetraps, purses and pouches; hawkers, peddlers and costermongers touted their wares: ribbons, brushes, bells, pails and knives. Year by year, a huge variety of popular amusements were added to the spectacle: exhibitions, theatrical booths, tumblers, stilt-walkers, acrobats, mummers, mountebanks and 'merry-andrews'. In Peter Ackroyd's words: 'From the beginning of its fame there were puppet-shows and street performers, human freaks and games of dice and thimble, canvas tents for dancing or for drinking, eating-houses which specialized in roast pork.'

By the 14th century the murmurs and exchanges of earnest cloth-sellers and cattlemen were completely drowned out by the spectacle of jousts, tournaments and archery competitions. The site of the fair became the time-honoured place for duels and ordeal by battle. As in much of London pleasure-seeking, where there was delight, death soon played a hand. The site was also used for the public executions of popular enemies of the state such as William Wallace and Wat Tyler. After Henry VII had legalized 'boylinge in oyle' as a means of execution, a cook of the Bishop of Rochester's household was publicly boiled to death at Smithfields.

After the priory was dissolved in 1546, the almost ludicrously named Sir Richard Rich – later Lord Rich the Lord Chancellor – bought this once holy sanctuary and the place of numerous alleged miracles in earlier times. He paid a princely £1064 11s 3d for it and converted it to a town-house. Much of the site of the annual Cloth Fair was developed into a lattice of streets as London expanded at this time, but this was still the place where Londoners came in pursuit of pleasure for another 250 years and more.

By the time of the Restoration, Bartholomew Fair – celebrated for its joyous outrages in Ben Jonson's drama of that name in 1614 – was an extravaganza that lasted 14 exhausting days. Actors had their own enclosures and special theatrical booths and some of the actors were among the best in town because the theatres had to close during this particular fair, such was the competition. The plays themselves were often elaborate affairs involving complex mechanics to ensure that even the least cerebral in the crowd would be amazed and would pass on the word. Like today's Edinburgh festival fringe performers, players at the 18th-century London fairs strutted in costume in front of their tents advertising the next showing with improvised comic dialogues, or by doing mimes. The fine actors and mimes in Covent Garden today – where painted figures masquerade as statues which change attitudes when a coin is dropped – would have been at home at Bartholomew Fair.

One of the more famous of the itinerant showmen of the late 18th and early 19th centuries was a man called John Richardson, whose favourite haunts were Bartholomew Fair and Greenwich. He began life in the workhouse at Great Marlow and after graduating to cleaning cow-stalls in Islington, achieved fame in the capital as the developer of an impressive mobile theatre. Far from being a travelling wagon containing a few props to be wielded by scruffy actors, this was a splendid affair with upper and lower stages – one for the actors, the other for the dancers. There were painted sets and an excellent orchestra produced the solemn atmosphere so apt for Richardson's plays – usually tragedies. The actors themselves were first class and a number of them, including the legendary Edmund

Kean, later rose to distinction in the established playhouses having started their careers with Richardson.

Other canvas tents at Smithfield were set up by brazen or semi-discreet prostitutes depending on the degree of sanction of the day. These particular 'Bartholomew's babies' did good trade. But tent or no tent, punters could always find pleasure with the alfresco fruit ladies in nearby Cock Lane.

Other forms of low life gathered in plenty at Bartholomew Fair, including many pickpockets, or cut-purses. Visiting Frenchman César de Saussure was astonished and horrified by the fair: 'for the noise and uproar is so continuous and overwhelming, besides you run a perpetual risk of being crushed to death and also of being robbed, for I think that no cleverer pickpockets exist than in this country, and in every crowd you must beware, else your pockets will soon be picked and emptied'.

The 'exhibitions' and 'theatrical booths' referred to above included numerous freak shows: strongmen and women, dwarfs and giants, pie-eating fat boys, stuntmen who could dance on tight-ropes as well as the five-legged bull, the three-legged man and the Siamese twins. Jonson records that there was a sign displayed at the 'Shoe and Slap' that promoted 'THE WONDER OF NATURE, a girl about sixteen years of age, born in Cheshire, and not above eighteen inches long . . . Reads very well, whistles and all very pleasant to hear.' There was a 'Man with one head and two distinct bodies'. Among the freak shows, Jonson also records a 'Giant Man' and a 'Little Fairy Woman'. Later, Pepys, who loved this fair and its freak shows above all others in London, gives an account of a woman with three breasts who would suckle three babies at a time and offered to hire herself for this purpose at private entertainments.

Opportunistic mountebanks were always ready to lead the London crowd by the nose, wherever they gathered. An 18th-century handbill offers a real feast for the ghoulish. It invites spectators to:

the Commodious Room opposite the New Inn, Surrey side of Westminster Bridge, where for a shilling . . . the Ethiopian savage: this astonishing animal is of a different species from any ever seen in Europe, and seems to be a link between the Rational and Brute creation . . . also the Orang Outang . . . a calf with eight legs, two tails, two heads and only one body . . . and an extraordinary exploit done by a white mouse . . .

The charlatans who ran these shows would surely have been excited by the potential of genetic manipulation to add piquancy to such exhibits.

The early Victorians were just as keen to see what was on offer at Bartholomew Fair although this was by now the acknowledged home of low-life festivities with its attendant whores, thieves and appalling smells; not the place for the gentility. One famous handbill, passed round the streets of London in the run up to the Smithfield fair in 1842, reflects how openly the showmen raked the embers of popular taste:

EXTRAORDINARY PHENOMENON!!! This Greatest Wonder in the World. Now exhibiting Alive at the Globe Coffee House . . . a FEMALE CHILD WITH TWO PERFECT HEADS . . . Born at Wandsworth, Surrey, April 17th 1842. The public is respectfully informed that the child is now Living; and hundreds of persons has been to see it, and declares that it is the most wonderful Phenomenon of nature that they'd ever seen. Admission Id each. No Deception; if dissatisfied the Money Returned.

While freak shows took the fancy of some, the marvelling crowd was often silenced by an astonishing act of derring-do. David Kerr-Cameron's rich account of London excesses in *London Pleasures from Restoration to Regency*, refers to a performer who was 'a fire-eater who 'chewed' hot coals, blew a hot coal on his tongue into life with a bellows and cooked an oyster on it – before swallowing the entire mouthful. As a pick-me-up he gave himself a libation of flaming pitch, sulphur and wax.' Kerr-Cameron also records a strongwoman at Bartholomew Fair in 1816 'billed as the "French Female Hercules", Madame Gobert would sit several people on an average-sized table and then lift it (and them) by her teeth'.

In the late 18th century, the Corporation of London had already sought a number of times to suppress Bartholomew Fair. In a reference to Bartholomew Fair in an 1860 edition of Chambers *Encyclopaedia*, the writer says that:

In 1798 the question of abolishing the fair was discussed by the corporation. It had long since ceased to be a place of traffic, and was only considered as a haunt of amusement, riot and dissipation. The fair had latterly been attended only by the keepers of a few gingerbread stalls; and, in 1839, measures were first seriously adopted for its suppression. In 1840, the exhibitions were removed to Islington. Wild-beast shows were allowed, but dwarfs and giants were excluded.

Bartholomew Fair was one of a number of London fairs that gathered a reputation for excesses of every kind. Our Lady's Fair at Southwark took place in the hive of alleys, houses and shops in what is now Borough High Street. Flocking over London Bridge, Londoners had much to look forward to: a monkey swinging on a high-wire carrying a jug of water and spilling not a drop; dancing donkeys; the usual run of fat boys gorging on puddings to the disgust and delight of the crowd; midgets, dwarfs, giants, bare-fist fighters and sword-swallowers. Regulars at Bartholomew Fair would notice that Southwark had many of the same entertainments, but there would always be something new. In 18th-century London perhaps it would be the figure of Robert Cadman, a famous tightrope walker in his day, moving nimbly above the crowd blindfolded and with baskets attached to his feet. Otherwise they saw the strange animals brought from overseas, promoted in sundry advertisements:

> The living alligator or crocodile, lately arrived from the coast of Guinea, will be seen during the time of the Southwark Fair at the Hand and Dial over against the Queen's Arms Tavern; and the Crown Bird, lately arrived, to be seen at the Lamb near St George's Church.

Coffee-houses, alehouses and taverns all competed during fair time to show freakish and strange things to attract customers. One newspaper advertisement promotes a 'prodigy of nature' as follows: 'At Painters Coffee-house, over against the Fountain Tavern near Stocks Market, is to be seen an Eel, the largest ever seen in London, being 68 inches long, 22 thick, and weighing 34 pound 3 quarters . . .'
Some London fairs later developed their own peculiar character

and attractions. 'None was more bizarre than Charlton's Horn Fair,' says Kerr-Cameron, 'an occasion of cross-dressing and gender-bending' and:

> as if this was not enough, the wearing of horns was almost obligatory. The women that day had a licence to be bold. Soon, though, the behaviour of the fair crowds, never genteel, deteriorated into a vicious debauchery that even the most broad-minded among the masses found unacceptable. They left the fair to the riff-raff and the untender mercies of the magistrates.'

Daniel Defoe wrote of the:

> yearly collected rabble of mad people at Horn-Fair; the rudeness of which I cannot but think, is such as ought to be suppress'd . . . The mob indeed . . . take all kinds of liberties, and the women are especially impudent . . . giving themselves a loose to all manners of indecency and immodesty.

These fairs were disreputable in almost every way but they were at least regular, annual events that ordinary Londoners could look forward to as a temporary escape from the drudgery and hardships of day-to-day survival. Occasionally the fairs were temporarily shut down by magistrates, or stopped by royal proclamation, because of the justifiable fears that they would spread capital-based epidemics of the plague to the country. Usually this meant that the citizens had to make do with the streets and taverns. But as the capital grew steadily, Londoners went further afield to the villages of Hackney, Edmonton, Stepney, Fairlop, Camberwell, Peckham, Mitcham, Bow, Edmonton and Enfield, for their pleasures. They queued for hours for ferries to take them to the Whitsuntide and May fairs; they even caught coal-carts to get them to Greenwich.

On Sundays when the streets were distinctly quieter and there was very little in the way of cockpits or prize rings or fairs to amuse the crowds, many would travel across to Bedlam at Moorfields and pay tuppence a head to enjoy the rantings and moanings of the inmates.

Bedlam was originally opened in 1247 at Bishopsgate as the Priory of St Mary of Bethlehem, right under today's Liverpool Street Station. Henry VII granted it a charter as a hospital for the insane in 1547. Since then it attracted hosts of insatiably curious Londoners. The practice of charging an entrance fee started at about the time of the hospital's move from Bishopsgate to Moorfields, just north of the ancient London wall at Moorgate, in 1675. This sad form of public entertainment was finally stopped in 1770, on a commercial basis at least, when the authorities felt that the sightseers 'tended to disturb the tranquillity of the patients' by 'making sport and diversion of the miserable inhabitants.'

For the rich and poor alike these kinds of entertainment – as well as the opportunity to join the throng at a pillorying, or hanging festivals (of which more later) – were amusements to be taken seriously and in full spirit. Sometimes Mother Nature herself offered London's inhabitants the chance of a more spontaneous carnival, The Frost Fair. The Thames flows faster today than it did in the 16th to 19th century when the winters were also colder – some even refer to the period as a mini-ice age. In the winters of 1683–84, 1788–89 and 1813–14 the Thames froze over so completely that it was possible to set up stall for weeks on end on the river itself. In 1788–89, the ice caked the river completely between Putney Bridge and Rotherhithe.

In the 1683^84 freeze, John Evelyn described how he 'went across the Thames on ice (which was now become so incredibly thick as to bear not only whole streets of booths, in which they roasted meat, and had divers hops of wares, quite across as in a town, but coaches, carts and horses passed over) . . .' and within a month . . . '. . . coaches plied from Westminster to the Temple, and from several other stairs to and fro, as in the streets; also on sleds, sliding with skates. There was likewise bull-baiting, horse and coach-races, puppet plays and interludes, cooks, tippling [and] lewder places, so that it seemed to be a bacchanalian triumph or carnival on the water . . .'

Charles II and Nell Gwynn were at home in this atmosphere. The Merry Monarch led his queen and entourage on to the ice and accepted a slice from the ox roasting on the river next to Whitehall. He later joined in the excitement even more heartily by building a royal pavilion on the ice, inviting guests to join him and Nell Gwynn for fine wine and a right royal knees-up.

From the 15th to the end of the 19th centuries London was a city that never slept and was voracious in the way it absorbed and churned the lives of its citizens. By the middle of the 18th century, London overtook Paris and Constantinople as the largest city in the world with over 700,000 inhabitants. Through international trade, the capital had more money available to it than any other city. By the time of the Frost Fair of 1814, it was the world's financial centre, with close to a million people. Everything was at full tilt. Kerr-Cameron aptly quotes Tobias Smollett's character Matt Bramble, who reports: 'The foot passengers run along as if they were pursued by bailiffs. The porters and chairmen trot with their burdens. People who keep their own equipages drive through the streets at full speed.' The river was full of watermen with their wherries, more than a thousand hackney coaches were for hire on the streets, while others paid a shilling a mile to be carried to their business in sedan chairs.

✿ BUCOLIC PLEASURES ✿

As London grew, Londoners never lost their love or basic need for greenery, fine private and public gardens, fields and open spaces. This desire for fresh air and vegetation, other than rotting matter in the streets, was hardly surprising considering the grimness and disease that marked some quarters of the city. It also reflects the nature of a population sucked in from all parts of rural England, Scotland, Wales and Ireland. There were young innocents who came to seek their fortune, displaced families and wealthy gentry and nobility who moved to their townhouses for the seasonal entertainments.

'Rus in urbe' – country in town – came into fashion as the city expanded. In Pepys's time in the early days of the Restoration it was still common to take a cab out to the village of Hackney to enjoy a syllabub and cream and to watch some hare-coursing. In the Georgian squares further into the fashionable west of the capital, residents sometimes introduced something of the countryside. St James's Square even supported a mangy flock of sheep for a while.

Parks, gardens, lawns, some quite extensive, were all part of the urban landscape in 17th-century London. As the new buildings went up, property-owners clung tenaciously to their personal swards of green. Fynes Moryson commented in his *Itinerary* of 1617: 'There is no country wherein the gentleman and lords have so many and large parks only reserved for the pleasures of hunting, or where all sorts of men allot so much ground about their houses for pleasure of gardens and orchards.'

Pleasure in the capital took on a bucolic nature. Two of London's most idiosyncratic large-scale public celebrations revolved around the green spaces at the edge of the new building. One was the pleasure gardens at Vauxhall, the other the hanging festivals that culminated at Tyburn, the area that is now Marble Arch.

After they opened in 1660, the gardens at Vauxhall quickly became the most fashionable and raciest of all the capital's pleasure spots. This was where the elegant ladies and gentlemen dressed in the increasingly complex and colourful fashions of the Restoration period would come to promenade. They would meet their friends and rub shoulders with peers as well as other ranks of society as they strolled along the Grand Walk beneath the elms, or sat and gossiped in the arbours.

Having spent at least half the day dressing themselves, some members of the coterie of London's fops or *beaux* would strut like peacocks in the gardens, disdainful of the occasional cry of 'French hen' by less polite passers-by. A Frenchman called Misson wrote of the fops: 'The play-house, chocolate houses, and park in spring, perfectly swarm with them: their whole business is to hunt after new fashions. They are creatures compounded of a periwig and a coat laden with powder as white as a miller's, and a face besmear'd with snuff, and a few affected airs.' Although he was by no means a fop, Pepys himself regularly spent four or five times more on his own clothes than on his wife's. In 1665 he records that he paid £24 on 'my new silk camelott sute, the best that ever I wore in my life'. So it should have been, given that this was about half a year's income even for a middle class family of the time.

But the gardens had much more to offer than elegant surroundings and space for meeting and parading. People could eat in style, drink to excess, dance and attend great open-air concerts and firework displays. They were offered a well packaged fantasy, put together purely as a money-making scheme but serving an important need. This was where many of them went to escape the bustle and, for many, the misery of the streets, and succumb, just for a while, to a highly stylized form of arcadia.

Initially there was no admission charge but later, following a make-over and the addition of new amusements, you would be levied a shilling, an amount modest enough to ensure that Londoners of all walks of society would come. A hundred years later, when the fortunes of the gardens were flagging as a result of competition and a reputation for unseemly activities, admission was still relatively modest at half a crown.

Vauxhall Gardens were at their most exciting from the middle of the 18th century onwards. You entered the twelve acres via a splendid river gate and then took your pick of the entertainments on offer. Typically of London, you could enjoy truly uplifting cultural events such as orchestral performances by some of Europe's greatest composers, or you could visit a freak show. During the early evening the atmosphere was relatively decorous. Strolling musicians, grottoes and temples, classical statuary, tea and syllabub were all available for your delectation. And, when darkness fell, a visit to Vauxhall with its fantasy of gas-lit promenades and 'love-exciting shady groves' was one of the hottest nights out in town.

James Boswell generally found the gardens to be 'delicious'. He refers to a visit there one early June evening in 1763 and describes how he was not in the mood for gaiety at all. He left his companions to their sport and managed to throw off his gloom by sitting bolt upright on top of his carriage home, chuckling inwardly as he adopted the guise of a footman.

Although he was a consummate pleasure-seeker, Boswell was not a boor in his pursuit of women, to whom he was slavishly devoted. But boorish behaviour at Vauxhall gardens was common in Pepys day, especially among congregating courtiers who became known as 'The Ballers'. Pepys was one of many who were disturbed by the behaviour of the young bucks in full, drunken cry; their language so lewd and brash that even Pepys was irritated by their 'mad, bawdy talk' and atrocious behaviour. 'How rude some of the young gallants of the town are become,' he wrote after one visit, 'to go into people's arbours where there are not men, and almost force the women – which troubled me, to see the confidence of the age.'

Everyone who was anyone – and everyone else – went to Vauxhall: the arch-seducer, Casanova, the Prince Regent, the nobility and aspiring gentry – and the contents of teeming London. This heterogeneity is vividly described by Tobias Smollett:

The different departments of life are jumbled together – the hodcarriers, the low mechanics, the tapster, the publican, the shop keeper, the pettifogger, the citizen, the courtier all tread upon the kibes of one another: actuated by demons of profligacy and licentiousness, they are seen everywhere rambling, riding, rolling, rushing, justling, mixing, bouncing, cracking and crashing in one vile ferment of stupidity and corruption.

Casanova describes how he was offered a ride in Lady Hamilton's carriage on his way back from an outing to the gardens and, stimulated by the gentle rocking of the carriage and the presence of a beautiful woman, he added her ladyship to a long list of conquests. On a different note, in 1749, an audience of 12,000 flocked to Vauxhall, their carriages jamming the whole south Thames area and some of the north, to listen to a rehearsal of Handel's *Music for the Royal Fireworks* performed by 100 musicians. This was an occasion reminiscent of the Three Tenors concert at Hyde Park or Prince Charles's own Party in the Park.

Pepys referred to the gardens as diverting and generally a cheap outing where you could spend as much or as little as you wanted. But just like in a modern fairground there was always plenty of temptation to spend more than you might wish to. The management made up for the free and later modest entry fee by fleecing its customers at every opportunity. A plate of meat cut thinly was expensive at a shilling. The value-added recreations were expensive too; at least they would have been to the lower class Londoners who, in time, became the gardens' most regular customers. Nevertheless, successive managers advertised and promoted new attractions with zeal and inventiveness. Sometimes, there were re-enactments of famous British battles, such as Vittoria and Waterloo attended by the great British generals who had won them, the Duke of Wellington included. A thousand or more foot and horse soldiers performed. Dancing in the pavilion and dining in the supper boxes were standard entertainments; the wines were good but expensive. Acrobats, magicians and circus performers would be booked to entertain, at a price; or you could see a ballooning exhibition at the extra cost of half-a-crown.

Vauxhall was also the scene of masked balls and masquerades, the rage of the period. Thousands came to a ball to celebrate 50 years of public support, for which the invitation, priced at half a guinea (about half an artisan's weekly salary), required the partygoers to dress as dominoes. Multitudes of Londoners would pay as much as a guinea for special balls. Costumiers provided every kind of disguise and set up temporary changing rooms close by. Caterers served a feast of pies, chickens, crayfish and prawns, and a truly mixed group from the Prince Regent, dressed as a waterman, to a hod-carrier dressed as a Harlequin, would mingle and make merry in disguise.

Inevitably, the democratic admission charge meant that pickpockets and highwaymen made themselves comfortable among the warm summer evening crowds. So did prostitutes, including many women whose dress and manner reflected a certain quality and discernment. They used the occasional visit as a means of engaging the attention of men in a subtle way, or of catching the eye of existing clients, parading with their wives, to signal their availability. On one occasion, Casanova himself, usually the initiator of amorous adventures, refers to being 'duped by a woman in a dark alley' at Vauxhall. But the gardens also offered the freedom of their soft spaces to young men and women who were interested in dalliance with less cost attached.

In the 1740s, Ranelagh Gardens, abutting Chelsea Hospital, set up in competition with Vauxhall and soon drew the in-crowd to its magnificent rotunda, supposedly one of the great wonders of the capital. In *Humphrey Clinker*, Smollett offers a vision of Ranelagh that has none of the jostling 'stupidity and corruptness' that he noted at Vauxhall. He wrote that these gardens were 'adorned with the most exquisite performances of painting, carving and gilding, enlightened with a thousand golden lamps, that emulate the noon-day sun; crowded with the great, the rich, the gay, the happy and the fair; glittering with cloth of gold and silver, lace, embroidery and precious stones'. In the rotunda, lit by chandeliers, visitors sat in the booths that surrounded the great dancing floor and drank tea or wine.

The jet set came to Ranelagh in droves. Horace Walpole, who likened the slow circular perambulations of the 'monde' to the movement of 'asses in an olive mill', wrote: 'you can't set your foot without treading on a Prince or Duke of Cumberland'. Ranelagh's celebration to mark the end of the eight-year War of Austrian Succession in 1748 was a great jamboree. It drew some 2,500 masked people thronging the tents and moving between the different bands of musicians in a celebration that would rival the grandest of today's May Balls.

There were other, relatively modest, pleasure gardens such as Island House Gardens in Southwark, or St Helena's Gardens in the east. Here there were a few gas-lights, some landscape gardening and a bar selling the fashionable drinks of the day (taking tea suddenly became popular). In this ambience you really could forget your cares and woes for a few hours. But there were other gardens that aimed to stimulate rather than tranquillize.

Older than Vauxhall, Marylebone Gardens, which opened in 1650, drew Londoners to wander among the trees in latticed groves and enjoy the long-standing London amusements of bull-baiting, bear-baiting, animal fights, bare-knuckle fights, cock-fights and throwing at cocks. The potential for paid sex or romance was on offer here as in most other venues, but Marylebone was primarily a draw for Londoners interested in savage sports. It also became notorious for highwaymen; even Dick Turpin put in an appearance. As the pleasure garden phenomenon took off, Marylebone was upgraded to include assembly rooms for balls and concerts, and there were also spectacular firework displays and fine food.

There had been pleasure gardens as early as the 1640s. One was opened in that year on a ten-acre site on Bankside. Building on the reputation for licentiousness and pleasure-seeking of Paris Gardens in this area, Abraham Cuper, the Earl of Arundel's gardener, opened Cuper's Gardens as an alcohol-serving retreat. The gardens soon became known as 'Cupid's Gardens'; the shilling entrance fee gaining you access to all kinds of privacy. Cuper's enterprise managed to run for 20 years before being closed down by the authorities because of its invasion by pickpockets and other low-lifes.

The last of the great gardens of the period, which opened in 1825, was Cremorne in Chelsea which had a grand entrance on the riverbank. Cremorne set out to provide a stylish environment like Ranelagh's but it soon turned into the 19th-century precursor of a modern theme park. Entry was ticketed and there were different 'experience' areas and an unremitting drive to meet the public demand for novelty with new shows and attractions every day. One handbill shows the range of amusements you might find:

Three Grand Bands / The Original Tyrolese Singers / Grand Fairy Ballets / Vocal and Instrumental Concerts / Bono Core, the Salamander or Fire King / Grand Cirque Oriental / Antonio Poletti (the Roman Wizard) / Cooke's Educated Dogs and Monkeys / Talented Company of Concert Singers / The Stereorama (the Most Splendid Exhibition in England) / Cosmoramic Pictures / The Savannah Minstrels / Elegant Acrobatic Displays / Balloon Ascents / Splendid Pyrotechnic Displays / Dancing on the Crystal Platform / Romantic Grotto and Fernery.

Like Vauxhall and several other gardens before it, once the evening turned to night, Cremorne became a place where high-class whores strolled in their finery. They served an enthusiastic clientele; literally hundreds of men each night toured the sights and made their arrangements in the dark groves by the river.

In the Regency period of early 19th-century London, there was a feeling that all who attended the gardens were being exposed to the latest fashions, sensations and artistic celebrities of the time. Clothes worn there were often extreme. Dresses could be so revealing they would turn heads today. The body-consciousness of Regency London was totally different from ours. The streets accepted and celebrated the female body; Gilray's cartoons show how figure-hugging many of the most fashionable outfits of the day were. One punishment for prostitutes discovered to have syphilis was to turn them out into the street in just their stays.

And just like night-spots in Paris at the beginning of the 20th century, Harlem in the 1920s and London at the beginning of the 21st century, the pleasure gardens were the perfect opportunity for a spot of bisexual experimentation or, perhaps, bi-curious tourism. An anonymous author makes it clear in his *Satan's Harvest Home* that expressions of affection between members of the same sex were often overtly public, reporting that when he sees 'two Ladies Kissing and Slopping each other, in a lascivious Manner, and frequently repeating it, I am shocked to the last Degree'.

All the anomalies that have made London so infinitely various were somehow condensed in the pleasure gardens. Opposite the lavish and ornate Cremorne Gardens with their mixture of genteel visitors and clients, were Battersea fields. This was a wild and rough area with little pretension to style. There were booths, shows and attractions to suit every taste. Here was another theme park in the making, growing out of the often sinister circus of London itself.

～ HANGING FESTIVALS ～

For some of the pickpockets, highwaymen and cadgers not quick enough to escape the scene of the crime on a night out at the pleasure gardens, celebrity of a different kind awaited them.

Corporal and capital punishment had been an intrinsic part of every Londoner's life from the foundation of Londinium onwards. Whipping, of prostitutes and other offenders were conducted in public and drew an interested audience; some jeering and laughing, others appalled. The use of the stocks for pillorying by the crowd was an ancient tradition and the format of this free show remained largely the same. The sentenced person was led by officers of justice to the platform where there was a thick hinged plank with three holes in it for the victim's head and hands. Lesser offenders were sometimes secured by a lower-set plank which had just two holes for the legs, thus allowing some leeway for self-defence. The mood and mercy of the crowd was important. Often what was intended to be a relatively mild disgrace turned out to be much more serious for victims of the pillory.

Even playful re-enactments of the pillory at today's school fairs or village fêtes – your chance to give the chemistry teacher one in the face with a wet sponge – can get a little out of hand. But a genuinely angry mob at liberty to hurl anything they wished at a well-known and hated victim often resulted in serious maiming, or worse. At some of these events, the crowd turned up well before the victim was secured in the pillory. They arrived with pails or came pushing carts containing an arsenal of dead rats, cats, dogs, rotted vegetables, stones and quantities of mud; also sticks and bottles. Once the offender was in place, the justice officers would step down quickly to avoid being caught in the firing-line of hard-hitting and obnoxious missiles. The officers had to stand nearby in order to clear the mud and filth from the nose and mouth of the victim when this became necessary to prevent suffocation.

According to Christopher Hibbert in *The Road to Tyburn* – a definitive account of crime and punishment in the 18th century – one contemporary newspaper report describes the fate of two men who were pilloried on St Margaret's Hill, Southwark:

One of them being of short stature and remarkably short necked could not reach the hole made for the admission of the head. The officers of justice forced his head through the hole, and the poor wretch hung rather than walked as the pillory turned round. Previous to being put in he had deprecated the vengeance of the mob and begged for mercy which in their exasperation for his crime, and their want of considering the consequences of their cruelty, they seemed little inclined to bestow. He soon grew black in the face, and the blood issued from his nostrils, his eyes and his ears; the mob nevertheless attacked him with great fury. The officers, seeing his situation, opened the pillory, and the poor wretch fell down dead on the stand of the instrument. The other man was likewise so maimed and hurt by what was thrown at him that he lay there without hope of recovery.

The crowd were reportedly furious on this occasion because these men had been found guilty of a homosexual offence, but they may equally have been carried away in the video-nasty of their own lives.

When the crowd were not disposed to anger – usually because they liked the pilloried victim – they could sometimes go out of their way to make the occasion as comfortable as possible. Daniel Defoe was sentenced to pillorying three times because of his anti-authoritarian views. This punishment appears to have been meted out in an attempt to get Defoe to betray certain Whig leaders. Londoners have always liked people who make a stand against the law, particularly if they show bravery and wit in the face of punishment. Although he was apprehensive about his punishment, Defoe had spirit enough to write a popular satirical poem, 'Hymn to the Pillory' (1703), and was greatly cheered when he found that his pillory was garlanded with flowers while the assembled crowd drank his health and bought copies of his poem in the streets.

In these extraordinary times, people who were brought in front of London magistrates could well be pilloried, whipped, fined, acquitted or sentenced to death – sometimes for the same type of crime. The conduct of justice was generally corrupt or inept. False witnesses made a reasonable living hiring themselves at the various courts to prosecuting or defending lawyers; the jury was corruptible or biased depending on whether they liked the defendant's manner or face; magistrates were often deeply corrupt too. One chief magistrate in the early 18th century was Colonel de Veil who dealt with the prostitutes who came before him according to their looks. If he liked them, he would often set them aside for an inspection 'in his private closet for the examination of the fair sex'. After the examination the prostitutes would be let off altogether, with an honourable discharge into the bargain. Curiously, for an unpaid city officer, de Veil managed to drum up an income of about £1,000 a year during his incumbency.

Many of the constables, who reported to the magistrates, were poorly paid deputies of the citizens who were supposed to be doing constable duty. They were invariably on the make and were seldom trusted, even by the magistrates. And at grass roots, or street level, the 'thief-takers' who were mostly responsible for bringing offenders to court, were paid a kind of bounty, often exceptionally worthwhile (£10 for a first offender in the mid-18th century). Sometimes thief-takers would work in pairs framing an innocent youth fresh from the country to make their money from a false charge. Fetching in known criminals and gangsters was far more profitable, but much more dangerous to the catcher in the event that the villains were acquitted, which was often the case.

As Hibbert says in *The Road to Tyburn*:

Numerous strange anomalies in the criminal system were suffered to remain without question. Attempted murder, for instance, was merely a misdemeanour, while to snatch a watch out of a man's hand and run away with it was a capital offence. To steal fruit from a basket was a felony, but to gather fruit and then steal it was a trespass.

Most magistrates tended to ignore the system and deal out justice according to their own discretion, sometimes kindly, sometimes appallingly. Many innocent people were hanged, but hardened criminals and murderers ended up on the gallows too. On one occasion, the crowd came from miles away to witness the dispatch of a murderess called Catherine Hayes. She had instigated and been present at the brutal murder of her husband by her two lodgers. They were given hanging sentences but because of her position as husband-killer, Mrs Hayes was convicted of both murder and petty treason. The penalty demanded for this was burning, and remained so until 1789. Usually, the executioner would humanely strangle the condemned before the faggots were lit, but on this occasion he botched the job and had to withdraw as the flames made his work impossible. An avid public witnessed Catherine Hayes's terror and agony as she tried to push away the flames.

A more serious punishment, for treason against the crown, was hanging, drawing and quartering – which sometimes involved disembowelling before the hanging. This was guaranteed to pull a big crowd, shrieking in horror or baying for a painful death if the victim's CV was distasteful to them.

Londoners were used to seeing death and were inured to it; on the approaches to the capital the gibbets were full of rotting flesh, left as a warning on the public roads. In London itself the spiked head of a hanged or beheaded convict was a common sight, especially at the Temple near the entrance to Fleet Street. The heads of those murdered would also sometimes be raised in this way, in the hope that someone might identify the victims. Until the early 19th century many children throughout the country would have witnessed a hanging at some point in their life. Even in small rural towns hangings were occasions of some pomp, usually attended by local officials. But it took London, with its appetite for mob assembly, to turn death into a carnival.

With so many people to accommodate, a large space was favoured. Tyburn was particularly popular. The site was on the Hyde Park side of Oxford Street where Marble Arch now stands. It offered the handy combination of standing and sitting room for the mob and the gentry, and a suitable build-up to the execution in the slow procession of the condemned from Newgate Prison.

The death route was lined with traders, hawkers, fruit-sellers, tumblers, jugglers – and pickpockets: gibbet fodder for the future. There were many thousands of spectators there who, depending on the popularity of the condemned, were either cheering them on or baying for blood. Ballad-sellers and pamphleteers were in abundance. Some opportunists very quickly put together mini-biographies of the condemned and most of these were the product of an excited imagination and nothing more. Thus, if you were a poor or inadequate person with no particular story to tell, wrongly accused of a capital offence, a fictitious street biography sealed your place in history as a demon.

Adding piquancy to what became increasingly monstrous and uncontrollable festivities, the big hanging or beheading days were public holidays for many of the labouring classes, including apprentices. They usually took place on a Monday, after a Sunday spent quite literally resting, because on Sundays London closed down. All work and all but illicit play stopped; all shops and manufacturers, lace-men, shoemakers and sellers, drapers, mercers, tanners, weavers, dockers, merchants, notaries, clerks, magistrates and lawyers closed offices and premises. A day off and recovered energies usually meant that the crowd was in a fever of anticipation for the morning execution.

After leaving his or her cell at Newgate, the prisoner's journey to the gallows at Tyburn, through crowds that had been waiting since the very early hours, was a long one full of morbid symbolism and theatrical ritual. At the outset, the deep bell of St Sepulchre's opposite Newgate boomed ominously. It was only ever rung to accompany the condemned on their last earthly journey. Prisoners were offered 'a grate bowle of Ale to be their last refreshing in this lyfe' at the hospital chapel of St Giles-in-the-Fields. But they did not always have the stomach for it. Travelling in a cart, their hands bound tightly in front of them, they were accompanied by a minister whose job was to get them to repent for their sins if they had not already. The hangman was there too, squatting predatorily on the convict's coffin.

Another bell, inter-chiming with the great bell above, would be rung at the porch of St Sepulchre, and the bellman would offer a prayer that had the dual purpose of admonishing bystanders and providing comfort to the convicted. It contained the line: 'All good people pray heartily unto God for this poor sinner who is now going to his death, for whom this great bell doth toll.'

As the procession moved along, it was not uncommon for young girls or men, depending on the gender of the convict, to aim kisses or throw posies of flowers in the direction of the condemned. Other stops at alehouses were sometimes allowed and the taverns and gin stalls along the way did a great trade. A poignant custom was for the prisoner to have a 'last drink' with the hangman, promising to repay him on his way back. As the procession drew towards the gallows, the 'fatal tree', the condemned were greeted with a forbidding sight, which often put an end to the false cheerfulness many of them adopted on the occasion. Some gallows would take up to 21 people to be hanged simultaneously.

James Boswell, always determined to milk every last ounce of experience from his stay in London went to a hanging where a fraud-ster, a woman guilty of theft and a handsome highwayman called Paul Lewis were top of the bill. Just as he displays initial self-questioning about trying out whores of various calibre, he is doubtful about his own intentions on 4 May 1763: 'My curiosity to see the melancholy spectacle of the executions was so strong that I could not resist it, although I was sensible that I would suffer much from it . . . I also wished to see the last behaviour, the handsome fellow [the high-wayman] whom I had seen the day before.' Boswell's reference to seeing the handsome fellow before, refers to a visit out of curiosity to Newgate, where he also saw the woman to be hanged, called Hannah Diego, 'a big unconcerned being', but he was taken with Paul Lewis, who was a 'genteel, spirited young fellow' whom he called 'just a young Macheath'.

Appalled by what he witnessed as a gawper among the 'prodigious' crowd, Boswell was thrown into melancholy and decided never to go to a hanging again. As with his resolutions about whoring, he was nevertheless up with the lark on another occasion to see the simultaneous 'scragging' of 15 men outside Newgate. On such an occasion, because the hangmen had only a rudimentary knowledge of anatomy, the length of fall intended to ensure quick strangulation was not always enough. The prurient crowd would then have the additional ghoulish excitement of watching the close friends or relatives of the hanged pulling on their legs to end the ordeal. When the gallows involved trapdoors through which the hanged fell, the hangmen or other officers of justice provided this service, appearing like jack-in-the-boxes from below.

This was popular entertainment on a grand scale. At the execution of Jack Sheppard, one of the most charismatic of early 18th-century criminals, eye-witness accounts estimated the crowd at around 200,000. Men and women crammed on to rooftops right along the route. The wealthier members of the audience paid good money for prime positions at the first and second-floor windows. Aged just 22 at his death on 16 November 1724, Sheppard had attracted the attention of the crowd as an infamous jail-breaker following a life of mostly petty crime. He had been seized and committed to St Giles Roundhouse in April 1724 and had easily escaped. After more thefts, he was again caught and incarcerated in New Prison, where he escaped on 25 May by ridding himself of his irons, cutting through bars, descending one wall and scaling another. Further thefts and robberies continued until, betrayed by London's master informer and crime lord, Jonathan Wild, he was captured on 23 July. Tried and condemned to death, he again escaped with the help of his girlfriend, Poll Maggot. Seized once more on 10 September, he was housed in the most secure part of Newgate Prison. Although manacled to the floor, he smashed his chains, climbed a chimney, broke through several bolted doors, returned to his cell for a blanket to use as a rope, went back to the upper levels and descended a wall to freedom. More pilfering and burgling the next day, followed by a drunken bout, led to his capture and return to prison for the last time. By the time of his execution he was a national hero. The apparently invincible Jonathan Wild travelled the same route on 24 May 1725.

Despite the sometimes hostile behaviour of the crowds some of the convicts appeared almost to relish their extraordinary position as the stars of these capital extravaganzas. They dressed in their finest clothes, smiled and joked with the crowd, greeted friends or sardonic well-wishers as they processed. Some had suits tailor-made for the day, always a bonus for the hangmen who traditionally had the right to the victim's wardrobe after his death.

A particularly resourceful woman called Madame Proctor made very good money out of the Tyburn hangings. She was fortunate in owning the field where the gallows were set up. A few shillings, and more on special days, would buy a ringside seat in one of Proctor's pews. She was said to have made more than £500 on the day that Earl Ferrers was hanged in 1760 for shooting a servant. This was a particularly popular occasion and it took three hours for the condemned, his cart and coffin to get from the Tower of London to Tyburn. Such was the crowd that a little boy was trampled to death by a horse and a girl somehow managed to strangle herself with her bonnet.

Oblivious to such goings on, Madam Proctor provided a useful service to the men of fashion, few of whom would miss the opportunity of a good hanging. George Selwyn was one of the keenest members of the cult of execution-goers among the wealthier members of society. An elegant man of wit and fashion, he particularly hated to miss a major hanging. A trip to Paris unfortunately meant that Selwyn missed the hanging of Lord Lovat, one of the key conspirators in the 1745 rebellion against the crown. But he asked his good friend Horace Walpole to attend and to write him an account of the proceedings. Enough to say that Lovat acquitted himself in style, as many were determined to do if this was to be their fate, some of them demonstrating extraordinary bravery and equanimity in the last few minutes of their lives.

As the fashionable people of London gradually took over new residences towards the west, the procession to Tyburn and the mobs that gathered there were starting to impinge on the new neighbourhood of the wealthy. From December 1783, the procession was cut and the hanging shows were continued directly outside Newgate Prison. The 'new drop' method was also introduced, involving a fall through a trapdoor. This was intended to dispatch people efficiently and quickly and often did. But the glamour and suspense of the procession to Tyburn, or to anywhere else, was completely curtailed. The urbane Dr Johnson, in the manner of an elder being overtaken by the speed of events, told James Boswell that 'Tyburn is not safe from the fury of innovation ... No sir, it is not an improvement: they object that the old method drew together a number of spectators. If they don't draw spectators they don't answer their purpose.'

At Newgate, there was only enough space for about 30,000 people to congregate physically, but the spectators still came and they were up very early in the morning to secure a place. If the victim or victims were notable, some gallants would make a night of it. The gentleman and gallants often hired rooms on the first and second floors of surrounding houses, paying as much as £25 for this accommodation which enabled them to hold eve-of-hanging parties and get mightily and merrily drunk. Thomas Ingoldsby in the first series of the *Ingoldsby Legends* (1840), records in verse how 'Lord Tomboddy' laments the ending of a hanging:

What was to be done? – t'was perfectly plain
That they could not well hang the man over again;
What was to be done, the man was dead!
Nought could be done – nought could be said;
So – my Lord Tomboddy went home to bed.'

There was surprised comment when the Marquis of Waterford, a young and rakish gallant and head of the Beresford sporting clan did not attend the hanging of a man called Courvoisier. He had murdered his employer in 1840 and this had caused a great stir. On the same occasion Thackeray waited for four hours on the cobbles outside Newgate prison and he recorded that the mob 'was extraordinarily gentle and good humoured'. This was not the view of Charles Dickens who also attended. Nine years later Dickens was also present at the execution of the Mannings, a husband and wife team, hanged at Horsemonger Lane Prison. Afterwards he wrote to a friend: 'The conduct of the people was so indescribably frightful, that I felt for some time afterwards almost as if I were living in a city of devils.'

Even after the convict was dead the body exercised a kind of totemic appeal. Women would hold the hands of the corpses – sometimes still twitching – to their faces. In one account by a French visitor, a young woman pulled down her bodice to put the dead man's hand on her breasts. And the hangmen would often retire to a local alehouse to sell the rope at sixpence an inch.

As Dr Johnson implied in his comment to Boswell about the purpose of spectators, deterrence was the overt reason for allowing – and even encouraging – the population of the city, young and old, to witness these executions. Anyone who visited a hanging festival would have born witness to the charged atmosphere, sometimes close to riot. But the crowds were not were not generally cowed by what they saw, although sometimes they had genuine pity for the person condemned or were horrified and greatly angered when a hangman bungled the job. The executions were all part of the reality of their lives; they were a show of death and a time for celebration, perhaps because the crowd were still alive to celebrate, whether they were aloof from the common herd or crushed in its middle.

But as Dickens and others witnessed, the mobs attending these executions often got out of hand. Whether or not the hangings deterred potential law breakers was less the concern of the authorities than fear of disorderliness, violence and even riot. The spectacle continued until 1868, when the Capital Punishment Amendment Act withdrew the business from the public eye and continued the hangings within the walls of Newgate Prison.

∽ PENNY GAFFS ∾

The debate about how children should enjoy themselves is one that looks set to continue to rage ferociously in the future. When should a child be exposed to adult tastes? What is the difference between exposure to factors that will assist development, and corruption? Do children have hedonistic adult urges that need to be repressed, or do they develop tastes for pleasure if they have access to extreme means of enjoyment?

Historians such as Nicholas Orme have shown that the notion that 'childhood' was non-existent before the Victorian period is totally inaccurate. His work on the medieval period indicates that children were not just miniature adults, but enjoyed their childish pursuits and child-orientated world with gusto. In Victorian times, childhood was determined primarily by the wealth or poverty of the family to which you had the good fortune or otherwise to belong. If you were poor, you had to work as a child; if you were rich, you did not. Until the Mines Act 1842 was passed, children under ten were still employed underground in mines. The Factory Act 1802 had already embarked on the road to progress by banning the employment of 'parish apprentices' (pauper children hired by factory workers) and provided for their basic schooling. In 1819 another such act aimed to protect 'free' children who were hired out by their parents and banned the employment of those under nine, and for those between nine and 16 for more than 12 hours a day. It was the campaigner Richard Oastler who made real progress by pushing for the Factory Act 1833 which secured a maximum 48-hour week for children between the ages of nine and 13 and a 68-hour week for children from 13 to 18. However, in London and other major cities of the times, the employed were often the lucky ones. Many others scraped by or died by the wayside.

A better candidate for 'lost childhood' would therefore seem to be the pre-teenage and teenage poor in cities such as London, Liverpool, Bristol, Cardiff and Glasgow. Those that made it to some degree of self-preservation frequently sought solace and escape in the Penny 'gaffs'.

Penny gaffs, also known as penny theatres – or occasionally in dockland areas, 'penny dives' – were semi-permanent hang-outs for kids between the ages of around nine and 16. The entertainment on offer was usually a short 20-minute play, followed by a comic-song or duet, and then another 20-minute play. The plays were abridged versions of the classics – *Julius Caesar, Othello, Richard III, Hamlet* or *Macbeth* – or of the popular melodramas of the day such as *Sweeney Todd* or *Maria Martin and the Red Barn*. On the face of it this was the perfect Victorian entertainment for the working classess – cheap, mind-expanding fare.

Reality was rather different. One contemporary journalist who provided a rich account of the penny gaffs and their juvenile clients was Let James Grant, a former editor of the *Morning Advertiser*. He wrote that: 'Respectable parents would never allow their children to visit such places. Their great patrons are the children not only of poor parents, but of parents who pay no attention to the morals of their offspring.'

Picture the scene. The gaffs were usually customized empty buildings . . . shops, warehouses or stables hastily converted for that use. The stage was assembled on planks roughly at one end of the room; they were nailed together and then secured on the top of about half-a-dozen 80-gallon beer barrels; sometimes an internal wall would have been pulled down to afford more space. The 'green rooms' were little more than oversized skirts behind which the raucous audience could easily hear the arguments and other noises of the performers.

The shows were turned out like a looped video. There could be five or even six performances a night – each to a new crowd, the previous house being unceremoniously bundled out by the proprietor who would be calling to 'make haste out of the way, to let in my fresh audience'.

The audience that surged in to try to get the best seats, contained all those 'streets of London characters' drawn so poignantly by artists such as Gustave Doré and interviewed so assiduously by writers such as Henry Mayhew, whose book *London Labour and the London Poor* is a profound contemporary reference. Twelve-year-old prototype Artful Dodgers could be found smoking the fashionable short-pipes 'each with (we must add)', wrote a paper in 1838, 'his prostitute'. There were teenage mothers breastfeeding their illegitimate babies; chipper gangs planning their next robbery, or dividing the spoils of the last. These were damaged children who looked on the world with knowing eyes. Blanchard Jerrold was the writer whose dispassionate and observant text accompanies Doré's engravings in *London*. Jerrold describes the look of these members of a lost world: 'Some have the aspect of wild cats. The lynx at bay has not a crueller glance than some I caught from almost baby faces.'

These children flocked in droves to the penny gaffs, their numbers occasionally enhanced by a passing coalman or street-lighter who dropped in for his 'pennorth' of fun. Most venues held at least 200 to 300 people, and as Let James Grant described, 'the average is 450 . . . one . . . in Paddington, is capable of containing 2,000 persons'.

They were the raves of their day, bordering on legality; their tendency to get out of hand led sometimes to police raids. London offered so many destitute buildings and abandoned shops that, when there was a raid, the proprietors and actors would usually be back in business within a day or two at a different venue.

In Grant's own estimation the average weekly attendance 'on the Penny Theatres of the metropolis' was about 24,000, mostly children. Given that there were more than 80 gaffs of this kind in the East End alone by the middle to late Victorian period, some opening only one night a week, others open five or six nights, Grant's account is highly credible. A chapter on the Penny Theatres in Grant's *Sketches in London*, published in 1938, offers a vivid account of the kind of antics that went on. In particular, you have a sense of the bickering crowd warming themselves in the huddle; a host of faces illuminated, no doubt dangerously, by no more than six candles 'at a penny each'. He describes the smallness of the stage, 'it being desirable, in the estimation of the proprietors, that as much space as possible should be set apart for the accommodation of the audience ... In some places, the stage is so small that the actors must be chary of their gesture, lest they break one another's heads.' The provision made for scenery was equally spare: 'They have usually some three or four pieces of cloth, which are severally daubed over with certain clumsy figures or representations; and these are made to answer all purposes.' And as for the costumes: 'The same dresses, in many of the establishments, serve for all pieces, no matter what their diversity of character.'

And the entertainment on offer itself only went down well with the audience if it was gruesome, raucous or lewd. Once again Grant paints the atmosphere evocatively.

They are not only fond of extremes, but will tolerate nothing else. Comedy is completely proscribed by them; they must either have the deepest tragedy or the broadest farce. In the tragic way, they evince a remarkably strong predilection for 'horrible murders'; and the moment that accounts of any such occurrence appear in the newspapers, a piece embodying the most shocking incidents ... is got up for representation at these establishments.

Henry Mayhew wrote about the sexually charged atmosphere at the penny gaffs:

> The most obscene thoughts, the most disgusting scenes were coolly described [in the plays], making a poor child near me wipe away the tears that rolled down her eyes with excitement of the poison . . . a ballet began between a man dressed up as a woman and a country clown. The most disgusting attitudes were struck, the most immoral acts represented, without one dissenting voice.

And again, 'a lad near me and my companion was asked if there was any flash dancing. With a knowing wink the boy answered, "Lots! Show their legs and all, prime." '

Some shows had vivid titles: 'Starving Poor of Whitechapel', 'The Horrible End of Emma Twinn', 'Bloodstained Jewels', 'The Ghastly Murders at Cutler's Row'. Many of the children at the penny gaffs were watching their own lives played out in front of them, farcically magnified. This is a short extract from one play (which lacks a title), courtesy of Grant's researches. He found the play at a Lambeth penny house and refers to it as one of the 'most successful pieces':

Enter TOM SNOOKS, HARRY FINCH, and NED TIMS.

TOM SNOOKS: I say, Harry, will you lend me a tanner till tomorrow?

HARRY FINCH: I would if I could, but blow me tight if so be as I've got one.

TOM SNOOKS: I say, Ned, old 'un, can you do anything?

NED TIMS: Woy, Tom, may I never smoke another pipe o' baccy, if I've got a stiver in the world.

TOM SNOOKS: I say, chaps, as we are all poor alike, wat do you say to goin' a robbin o' some old rich fellers?

HARRY FINCH: Capital, Tom, nothing could be better; don't you think so, Ned?

NED TIMS: Woy, yes, if it were not for wot follows.

TOM SNOOKS: Wat do you mean?

NED TIMS: Wat I mean is this 'ere, that I'm afear'd we might all three get scragged.

TOM SNOOKS: Pooh, pooh! All nonsense.

HARRY FINCH: Well, Ned, I'm bless'd if I ever thought you were such a coward.

NED TIMS: Well, dash my wig if I cares wat be the consekence – I'll go. I say, chaps, hush – I'm blowed if there be not an old feller on the road there: let's begin with him.

TOM SNOOKS: Done, Ned, done.

HARRY FINCH: Come, Ned (*patting him on the shoulder, and looking him coaxingly in the face*), may I never have a button to my coat if you ben't a regular trump.

The stranger is accosted and proves to be hopeless quarry, confessing himself 'to be quite as destitute of brains as money'. And so on. This was the soap of its day, not completely unlike a scene from Albert Square when Phil turns nasty, but with less attempt at characterization.

The evenings were intensely emotional affairs which stirred all kinds of passions. Paul Sheridan, to whom the author owes most for this account, describes in *Penny Theatres in Victorian London*, how 'at one gaff, strong wire netting had to be strung across the stage immediately the audience began to grow restive'. Vegetables and empty bottles were frequently hurled at the actors if the spectators did not approve of the show that was set before them. On one occasion, when the proprietor had tried to outdo his competitors by offering a free carrot with every ticket, the company of actors found themselves bombarded with 300 carrots in one throw. Luckily one of the actors was a donkey, and may have appreciated the audience's high spirits.

The action itself would often be interrupted by fierce disputes between the actors. Grant talks of violent quarrels on stage as well as off – often about the fact that the actors had not been paid or, more poignantly, about which performers should get the chance to eat the bread used as a prop.

Blanchard Jerrold, accompanying Doré's illustrations in *London*, points out that the audiences' sympathies in the marginally smarter theatres, such as the Garrick, were always with the underdog: 'they leant to the starveling, and the victim of fate'. Aggression was not the only emotion you would find in the gaffs. In many ways the atmosphere in these places must have been affirming and comforting to the young members of the audience; street urchins willingly used gaffs to escape into a world of fantasy in the company of fellow sufferers. The actors were typically from the same social class and age group as the audience. Grant cannot imagine how some of the players could bear to perform in these 'miserable' places, particularly after some had acted in the 'larger houses'. But as many actors today will tell you, a job is a job, and the alternative in Victorian times – unemployment – did not have the fall-back of dole money. Also the nightly round of five or more performances may have been exhausting but with such an involved and impressionable crowd the actors might also occasionally have enjoyed themselves.

The characters they played were frequently aristocrats and royalty so night after night the young actors could imagine themselves as powerful and rich movers and shakers. They were paid only between ten pence and five shillings a week, and sometimes they had a half-starved, newborn child wailing for its next insubstantial breastfeed from behind the tattered curtain – but in everyone's eyes for a few moments they were heroines, sex goddesses, even queens.

Grant describes how: 'With thousands, the desire to witness the representations at the Penny Theatres amounts to an absolute passion. They are present every night, and would at any time infinitely sooner go without a meal than be deprived of that gratification.' He then goes on to add, with typical Victorian censure, that 'there can be no question that these places are little better than so many nurseries for juvenile thieves'.

This was the youngsters' secret world where some even had their own code of speech; a speech that would probably not have been immediately understood by their parents or other adults in the ghettoes of London. Mayhew overheard one asking for a 'yennep' to get a 'tib of occabot'. We could compare it with the 'nadsat' language spoken by Anthony Burgess's more recent delinquents in *A Clockwork Orange* (1959).

Apart from the sex, drink and peer group comfort of the gaff, there was a higher-minded reason for these kids to want to spend their hard-earned cash there. Though the interiors of most gaffs were of bare boards and bricks, the performance aimed to help the audience to forget the drudgery of their 12-hour days and the squalor of their lives. Mayhew describes how the young spectators 'were dressed in showy cotton-velvet polkas, and wore dowdy feathers in their crushed bonnets'. Blanchard Jerrold believes himself incapable of describing the atmosphere of these places but nevertheless makes a good fist of it:

> An overwhelming cocked hat, a prodigious shirt collar, straps reaching half way to the knees, grotesque imitations of that general enemy known to the Whitehall loafer as a 'swell', caricatures of the police, outrageous exaggerations of ladies' finery, are conspicuous in the wardrobe of the penny gaff. What can that wardrobe be? An egg chest, an old bedstead, a kitchen drawer?

Fluffy white clouds and blue sky were painted on the ceiling of one gaff. But quite apart from the escape into fantasy, some of the children present were enthralled by the intangible buzz of the theatre. Today, touring education companies still work magic, introducing theatre to schools and clubs in areas where there are marked social problems. Interestingly, their chosen genre is often the energetic and robustly devised piece of the kind that Victorian penny-gaffers would have watched. But as one older coster-monger pointed out to Henry Mayhew: 'It's all stuff [o' nonsense] talking about them preferring this sort of thing. Give 'em good things at the same price, and I know they will like the good better than the bad.'

The parallels with today's raves are interesting. One of the 'problems' of both is perceived to be the threatening presence of a charged crowd outside the venues. Mayhew describes how: 'The crowd without was so numerous, that a policeman was in attendance to preserve order, and push the boys off the pavement – the music having the effect of drawing them insensibly towards the festooned green-baize curtain.' Whereas our ravers have ecstasy, crack, amphetamines and coke to keep them high, their Victorian equivalents relied on opiates and gin. The comparisons break down of course. The effects of the gin and opiates, even on hardened constitutions, were intensified by the near-hallucination that many experienced because they were on the point of near starvation.

Like raves, penny gaffs attracted plenty of opprobrium from those outside the sub-culture. Grant comments: 'If they continue to increase as rapidly as they have done for the last five or six years, they cannot fail to attract the attention of the magistrates, if not the legislature itself . . . my purpose is to impress, if possible, on the minds of the civil authorities, the propriety of shutting up the Penny Theatres.' They did increase rapidly.

After a considered study of a number of gaffs, Mayhew wrote:

> Here the stage, instead of being the means for illustrating a moral precept, is turned into a platform to teach the cruellest debauchery . . . so precocious are the little things, that the girl of nine will, from constant attendance at such places, have learnt to understand the filthiest sayings, and laugh at them as loudly as the grown-up lads around her . . . How can the lad learn to check his hot passions and think honesty and virtue admirable, when the shouts around him impart a glory to a descriptive song so painfully corrupt, that it can only have been made tolerable by the most habitual excess?

Gaffs were a sub-culture and a home-from-home which served a need and fetched a response in their audiences' own mostly bleak lives. Lives which Mayhew, Grant and many other benevolent Victorians had the very best intentions in trying to document and understand, but it is only ever the change brought about by not being poor that really counts. In the 1970s and 1980s, Mary Whitehouse was an ardent campaigner against bad language and depictions of sex or violence on television. She may have been attacking a different kind of poverty, or maybe not. Her voice was heard a lot, enjoyed greatly, and mostly ignored.

SPORT AND GAMBLING

❧ A NOTE ABOUT 'SPORT' ❧

'**L**et us now come to the sport and pastimes, seeing it is fit that a city should not only be commodious and serious, but also merry and sportful.' So wrote 12th-century chronicler William FitzStephen, who was busy painting a very pretty picture of London at almost exactly the same time as Richard of Devizes wrote his extremely acid account of the capital, quoted earlier. As 'merry and sportful' as it was on many occasions, much of London sport was less dainty than this.

Like many words in the English language, 'sport' has various meanings but as far as Londoners over the centuries are concerned, two versions will do. The first is 'sport' in its broadest sense, meaning almost anything that is not to do with work or a serious purpose. It includes pastimes, amusements, pleasures and diversions, literally of any kind. Physical exertion and technical skill may be involved but they are by no means requisites; sport of this type can include anything that offers pleasure. So every London pleasure mentioned in this book – love-making and whoring, idling and primping in the gardens, baying for blood at hanging festivals, eating excessively, gaming, card-playing, throwing dice and betting, drinking interminably and being out of your mind in an opium den – is sport in its way.

Londoners have a truly rich and varied history in sport of this kind; they are the fathers and mothers of invention when it comes to creating diversions and enjoying them to excess. The audience at the Globe, who also dallied happily at the the pastimes of bear-baiting, bull-baiting and cockfights, thoroughly understood the twisted implication in the line from Shakespeare's *King Lear* (1606): 'As flies to wanton boys are we to the gods, they kill us for their sport.' The very same audience was equally at home with the invitation to Celia in Jonson's *Volpone* (also 1606): 'Come, my Celia, let us prove,/While we can, the sports of love.'

A little later than this, in 1618, James I of England drew up a Declaration, known as the Book of Sports. Its intention was to signify the king's pleasure that on Sundays, after divine service, 'no lawful recreation should be barred to his good people, which should not tend to the breach of the laws of his kingdom and the canons of his church'. The sports specified as 'lawful recreation' were dancing, leaping, vaulting, May-games, Whitsun-ales, Morris dancing and the setting up of Maypoles, but it was James intention that, provided his people went to church on Sundays, they should afterwards do pretty much as they pleased.

The Declaration was not in fact directed at Londoners but it gives us an idea of how the monarch perceived his role in 'controlling' the leisure of his subjects. It was drawn up because of some discontent in Lancashire where the authorities saw fit to suppress rather than regulate the people's pleasures. This was giving the Reformed or Protestant Church a bad name and therefore strengthening the influence of Roman Catholicism, which James I did not want. In the event, the Book of Sports was published but not widely issued until Charles I reissued it in 1633, with the same intention of getting people to go to church and then sport as they wished, within reason.

But with the king's blessing or not, the English have always loved to gather in a crowd and sport together – the more boisterous the better.

Sportsman and sports historian, Peter Radford, interviewed for the *Sin City* television series, gives a colourful account of the easy-going rough and tumble of medieval leisure time:

On saints days and festivals, when people had time off they flocked to the open spaces, enjoyed themselves, frolicked, boozed undoubtedly, raced, played ball games and, if there was a slope, the girls would roly-poly down them with their skirts round their ears much to everyone's delight. Later on they would put more organization into these events so that they could get more of a laugh out of it. They would put a prize – a bacon or a fancy hat – on top of a pole and grease it; the prize went to the one who could climb it.

In this way, the more communal the amusement or diversion, the more it leads us to 'sport' of the other kind; the kind that involves physical exertion and competition: athletic performance, semi-formal games and eventually teams. Londoners in Roman Londinium enjoyed plenty of games of the more organized sort. The gladiatorial combats already described were occasions of great sport; so were the chariot races and horse races that we know took place in the circuses of Rome and various major towns in the western and eastern empires. Some of these must have taken place in Londinium too but it is difficult to gauge the level of participation involved. We know for sure that early Londoners had plenty of opportunity to join in a bellowing congregation in support of their own superheroes, athletes, performers, acrobats; men and women who combined grace with daring, and often immense bravery in the face of death. After the Romans, this degree of administered and organized sport following strictly applied rules largely disappeared until very much later.

In the meantime, Londoners were avid football players from early medieval times and they developed all kinds of sporting pursuits that suited their tendency to escape from the mundane or miserable into unruly excess. London's streets and fields were the venue for activities that we could loosely describe as sport but, in the view of many contemporary observers and bemused foreign visitors, were sometimes closer to riot. More formally, there were feats of strength and skill such as wrestling, jousting, archery – the sports that helped to train young men for warfare. These involved the adroit combination of fitness and technical skill; the show of daring and bravery in pseudo-battle and the championing of heroes – some of the earliest models for the relationship between today's sporting superheroes and their fans.

And later still, Londoners developed their own games, strange crossovers between golf, croquet and billiards; their own very peculiar form of tennis. They hurled and skated on London's frozen Thames. They were boundlessly creative with sticks, balls, hurdles, and 'hazards'. They went to great expense to build the courts and venues for these games, some of which were never played outside the capital – because the capital was a club full of people who were pathologically disposed to club.

More formalized sports – the ones that required rules that most people understood and which were even committed to print emerged only later still in London's history. This was owed to the intervention of the Victorians and the focus on good clean fun, playing the game, fair play, referees and umpires. Peter Radford believes that the move towards amateur sports and rule-making was a cloak for something more sinister.

It was the cloak to hide the fact that the people who were making the rules were the privileged that could afford to give their time and not be paid for it. It was a way of keeping out the people who were good at sport; it was a way of keeping out the watermen who were on the river because they did it for a living and they would be good at it. It was a way of keeping out the labourers because they were fit and strong and they dug ditches and you wouldn't want them in a sport where strength and fitness were involved. So it was a less than subtle way of making sure that the gentlemen of the middle class had sport to themselves and kept out the people who could beat them.

Before the Victorians took over, sport was inventive and often anarchic – a chaotic adventure of communal pleasure-making coupled with some of the most extraordinary physical feats known in history.

Whether as participants or spectators – distinctions that were often thinly divided – Londoners were famous for their excesses in all these sports, also for the way they have honed the arts of brinkmanship, connivance, duping, doping and hocusing that have for so long formed the underbelly of London sporting life. Money, the clink of coins and the fiduciary wedge, is a commonly shared theme between sport the diversion and sport the game. To Londoners, from monarch to poor apprentice, a quick and speculative kill on a game, a fight or a race has been their most serious sport of all. Sport and gambling are joined at London's hip.

So then on with the first game.

✑ FOOTBALL ❧

Londoners love football and they always have; some are obsessed by it. They have also always enjoyed the internecine and tribal pursuits of fighting, betting, drinking, vandalism and hooliganism that have been attendant on the 'Game'. It would be specious to claim that this sport, or its earlier antecedents, started in the capital; ball games of every kind have been played in Britain since the Roman occupation. But as in all instances of pleasure taken to excess, Londoners are jealous of their ownership of the game and have contributed in a major way to its development right through to the time that the foot-only kind split into football and various versions of handing and running with the ball, including rugby and American football.

Writing about life in London at the time of Henry II, William FitzStephen once again offers a very early reference to what was clearly some form of football in the late 12th century. He wrote that the boys in London 'annually upon Shrove Tuesday go into the fields and play at the celebrated game of ball [*ludum pilae celebrum*]'. The 'celebrated game of ball' he refers to is not actually specified as football but, for generations afterwards, the Shrove Tuesday is recorded as being the time when a form of football was played, by schoolboys particularly, all over the country, so it is likely that FitzStephen is referring to football in this instance.

According to legend and to Vernon Bartlett's account of it in *The Past of Pastimes*, the first football used in Chester in the ninth century was the head of a Dane. But this would have been clumsy, painful to use and would have bounced poorly. For the most part, from as early as the second century BC Greece (as recorded by Galen) to as late as the middle of the 19th century, the ball more commonly used was made of inflated pig or ox bladders. In ancient times, the ball was shaped by dipping it in hot ashes and rubbing it, a ritual apparently accompanied by songs.

Soon football was no longer confined to Shrove Tuesday but was played at other times too throughout London, and it became associated with disorder, property damage and violence. There was no fast traffic to impede the scores of young men – once again the 'apprentices' out for larks – who crashed through the narrow streets and the open spaces of London, putting paid to peaceful holidaying and frightening pedestrians out of their wits. Peter Radford says:

> Of course, the pitches were not pitches as we know them now. They were enormous; sometimes one end of a street to another. Sometimes there was a game of 'camp ball', a cross between football and hockey which went for miles when the territory might have been one church steeple to another. And the teams could have several hundred people in them so the game could last for quite some time.

In time, football became synonymous with the worst sort of rowdiness. According to the royal proclamations and local authority injunctions uncovered by Bartlett and other historians, it was banned several times in the 14th century. Edward II put a stop to it in 1314, 1331, 1349 and 1365. Bartlett suggests that some of the bans were because this form of mob football interfered with archery practice so a number of people were killed. With firmer controls in place, the over-excited football fans of modern day London can count themselves lucky for not being picked off by deadly arrows.

The banning continued at a steady pace. Richard II in 1388; Henry IV in 1401, 1409 and 1410; Henry V in 1414; Edward IV in 1474; and Henry VII in 1496. Local authorities and magistrates all seized their opportunity for zealous banning in various parts of the later medieval capital in 1477, 1478, 1572, 1581 and 1615. Clearly the game was a menace.

It is no surprise that there was a ban in 1581, given the likes of Sir Thomas Elyot, who was clearly fishing hard for a permanent one when he described football in *The Governor* as 'nothing but beastly fury and extreme violence, whereof proceedeth hurte and consequently rancour and malice to remain with them that be wounded, whereof it is to be put in perpetual silence'. And no account of London's unique sporting pleasures would be complete without the chirpy voice of Richard Stubbes (once again from *Anatomy of Pleasures*, 1583) who gamely denounced the sport as 'a develishe pastime . . . and hereof groweth envy, rancour, malice, and sometimes brawling, murther, homicide and great effusion of blood'. Rumour has it that Stubbes was an erstwhile Millwall fan.

Thankfully for the continuance of the sport, contemporary opinion was divided about the merits of the game. In 1581 Richard Mulcaster, headmaster of Merchant Taylor's and later St Paul's schools, and author of *Positions*, wrote that football 'could not have grown to this greatness that it is now at, nor have been so much used, as it is in all places, if it had not had great helps both to health and strength.'

It was the dissenters, however, who left most of the written records. Football became part of a much larger sporting subculture involving ragged assemblies of people. Those who were most appalled by them seriously questioned whether they were legal. According to Norman Wymer in *Sport in England; A History of Two Thousand Years of Games and Pastimes* (1949), John Northbrooke demanded an inquiry in 1577 into the legislation covering these sporting gatherings, describing the people who took part in them as 'loitering idle persons, ruffians, blasphemous swingebucklers and tossepots.' He makes no reference as to whether these were the 'away' games.

Playgoers in early Jacobean London would have spotted Shakespeare's meaning instantly when Kent in *King Lear* calls Oswald 'a base football player'. An earlier Shakespeare play, *A Comedy of Errors* makes it clear that the rounded pig or ox bladder previously referred to was cased in leather by this time; in the same breath he gives us a neat description of football's long famous 'one-two' move to get round an opposing player:

> Am I so round with you as you with me
> That like a football you do spurn me thus?
> You spurn me hence, and he will spurn you hither;
> If I last in this service you must case me in leather.

A little later, the London playwright William D'Avenant, pretending to be a snooty Frenchman, wrote a sarcastic piece about football on the streets, taking another favourite London pastime in his stride:

I would now make a safe retreat, but that methinks I am stopped by one of your heroic games, called football; which I conceive, under your favour, not very conveniently civil in the streets; especially in such irregular and narrow roads as Crooked-lane. Yet it argues your courage, much like your military pastime of throwing at cocks. But your mettle would be more magnified (since you have long allowed these two valiant exercises in the streets) to draw your archers from Finsbury and, during high market, let them shoot at butts in Cheapside.

A real visiting Frenchman, César de Saussure – already quoted for his squeamishness about the pickpockets at Bartholomew Fair – offers a far from tongue-in-cheek account of what he saw in 1728: 'In cold weather you sometimes see a score of rascals in the streets kicking at a ball, and they break panes of glass and smash the windows of coaches without the slightest compunction; on the contrary they will roar with laughter.'

Gradually, though, the game became codified and even gentrified. Once football had been taken up by the major public schools of the 18th and 19th centuries, where it was initially played with as many different sets of rules as schools, there was a steady move towards formal, agreed rules and teams of equal numbers. In late 1863, London was the scene of heated debates among the players who had moved on through public school to universities in Cambridge, Oxford or London. They held a series of meetings to try to determine not only the rules of the sport, but the future of the game. Those preferring to run with the ball in their hands shouted down those who preferred the foot-only variety, but the latter won the day and the former went off and squeezed their ball into a different shape. Thus rugby and soccer went their different ways and the Football Association was formed in London, with ten clubs.

By 1871 there were 50 football clubs in England, and by 1905 there were 10,100. This extraordinary rise was mirrored by the attendance at FA Cup finals during the later Victorian period. Attending Kennington Oval in 1872 there were 2,000 spectators; in 1881 there were 4,000; in 1891 there were 23,000. In 1901, the FA Cup Final was watched by a staggering 110,802 people, this time thronging Crystal Palace. It is nothing compared to the millions who watch it on television today but it is evidence of the enormous popularity of the game at that time.

✆ PALL MALL AND OTHER BALL GAMES ✆

Exactly 200 years earlier than the formation of the Football Association – which to some people is the beginning of history itself – Samuel Pepys was taking a stroll in 'the Park', by which he meant St James's Park near Buckingham Palace. It was a fine day in the middle of June and the gregarious and inquisitive Pepys fell into conversation with the keeper of Pall Mall, who was proudly sweeping this elegant stretch of terracing in the heart of London. Following their conversation, Pepys recorded for posterity 'that the earth is mixed that do floor the Mall, and that over all there is cockle-shells powdered and spread to keep it fast, which, however, in dry weather turns to dust and deads the ball'.

Just about everyone who has ever played Monopoly – and there are many millions of us all over the world – rightly think that Pall Mall is one of the smarter of London's decorous royal avenues. But following the Restoration, the merry monarch had this half-mile long stretch of raddle-coloured road created not for conveying carriages and horses, but for playing a particularly unusual game. This was not a game for apprentices or the lower orders but one for the king and his courtiers and others occasionally, by invitation only.

Pall Mall or Pell Mell probably derived from *Paille Maille*, a sort of early French croquet. The London version was clearly a sophisticated game that sport historians believe to be a mixture of croquet, golf and a rudimentary form of billiards. It required expensive facilities which in turn involved considerable expenditure to maintain. Powdering 11 million cockle-shells, or however many may have been enough to cover the long Mall, was a grind in itself; collecting, transporting and spreading them evenly was another business altogether. A low wall had to be built all the way round the extensive playing area to protect the attending gallants and their ladies and to keep the ball in play. We know the game was dangerous when it was played recklessly. As the Pell Mell version of the name suggests, it was a game requiring speed (as well as skill): according to the *Oxford Reference Dictionary* 'pell mell' means 'headlong, recklessly'.

A former Pall Mall court, believed to have been set up inside the gardens of St James's Palace itself, was built over during the Commonwealth period. Whether this had something to do with the quality of the game, or was for another reason best known to the former Parliamentarians, remains uncertain, but Cromwell was clearly suspicious of many sports, particularly those initiated within royal circles. Cromwell had certainly tried to ban tennis because he was concerned about the excessive gambling that went with the game; but he was less successful there. Charles II's action of restoring Pall Mall on such a grand scale in the centre of London can be seen as evidence of his desire to cock a snook at his puritanical predecessors.

The ball for Pall Mall was hard and about one foot in circumference. Made of boxwood, it was 'beaten to a proper surface' by continual hammering. The mallets (or malls) were about four feet long and their heads were curved slightly upwards at each end. The handles were covered with soft leather to improve grip and reduce swing. According to a contemporary instruction manual, there is one way, and one way only, to address the ball. Using the heaviest mallet the player should 'get an even swing behind the drive, make full use of the hops and refrain from hitting at the ball'. As in golf, the aim was to drive the ball down the alleys in as few strokes as possible. Unlike in golf, and more like in croquet or king-size billiards, the player had to go through a number of iron arches, known as 'hazards'.

'Hazard' is an ancient word, drawn from the French but, according to the *Old English Dictionary*, probably deriving from a game of dice played in Arabia. At the time of Restoration London, hazard already had several meanings. For example, it referred to a very popular game of dice which drew most of the smarter people of the capital to the table in an orgy of gambling, sometimes involving the exchange of fortunes. In tennis, by which we mean royal or real tennis, the 'hazard-side' was the side of the court into which the ball was served. Thus, in Shakespeare's *Henry V*: 'We will in France . . . play a set, shall strike his father's crown into the hazard.' In billiards in this period, hazard referred to some of the holes or pockets around the edge of the table. In golf, the hazard was commonly a reference to the bunkers, furze, woods, water or other obstacles that still induce so much hernia in players. And, of course, hazard also meant chance, the possibility of loss or peril. Most of all, that carried the implication of fleeting lives at play; hazard was a fine London sporting word. And so back to the hazard of the Mall.

At the first arch, or iron ring, that the Pall Mall player approached he would swap his boxwood ball for a carefully selected small steel one and choose another mallet to hit onwards. After some rain the ground would be just right; the powdered shells lying solid on the ground. At such times the ball flew, in the opinion of one observer called Edmund Waller 'as from a smoking culverin 'twere shot'.

The etiquette of the game was important and any deviation from protocol could excite the players, as Pepys noted when he visited St James's Park another time in January 1664:

> Afterwards to St James' Park, seeing people play at Pell Mell; where it pleased me mightily to hear a gallant, lately come from France, swear at one of his companions for suffering his man, a spruce blade, to be saucy as to strike a ball while his master was playing at the Mall.

Different versions of Pall Mall were played to suit different occasions. Some courts were seven to eight hundred yards long; others had high walls or fences; some were divided into alleys; later courts were circular. Modern minds tend to have a solid, post-Victorian view about this sort of thing. Imagine nowadays journeying to a friend to play a game of croquet, a game you cannot help but acknowledge being particularly good at. You arrive to find that on the scratch of grass he calls his London lawn, your chum has gone inventive. He is using different size hoops, odd-size balls, one of which bounces and has to be taken through a hoop stuck halfway up a tree trunk. Worst of all, your host is a stickler about his peculiar rules which, to your added consternation, involve a certain amount of hopping between the hoops. It is just not playing the game!

A picture in a book called *An Illustrated History of Ball Games* by Nigel Viney and Neil Grant, shows men playing Pall Mall being watched by a group of women. In this there is a ring suspended about

12 feet off the ground – small wonder the mallets were bent upwards at either end of the hammer, with the end sections called 'lifters'. Yet another version of this highly flexible game, involved a court with only a ring at each end of the malls and no interfering hoops or other hazard in between.

The game seems to have mostly died out by the early 18th century, probably because of the expense of maintaining the courts and the premium on land in fast-growing London. But embers appear to have remained and to have been rekindled. Brian Jewell in *Sports and Games – History and Origins* suggests that the last version of the game played in London took place on a circular court on the grounds of the Freemason's Arms in Hampstead as recently as the 1970s.

∽ CRICKET ∾

With a circular pitch in mind, it would be churlish not to move directly on to cricket, one of the other great British sports which experts repeatedly claim originated in England, and may have done. But London cannot have this one to itself entirely. The first recorded semi-official 11-a-side game of cricket was played in Sussex for a wager of 50 guineas (a little over £50) in 1697. So Sussex wins out in the 'first-recorded' stakes. But it was London, as ever, that ran for the ball in cricket's development. Since the late 18th century, Marylebone Cricket Club (MCC), based at Lord's Cricket Ground in North London, has been at the heart of the game in Britain and still takes the lead in framing the laws of cricket today, wherever they are applied.

But back to 1697 where a 50-guinea bag – evenly divided between 11 players – was a high enough stake to have involved a considerable number of punters and a fairly large crowd. It would have been a busy and highly involved crowd too. Just a little later, cricket in 18th-century London was nothing like the pleasant activity – a distant tock and a spatter of applause from a mostly inattentive audience – that we watch on Clapham Common, or at Hampstead, Kew, Chiswick or Barnes today. In true London fashion, cricket became almost a fairground extravaganza once the 18th century had pressed it into action.

The most popular and best known venues for the big cricket games at this time were Lord's and the Artillery Grounds in Finsbury Park, but there were others, including Moulsey Hurst, Kennington Common, White Conduit Fields in Islington, Walworth Common and Tothill Fields. When a big game was advertised, by word of mouth and handbills posted all over the city, sometimes as many as 20,000 people from all walks of society would flock to the grounds. In their day some of these matches might have resembled an FA Cup tie at Arsena, but without the police to cordon and control the crowds. The streets would gridlock with carriages and pedestrians and, with some matches lasting up to three days, there would have been many traders servicing the needs of the crowd. Fast-food suppliers would set up stall; carriers would bring huge panniers to provide drinking water. There would be plenty of alcoholic beverages, too and ice (prepared by means of freezing mixtures or in earthenware vats covered with ether-soaked cloths to assist evaporation and cooling). Lavatory facilities and even beds had to be provided for those who had come the furthest.

According to Richard Underdown in his book *Start of Play – Cricket and Culture in Eighteenth Century England*, games of cricket could inflame players and spectators alike and some matches were hotbeds of contention. In 1718 there was a serious dispute about a cricket match played at White Conduit Fields. As always, there was a wager attached. The game between 'a London XI' and a team from the Punch Club Society of Rochester who called themselves 'Kent', was being played for half a guinea a man. After four hours of play in front of a large crowd it began to rain. 'The violence of the rains which fell so heavy, it was impossible to continue the game.' By this stage the Londoners were well on top and several members of the Punch Club decided to walk off. According to the Londoners they were 'hoping thereby to save their money', which was not part of the deal.

You can imagine the scene. The London team were fired with righteous indignation and the Kent team were equally angry at the accusation. It was only the weather stopping play, they said. The spectators were probably the most unhappy of all. It ended with the Londoners suing the Punch Club Society to get their stake money back. The case was heard before Lord Chief Justice Pratt, who

ordered that the game 'be played out'. Thus, the match was recon-
vened in July 1719 when London won by 20 runs. There was bad
feeling between the teams, but this did not stop them reconvening for
another match the following year. One witness, quoted in *A History
of County Cricket – Kent*, by R.L. Arrowsmith, gives the flavour of the
match, clearly devoid of the bucolic soft-focus lens with which so
much English cricket is stereotyped today:

> . . . The Kentish men having the Wickets, two Londoners
> striving for Expedition to gain the Ball, met each other with that
> Fierceness, that hitting their Heads together, they both fell back-
> wards without stirring hand or foot, and lay deprived of Sense
> for a considerable Time, and yet 'tis not known whether they
> will recover.

The atmosphere between the teams may well have been fiercely
competitive, but the tension among the spectators is likely to have
been even more dangerous. The concept of crowd control in
London's history is a comparatively modern one. Even after the Peace
Preservation Police, or 'peelers', came into being in 1815, crowd
control was not their first objective. As Radford says:

> The history of sport in England is sometimes as much about the
> crowds that gathered to watch it, as about what they watched.
> Freeborn Englishmen and women did not like to have their lives
> and pleasures interfered with. They never liked being controlled
> and sanitized. As a result, the English sporting crowd has
> always been a fearsome thing.

According to Underdown, in 1764, the magistrates complained about
the 'swarms of loose, idle and disorderly people' to be found around
cricket matches in London. The crowds themselves were often
described in similar ways, but as bodies of supporters they were
alternately fiercely loyal to each other and mutually hostile in ways
that modern football if not cricket fans would understand. At a
match in 1736, when Surrey were playing Kent on Kennington
Common, three soldiers arrived to apprehend a deserter, but the
crowd rescued him and inflicted 'a severe discipline' on the soldiers.

There are several other reports of incidents at cricket matches in London in the 1730s; sometimes the crowd threw stones at anyone who tried to jump the queue to get into the ground; a man died from such a blow. Eric Cantona's famously aggressive boot-in-the-head response to an insulting spectator has a long precedence. People in the crowd occasionally came to blows and sometimes the teams on the pitch joined in. At other times the games had to be stopped because the crowd disputed an umpire's decision and threatened even more serious disorder. The arguments surrounding betting compound this picture; there were often complaints about thrown matches.

Many spectators were social misfits and members of the criminal or sporting class of the 18th-century underworld. But others were members of the aristocracy, the social strata that was later the core of London's sporting and betting elite known as 'The Fancy'. In 1735, Frederick Prince of Wales and his friend Lord Middlesex – at the very pinnacle of noble society – promoted two cricket matches for £1,000. Frederick's death at the age of 44 is attributed to a blow on the head by a cricket or tennis ball; the former seems more likely. (Perhaps it was propelled by a sportsman hired for the purpose by Frederick's father, George II who had plenty of reason to find his eldest son repellent.)

This mix of social extremes is represented in many of London sports in the 18th century, and to some extent in the 19th too, particularly in sports that attracted the biggest betting. But in cricket more than in any other game the extremes of social class are represented on the playing field as well as in the crowd. Not only would the lord be playing with the gardener but in an inversion not witnessed in society before (perhaps with the exception of carnivals involving the 'Lords of Misrule'), the gardener could also be captain of a team which included his lord and master. Those in society who represented the respectable, middle ground sometimes complained that cricket was far too much of a social leveller and therefore dangerous to the proper order of things. In 1743, *The Gentleman's Magazine* carries the distinct grumble that 'great and little people, baronets and butchers, went out to field together'.

It may not have have been just the dangers of social levelling that stimulated this kind of comment. Given the crowds and the need to attract them in order to fill the money pots, the unruly matches were sometimes the occasion for other types of visitor attraction. Sometimes these happened without planning. Dogs were known to spoil the fun for players and increase it for spectators by running between the players legs and tripping them up. They also chased players in pursuit of balls or got to the balls before them. Such was the problem that organizers announced that any dog allowed to run loose onto the ground would be shot.

Far more of a crowd-tickler than an ad hoc dog on the pitch was racing by topless women. There are several contemporary reports that reveal that these races were arranged by the cricketers themselves to ensure the presence and amusement of the crowd. They took place during the interludes as the players changed ends, or were enticements that the crowd could look forward to after the match finished. The topless women racers were the forerunners of the streakers of post-1960s Britain, when so much cleavage – and occasionally other parts – was aired to millions courtesy of televised sporting events.

In 1744, *The Penny London Morning Advertiser* reported a cricket match on Walworth Common in which the players had each subscribed for a prize of a Holland Smock, worth one guinea, to be given to the best of 'two jolly wenches' who were to 'run in drawers only'. On 24 June 1748, the same paper reported another race between two women, Mary Weaver and Sarah Lucas, this time stark naked. The race took place after a cricket match held between High Kent and the Black Swan Club.

Radford's intriguing research shows that topless racing was already well established by the time ingenious cricket promoters co-opted it as a crowd puller. *Mist's Journal* reported on 23 October 1725 that 'a vast number of the lower class Gentry' had gathered somewhere in London expecting to see a race between young women 'in puris naturabilis' – i.e. starkers. The prize was two guineas. But as it turned out the girls were made to wear 'white waistcoats and drawers but without shoes or stockings.' Another paper, *The Daily Post Boy*, reported in August 1735 that two women ran almost naked in Stepney Fields for 'a guinea, a Holland Shift, an Apron and a pair of stockings'. But there is some finger-wagging attached. The account goes on to state that, for the sake of decency, in the future racing women 'will be obliged to have on White Drawers, and a White Waistcoat'.

Not to be outdone, by 1787 men had also got in on the act. On 20 December that year, *Jackson's Oxford Journal* reported that a runner by the name of Powell 'made a trial of a mile' on Moulsey Hurst, near Bushey Park running 'entirely naked'.

In no time the sport of naked running moved from the outskirts to the streets of busy central London. In September 1790, *The Craftsman* reported that two runners named Wood and Harper competed in a one-mile race along Tottenham Court Road. They 'stripped quite naked' and 'at about 6.15 started from the Turnpike Gate'. It is common knowledge that early morning is a good time for naked running, even in the blue darkness of winter. According to *The Sporting Magazine* in November 1792, one morning at seven o'clock, 'two waiters from the Cannon Coffee House raced stark naked' in St James's Park, 'to the amusement of a great number of spectators and the delicate nymphs of the Horse Guards'. The language here is gentle and consensual, evoking an event which was good fun for everyone involved.

The mood surrounding sport in London was not always so breezy; indeed it ranged from mildly cruel to what we would consider excessively violent. We should bear in mind that the accounts that follow involve people who are very much like us in many respects, except one. They lived at a time when betting on human or animal blood sports was acceptable, and reflected many aspects of their lives. They expected hard treatment themselves and often received it. Maureen Waller in *1700 Scenes from London Life*, wrote: 'There was no doubt that Londoners had a taste for cruel and ferocious sport, which reflected their own lives: nasty, brutish and short.'

And so to bulls, bears, cocks, rats, dogs, torn bodices and knuckle fights, once the stuff of the seamiest London pastimes.

ஸ் BULL AND BEAR-BAITING ஓ

By the time it reached its heyday in the 16th and 17th centuries, this particular pastime had been going on in London since time immemorial. Under the management of impresarios such as Philip Henslowe and Edward Alleyn, not only was it very popular, but it took place in legal, purpose-built establishments. These were the Bear Gardens and they were prominent in the London landscape, particularly in Bankside and nearby Paris Gardens. In their day, the amusements of bear- and bull-baiting were by no means sordid or squalid affairs and we know that the same audiences who understood the subtleties of *As You Like It* or *The Tempest* also enjoyed 'nature, red in tooth and claw' at the Bear Gardens.

The actual baitings were often the central part of organized shows, almost like modern circuses. Their presentation and content were probably the nearest in form to the extravaganzas that took place in London's amphitheatre and in others throughout former Roman Europe.

Not only the nobility, but the kings and queens of England enjoyed this sport, particularly from the 14th to to 17th centuries. Some noblemen even had their own bear-keeper, the 'bearward' as part of their household. The fifth Earl of Northumberland, who died in 1527, is recorded to have paid 20 shillings a year to his bearward, 'when he comyth to my lorde in Christmas, with his lordshippe's beests for making his lordschip pastime the said twelve days'. And just as a senior foreign dignitary or statesman today may be entertained with a visit to a Centre Court match at Wimbledon, a visitor to the Elizabethan court would come to a bear-baiting. In 1561, a 'grett bayting of the bull and the bare' was put on in Whitehall for the French ambassador, attended by the noblest lords and ladies in the land in all their finery. A later record, in 1623, offers an entirely new twist to the display when the Spanish ambassador was entertained to a spectacle at which they 'turned out a White Bear into the Thames, where the dogs baited him swimming'.

There was a specific Bear Garden built for more standard bear-baiting displays in Whitehall; the place was known by this name until the early Victorians removed any allusion to the sport from the heart of London.

Visiting dignitaries have provided wonderful eye-witness accounts of this sport, as of many other pastimes. A German traveller, Lupold von Wedel, describes the Bear Garden in Southwark following a visit in 1584:

There is a round building three storeys high, in which are kept about a hundred large English dogs, with separate wooden kennels for each of them. These dogs were made to fight singly with three bears, the second bear being larger than the first and the third larger than the second. After this a horse was brought in and chased by the dogs, and at last a bull, who defended himself bravely. The next was that a number of men and women came forward from a separate compartment, dancing, conversing and fighting with each other: also a man who threw some white bread among the crowd, that scrambled for it. Right over the middle of the place a rose was fixed, this rose being set on fire by a rocket: suddenly lots of apples and pears fell out of it down upon the people standing below. Whilst the people were scrambling for the apples, some rockets were made to fall down upon them out of the rose, which caused a great fright but amused the spectators. After this, rockets and fireworks came flying out of all corners and that was the end of the play.

In *A History of London Life* by RJ Mitchell and MDR Leys, we learn that on Sunday 18 August 1604, James I put on a banquet and entertainment at Whitehall Palace for the Constables of Castile. There was fine food, elegant dancing and everything was in exquisite taste. When this was over 'all took their places at the windows of the room that looked out upon the square, where a platform was raised, and a vast crowd had assembled to see the king's bears fight with greyhounds. This afforded great amusement.'

By the end of the 17th century there were Bear Gardens, as well as bear and bull-baiting arenas of a rudimentary kind, all over London. The sport was held every Monday and Thursday at Gray's Inn; and also regularly at Marylebone Fields, Soho, Tothill Fields in Westminster, and at Hockley-in-the-Hole that was in Clerkenwell.

Peter Radford has done considerable research in this area. He reports: 'To get the best out of a baiting, the bears were tethered and their teeth were usually ground down so that they had to use their forelimbs to fight off the dogs. The dogs' owners paid a shilling to set their dog on the bull, but I have never been able to work out what the dogs' owners stood to win.' If one could hazard a guess, the winnings may have been in the form of a wager made on the basis of the dog's savaging abilities, or it may have simply been a means of boosting the owners' standing and self-respect.

Inventive as ever, the London promoters would tempt their audiences with increasingly novel baiting entertainments. A 17th-century printed advertisement offers a feast of activities to draw in the punters:

> At the Bear Garden, at Hockley-in-the-Hole, at the request of several persons of quality, on Monday, the 11th of this instant in June, is one of the largest and most mischievous bears that was ever seen in England to be baited to death, with other variety of Bull-baiting and Bear-biting; as also a wild Bull to be turned loose in the Same Place, with Fireworks all over him. To begin exactly at three o'clock in the afternoon, because the sport continues long.

This kind of show would have been exceptional because bears were valuable and the sport was usually stopped before too much damage was done. Some of the bears were local celebrities and they were recognized and known by name: 'Harry Hunks', 'Tom of Lincoln', 'Blind Robin', 'Old Nell of Middlewich' or 'Sackerson'. Their owners were probably extremely fond of them; after all they were their living. According to Brian Jewell in *Sports and Games – History and Origins*, Old Nell of Middlewich used to be taken into a nearby tavern for refreshment after a bait.

The bull-biting or baiting, sometimes also known as bull-hanking, often involved dogs being tossed high into the air by the defending bulls. The dog's owners carried long sticks that were used to break the fall of the fighting mastiffs. (In bear fights similar poles or sticks were used to lever the jaws of the mastiff when he clutched his victim too tightly.) Contemporary engravings show dog owners wearing large aprons in which they attempted to catch the dogs before they hit the ground. This alone must have been an interesting part of the entertainment.

John Evelyn was one of several contemporary chroniclers who clearly disapproved of these sports, having witnessed them first hand. After seeing one bull-baiting on Bankside he records the extent of the dog-flinging that sometimes occurred: 'One of the bulls tossed a dog full into a lady's lap as she sat in one of the boxes at a considerable height from the arena. Two poor dogs were killed and so all ended with an ape on horseback.'

By the end of the 17th century, general enthusiasm for bull- and bear-baiting was waning and during the reign of Queen Anne at the beginning of the 18th century, the three bear gardens that remained were poorly attended. Records indicate that impromptu bull-hankings sometimes took place and still attracted crowds at that time. The most popular place for this was Bloomsbury Fields behind the house of the Duke of Bedford. On one occasion some 2,000 people turned up for a hanking with dogs. But they were dispersed before the event got underway by officers of the guard under orders from the Duke who was not keen on the rabble in his back yard.

Liza Pickard in *Dr Johnson's London* records another bovine sport, enjoyed on market days at Smithfield when gangs of men and boys gathered round a herd of bullocks brought in for slaughter. They would whistle and shout, brandishing sticks before picking on a game bullock and literally chasing it round the streets until it was too tired to run; London's very own Pamplona but without quite the style or ceremony. A drover's boy would catch the exhausted animal and take it to the slaughterhouse.

By this time the bull and bear fights were history, or had been driven underground, in London. But animal fighting certainly did not stop there. The descendants of the mastiffs once used against the bulls and the bears were brought out again in dog fights; savage and illegal affairs carried on in the sporting taverns of the city.

Less of a problem from a legal or indeed humane point of view was the 'ratting' that went on in the Victorian period. Again, the taverns were at the centre of the action. Rats were bought for as much as a shilling each, although more typically half-a-crown would secure a dozen. There were notices in the streets: 'Rats Wanted' and 'Rats Bought and Sold'. Jimmy Shaw, a publican ex-pugilist who owned one of the more popular rat houses, told Henry Mayhew, one of the foremost documenters of the London poor in the 19th century, that he took delivery of between three and seven hundred rats in a week and kept 2,000 alive on his premises. He said that 20 families were engaged in supplying his needs.

In these dim and fetid environments, the swells and the low-life of London gathered close together round the rat pits to bet on how many rats a particularly well trained and fierce dog could kill in an hour. One contemporary picture shows 'Tiny' sportingly dispatching rats at a rate of 200 an hour in the pit at the Blue Boar in Bunhill Road, watched by an eager crowd.

Rats are not high on the list of animals beloved by humans. Even so, killing on this scale for fun has no equivalent in today's London pubs; the worst one generally finds is a raucous bowling match or blood running high at a closely fought darts fixture. Peaceable betting at dominoes does not count. Even the ancient English art of cock-fighting appears almost paltry by comparison.

⚬ COCKFIGHTING ⚬

This was England's national sport before football. There are claims that it first came with the Phoenician traders or with the Roman invaders but it may have been a native pastime. Every small village, every different community of England's larger towns, had a cockpit. Both cockfighting and throwing at cocks were enter-tainments that involved people of all ages at every level of society. The former was a battle between fighting cocks; the latter consisted in throwing sticks at a tethered cock, with the person who knocked it 'dead on' winning the fowl as a prize. Heavy sticks such as hawthorn were favoured.

In early times, the sport was considered a way for young boys in particular to develop their targeting abilities as a preliminary to more formally organized archery practice.

Cockfighting was a particularly prominent activity at the Shrove Tuesday carnivals. Again we have William FitzStephen to thank for his late 12th-century description: 'Every year also at Shrove Tuesday . . . the schoolboys do bring cocks of the game to their masters and all the forenoon they delight themselves in cockfighting; after dinner all the youths go into the fields to play at the ball.'

According to Vernon Bartlett, in *Past of Pastimes*, 'cocking' was very popular in schools for many centuries. Boys were given a special allowance to buy fighting cocks and the 'forenoon' play to which

FitzStephen refers was devoted to the 'mains', in which several birds fought until there was only one survivor. Parents were expected to pay their 'cockpence' on these occasions as a contribution to the teachers' salary. The teachers would have been grateful for the dead birds too, which they were allowed to keep.

By the 16th century, cockfighting was thought unsuitable for London schoolboys. When John Colet, chaplain to Henry VIII established St Paul's School in 1509, he stipulated that 'the scholars use no cock fighting nor Riding about of Victory nor Disputing at St Bartholomew's; which are but foolish babbling and loss of time'.

The freshly crowned 18-year-old king was surely glad that his own basic schooling had already finished for he revelled in just about all the items on Colet's forbidden list. He loved to attend cockfighting and he took part in almost every other sport too. By all accounts he was genuinely good at many of them before his expanding girth slowed him down. At his Whitehall Palace Henry VIII had himself built 'divers fair tennice courts, bowling alleys and a cockpit'. Diverse indeed: there were two open and two closed tennis courts at his palace in Westminster and another was built at Hampton Court, which remains the oldest surviving real tennis court in England.

Henry VIII was a great one for being the biggest and the best, even when it came to showing off the size of his calf muscles to his courtiers, and his cockpit was also probably the largest built in London. A record made by a man called Wilson in 1607 recounts that Henry VIII 'did take such pleasure and wonderful delight in the cocks of the game that he caused a most sumptuous and stately cock pit to be erected in Westminster, wherein his Majesty might disport himself with cock fighting among his most noble and loving subjects'. Historians are divided about the exact site of Henry VIII's stately cockpit; some believe it was in the area of the present-day Treasury in Whitehall, while others reckon that it could have been where 10 Downing Street stands today. Can we imagine two such different uses for the same site – one Cabinet discussions, the other fighting cocks?

After some assiduous ferreting through ancient ledgers, historian Walter Gilbey reports in *Sport in Olden Time* that there was no record of cockfighting in Henry VIII's Privy Purse Expenses, although there are details of losses at dice, cards 'tables', shovelboard (an old form of shove ha'penny) and the 'Pope July game'. There is also mention of shooting matches, falconers, pheasant breeders, horse trainers and riding boys. A more contemporary source confirms that Henry was an inveterate gambler and a good catch for hustlers: the King 'was moch entysed to playe at tennes and dice, which appetite, certain craftie persones about hym perceyuynge, brought in Frenchmen and Lombardes, to make wagers with hym, and so he lost moch money'.

In 1635 a distinguished poet, Gervase Markham, wrote a discourse called *Pleasures of Princes* giving detailed advice on 'the choice, ordering, breeding and dyeting of the fighting-Cocke for Battell'. Markham believed that 'there is no pleasure more noble, delightsome, or void of cozenage and deceipt than the pleasure of Cokynge'. Poets were clearly involved in the gaming scene. Another verser of the period, Charles Cotton, published his *Compleat Gamester* in 1675. In this he too places 'cocking' high above any other recreation and reports that it 'hath gain'd such an estimation among the Gentry'.

Markham instructs us that to prepare a bird for battle he should be fed only fine, white bread and spring water for three or four days. Cotton's advice is far more detailed. The cock should be given 'white sugar candy, chopt rosemary and butter mingled and incorporated together', after which they should be put in straw to make them sweat. 'Towards four or five a clock in the evening,' continues Cotton, 'take them out of their stoves, and having lickt their eyes and head with your tongue, put them into their pens, and having filled their troughs with square-cut manchet [white bread], piss therein, and let them feed while the urine is hot; for this will cause the scouring to work, and will wonderfully cleanse both head and body.'

This sport was by no means confined to princes and schoolboys. In 1570 when the court and the aldermen in the city were both concerned about an outbreak of the plague, they ordered that all 'masterless men' caught frequenting places of common assembly, such as gaming houses, cockpits and bowling alleys, should be banished from the city. But throughout the 16th and 17th centuries the sport raged on, despite the outright prohibition in 1654, once again by the Puritanical Commonwealth. The 'Cock pit steps' coming out of Bird Cage Walk by St James's Park indicate another Westminster site. Others were at Drury Lane (hence the old term

'Cockpit Theatre'), Horseferry Road, Shoe Lane and Jewin Street. These were clearly not big enough or available frequently enough so 'cockers' built the 'Royal Cock Pit' in Tufton Street. This is the one depicted in Hogarth's famous engraving, *The Cockpit* (1759).

Waller records in *1700 Scenes from London Life* how Zacharias Conrad von Uffenbach, another German traveller sampling London amusements, went straight from a fist fight between an Englishman and a Moor at Hockley-in-the-Hole to a cockfight advertised at Gray's Inn. The fighting took place on a table in the centre of a round tower where the spectators sat on tiered benches. Reports Uffenbach:

> Everyone begins to shout and wager before the birds are on view. The people, gentle and simple (they sit with no distinction of place) act like madmen, and go on raising the odds to twenty guineas and more. As soon as one of the bidders calls 'done' . . . the other is pledged to keep his bargain. Then the cocks are taken out of the sacks and fitted with silver spurs . . . As soon as the cocks appear, the shouting grows even louder and the betting is continued. When they are released, some attack, while others run away . . . and are impelled by terror to jump down from the table among the people.

Uffenbach says that the money waged on these fights had to be paid straightaway. According to Waller, defaulters would be treated to immediate ridicule such as being hauled up in a basket and dangled near the ceiling. In 1728, César de Saussure gives a similar account to Uffenbach, adding that he thought the cocks were ugly in their close-cropped state. He offers other details too: 'Some of these fighting cocks are celebrated, and have pedigrees like gentlemen of good family, some of them being worth five or six guineas . . . Cocks will sometimes fight a whole hour before one or the other is victorious; at other times one may get killed at once.'

While this sounds like a riot of feathers and general betting mayhem, cockfighting by this period had developed into a complex and precise game and punters were versed in every nuance. They wanted to know the age of the birds (two years was the best) and their precise weight so that they could be matched accurately, or paired off into 'byes'. A middling size was best, between three pounds six ounces and four pounds eight ounces. The young cocks, known as 'stags', that were within an ounce in weight of each other were said to 'fall in' and those which fell in went into the 'main'. This was no longer the schoolboy type referred to earlier, although similar. In these adult cockfights, betting was staked on each battle with so much put aside for the overall winner, or the winner 'in the main'. The 'byes' were matched with less heed to weight or age and attracted smaller bets. The training, trimming and fitting of silver spurs, or occasionally of steel ones, was a matter of great pride among owners and was deemed a high art. And so it remained for at least another 200 years, despite attempts to prohibit the sport.

Under Victorian law a hefty fine of £5 could be charged for every day that a man was known to have been involved in cockfighting, whether as owner, spectator or the landlord of premises. But the Victorian authorities could do little about it in London. They knew it still went on; as it does very occasionally and secretly in the manors of London today.

Not surprisingly, the imagery of cockfighting has always permeated the English language. A cock once referred to a beer tap or spigot on a barrel in taverns such as the 'Cock and Bottle', or it could signify a strutting and boasting type of person, once called a 'cockalorum'. There was also the empty-headed fop or 'cockscomb', and the 'cock-sure' leader who was 'cock of the walk', unless he threw badly at a game in which case he was 'cockshy'. This was a time when people 'lived like fighting cocks' and hoped 'to die game'. And today we are still occasionally 'cock-a-hoop', when we are not 'cocking a snook', or 'cocking an ear' or eye. Outside the realm of cockiness, we show 'a clean pair of heels' (meaning to run away without blood on your spurs); we 'pit' ourselves against each other or fortune and some-times 'ruffle a few feathers', but only if we are 'cut out' for the job (cocks were clipped and had their combs cut for battle).

In London, of course, there was, and always will be, the 'cockney'. According to *Brewer's Dictionary of Phrase and Fable*, the word derives from an earlier spelling of 'cokeney', meaning 'cock's egg', a nickname for the small and malformed eggs that are sometimes laid by young hens and a term that came to be used by country folk about townspeople in general because of their reputed ignorance of country life and customs. Some would consider this explanation a load of cock, but it is as good as any. There is also the explanation that the word derives from 'cocker' meaning to rock the cradle and generally to pamper and cherish. The idea goes that Londoners were the ones who had a pampered and cherished life compared to the hard-living inhabitants of the country; so Londoners were the cockers and eventually cockneys. Interesting. Others believe that the word derives from the cock on the weathervane of the steeple of St Mary-le-Bow since a cockney is traditionally anyone born within the sound of Bow bells. But perhaps the word derives from England's erstwhile national sport, taken to heart and to excess in the capital.

✺ MEN AND WOMEN FIGHTING ✺

Sir Richard Steele wrote in *The Spectator* of 16 February 1709 that several French writers had commented on British 'throwing at cocks' and other baiting of animals, 'much to our disadvantage', and had imputed this passion to 'a natural fierceness and cruelty of temper'. Perhaps the Frenchmen were right.

We have already seen that fighting, or at least unruliness – scrapping, bundling and boisterousness – often leading to violence, went hand in hand with football and cricket. You could not even have an innocent slide on the ice without coming to blows. In the 12th century FitzStephen records how when Moorfields froze over, the young lads were not content to do a bit of easy skating by fixing bones securely to their feet. They also armed themselves with sticks shod with iron and went out tilting at friends and rivals at full speed. A rough and dangerous game that led to bloody noses and broken limbs but this was all part of the toughening process of their lives. Scrapping of this kind was normal and even expected.

In his interview for the *Sin City* series, Peter Radford offers the opinion that people were cruel in the past.

Yet they led a life in which they didn't spare themselves either. For example, it was customary in every village in the country, and it was certainly true in parts of London, for young boys to face each other in single combat with stout sticks. The object was to hit the opposition on the head. But, of course, hitting the opponent over the head didn't get you a score. What got you a score was the fact that blood would run an inch . . . No one stopped the competition because a head was bleeding – that was the point of the competition.'

A few bleeding heads, a few bloody noses, the tussle 'and scrap' of growing up in tough circumstances and being prepared for it – this sounds reasonable enough. But more than a school of knocks, fighting of the human variety was also a London pleasure. A good fight that started by chance rather than arrangement was a real bonus in the day. When this happened the London crowds did not turn away or look for a policeman. They quickly formed around the event like a phagocyte enclosing a foreign body in the street's bloodstream. They yelled encouragement and usually someone suggested a wager. Says de Saussure of Londoners, 'the lower populace is of a brutal and insolent nature, and is very quarrelsome'.

Like de Saussure, Henri Misson was another keen French observer of British oddities, particularly as they were manifested in the capital. Back to boys fighting, he noted:

If two boys quarrel in the street, the passengers stop, make a ring round them in a moment, and set them against one another, that they may come to fisticuffs . . . And these by-standers are not only other boys, porters, and rabble, but all sorts of men of fashion, some thrusting by the mob that they may see plain, others getting upon stalls; and all would hire places, if scaffolds could be built in a moment.

Seating was indeed arranged for just this purpose at better organized fights, held in various venues around London, and these involved women as well as men. We return to César de Saussure who went to a fight which involved single stick and backsword bouts in which the men 'do not spare each other'. De Saussure starts us off with a graphic account of the women's contest:

Both women were scantily clothed, and wore little bodices and very short petticoats of white linen. One of these amazons was a stout Irishwoman, strong and lithe to look at, the other was a small Englishwoman, full of fire and very agile. The first was decked with blue ribbons on her head, waist and right arm; the second wore red ribbons. Their weapons were a sort of two-handed sword, three or three and a half feet in length; the guards were covered and the blade was about three inches wide and not sharp – only about half a foot of it was, but then that part cut like a razor. The spectators made numerous bets and some peers who were there made very large wagers. On either side of the two amazons a man stood by, holding a large staff, ready to separate them should blood flow. After a time the combat became very animated, and was conducted with force and vigour with the broad side of the weapons. The Irishwoman presently received a great cut across her forehead, and that put a stop to the first part of the combat. The Englishwoman's backers threw her shillings and half-crowns and applauded her. During this time the wounded woman's forehead was sewn up, this being done on stage; a plaster was applied to it, and she drank a good glass of spirits to revive her courage, and the fight began again, each combatant holding a dagger in her left hand to ward off the blows. The Irishwoman was injured a second time, and her adversary again received coins and plaudits from her admirers. The wound was sewn up, and for a third time the battle recommenced . . .

The poor Irishwoman was destined to be the loser, for she received a long and deep wound across her neck and throat. The surgeon sewed it up, but she was too badly hurt to fight any more, and it was time, for the combatants were dripping with perspiration, and the Irishwoman also with blood . . .

De Saussure gives an equally vivid account of the fight that followed between the men. They had shaven heads and wore green and yellow ribbons; they used the same weapons as the women but 'they showed more strength, vigour, and ability, if not more courage'. The men also stopped only to have their wounds sewn up; the fighting periods being the equivalent of modern boxing 'rounds'. Even the rewards of victory had to be fought for. De Saussure writes:

After every round the victor was thrown money by his backers; but he had to exercize great skill in catching the coins, for he had a right only to those he caught in his hands; those that fell on the ground became the property of some of the numerous rascals that were standing about, who hastened to pick them up and appropriate them. The two combatants received several wounds, one of them having his ear nearly severed from his head, and a few moments later his opponent got a cut across the face commencing on the left eye and ending at the right cheek. The last wound ended the fight and the entertainment.

Hellish as these accounts may seem to modern sensibilities, these were organized fights, attended by surgeons of a kind, and complying with rules that the combatants understood. The fighters often knew each other and were even members of the same family or close community; they fought for money and provided entertainment. The women fighters boasted of their prowess and strength in much the same way as Tyson or Lennox, when quizzed about a forthcoming fight, will do today. One notice put up as an advertisement in 1723 read:

> I, Martha Jones of Billingsgate, fish-woman, who have fought the best fighting women that ever came to that place, and hearing the fame that is spread about the Town of this noble City Championess, of her beating the Newgate Basket-woman, think myself as brave and stout as any, therefore invite her to fight me on the stage for ten pounds.

The story that William Hickey, another *bon viveur* and diarist, famous for his *Memoirs*, tells of his adventures as a young gallant in 1763, evoking a savagery that has little to redeem it. His account captures the sense of depravity, the descent into hell of lost souls, that Hogarth evokes time and again in his contemporary illustrations.

Hickey relates how he and his companions were 'brim full of wine when we sallied forth at the customary hour, went the old Bow Street rounds, from whence I was led into an absolute hell upon earth'. His destination that night was a place called Wetherby's in Little Russell Street, near Drury Lane. His party was admitted through a well guarded and bolted door and he was led into a room which was in uproar:

Men and women [were] promiscuously mounted upon chairs, tables and benches, in order to see a sort of general conflict carried on upon the floor. Two she-devils, for they scarce had human appearance, were engaged in a scratching and boxing match, their faces entirely covered with blood, bosoms bare and the clothes nearly torn from their bodies.

While this contest went on 'with unabated fury', Hickey took in another sight: 'In another corner of the room, an uncommonly athletic young man of about twenty-five seemed to be the object of universal attack. No less than three Amazonian tigresses were pummelling him with all their might, and it appeared to me that some of the males at times dealt him blows with their sticks.' In this instance, Hickey's companions intervened and managed to stop the fight 'after a few knock-me-down arguments'.

In all these accounts the commentators tended to be more shocked by the crowd than by the fighters and, as Hickey observed above, some of the spectators joined in, although in what appears to have been a cowardly manner. In the bare knuckle fights that were starting to be promoted in the mid-1740s in London, some wealthier members paid to sit in the ring with the fighters to get a real smell of blood and sweat, while the boxers were often subjected to clouts from ringsiders if they came too near them.

∽ BARE-KNUCKLE BOXING ∾

There is a great deal of evidence of formal boxing bouts in London much before the end of the 17th century. But the inhabitants of Londinium would most probably have enjoyed an ancestral form of the sport in their amphitheatre. This was based on an ancient classical form of boxing that, by 686 BC, had become refined and respected enough to be included in the Olympic Games. The matches were held outdoors with the spectators forming the boundaries, and the fight continued without pause until one combatant was unable to continue. The victors received good rewards including gold, livestock or trophies. The boxing evolved so that fighters would wear soft leather strips around their wrists and two-thirds of the way up their forearms as rudimentary protection. In the heyday of gladiatorial sports during the Roman Empire – which included the whole 360 years of Londinium occupation – hard leather hand bindings came to replace soft leather and this was more of a weapon than a protection. By the fourth century, the boxing that early Londoners may have witnessed had evolved another stage. The hard leather fists became studded with iron or brass nuggets and the boxers were compelled to fight to the death for the entertainment of the crowd.

Only many centuries later are there records of formal bouts taking place in London. The earliest of these was in 1681 and by 1698 regular pugilistic contests were held at the Royal Theatre. These early matches did not obey rules of any kind. They shared only the factor that the winner took the prize in the form of whatever purse was agreed, plus some of the stake money that was bet by the spectators. There was no weight classification and the fight continued until one combatant gave up or was pummelled to the ground. Alongside the punching there was plenty of wrestling, and there was no problem with hitting a man when he was down. These fights were illegal; and they attracted an audience of both men and women from the usual wide cross-section of London society.

One Londoner who caught the public's attention in the early period of the Prize Ring, as it became known, was James Figg. By 1719, this prizefighter was so popular that he was acclaimed as Champion of England, a distinction he held for another 15 years.

As a form of street show, Figg and others put up boxing booths in Oxford Street, then called Oxford Road. In time the matches shown in the booths moved from the street to other outdoor and indoor venues, including the Fives Court in St James's and the Tennis Court at Westminster. But they were most popular in the taverns, which fostered just about every kind of violent sport that could boost the number of drinking and gambling customers.

Figg's was one of the best frequented booths on Oxford Road; he called it an 'amphitheatre'. The writer Lady Mary Wortley Montagu had a certain fondness for James Figg, calling him an 'honest blockhead'. (Lady Montagu was daughter of the first Duke of Kingston, who sired a line of sportsmen on the London scene.) But Figg does not appear to have been much of a blockhead, nor overly honest. People flocked to see the men sparring in organized fights, sweat pouring and blood flowing – and they paid over the odds to do this. They were being fed just the kind of excitement that they loved, the better for the fact that the opponents were volunteers and there was money to be won.

The first rules of this sport were devised by one of Figg's pupils, a robust London waterman called Jack Broughton. In 1743, Broughton – known as the 'Father of Boxing' – established controls that laid the foundation for boxing as an acceptable athletic pursuit. Under Broughton's rules, the fight moved away from bar-room brawl to a technique depending more on the fists. Wrestling holds were permitted, but boxers could not grab opponents below the waist. When a man was down, he was allowed 30 seconds' rest after which he had to square off a yard from his opponent or be declared beaten; hitting him when he was down was forbidden. Out of the 30-second rest allowance, the more formal rest between bouts developed. Broughton even introduced 'mufflers', the forerunners of modern gloves, to protect hands and faces. But these proved to be ahead of their time. The London rules of the bare knuckle contest, and the tough 'professionals' championed in the Prize Ring predominated on the London circuit until the 1880s – even after the Marquess of Queensberry introduced his own rules in 1867.

Radford has closely researched the bare knuckle fights of the 18th century. Fights usually resulted in bloody noses, black eyes and broken bones, but their duration varied greatly. Some fights lasted six rounds; others could last 180; this was five minutes or a staggering three and a half hours. But rounds were much shorter than the three minutes allocated today; they tended to be an average of about 45 seconds with a 30-second break between them.

Bare-knuckle fights have been banned for more than 100 years because they are deemed too savage and harmful, but the evidence suggests that boxing in its modern form could actually be more dangerous. At the beginning of a bare knuckle bout the fighters would very rarely hit out with slogging punches carrying their full body weight. To do this risked serious damage to one's knuckles and sometimes dislocation of the forearms. Even the professional bare-knuckle fighters of the 18th and 19th centuries did not want to break their pickle-hardened fists prematurely on an opponent's thick skull. By the end of the long fights, the knuckles were often in a shocking condition, even after a fight consisting mainly of short jabs and knocks that sought to beat about the rib cage or to break open an eyebrow or lip. Ironically, the protection of the glove today encourages a far harder punch, and attracts more head punches of the type that can do long-term damage, or worse.

In his research for this book, Radford comments:

> Many of the fighters lived to be a good age and, despite the quarrels that the newspapers like to report, they acted as each other's seconds and bottle-holders over many years with very little long-term hostility and no apparent malice. They went to the theatre with each other, attended each other's weddings, and cried at their funerals . . . All was not as brutal as the puritanical souls and shock-horror merchants would have us believe.

Rules or no rules, fight-fixing was common. After Jack Slack beat Broughton to win the championship, boxing experienced a period of decline although men such as Daniel Mendoza, who published *The Art of Boxing* in 1789, and John Jackson, known as 'Gentleman Jackson', gave it back some respectability. Mendoza weighed only 160 pounds, but he was fast and had a famous left jab. Jackson had good connections among the wealthy of London which assisted in taking boxing out of its former, mostly low-life milieu. He won the championship in 1795 and retired undefeated in 1803, after only three defending fights. He later became a kind of early 19th-century personal trainer to the wealthy and famous of the day, Lord Byron included. These were the men of 'The Fancy', a loose grouping of rich sporting men who dabbled as part-timers in various sporting scenes but mostly the Prize Ring, before making their names as politicians, or writers, or retiring to the leisure of their estates.

In *The Celebrated Captain Barclay*, Radford provides an account of some of Lord Byron's personal training sessions with Jackson. Byron makes the following entries in his diary in 1814: Thursday 17 March 'I have sparred with Jackson for exercise this morning'; Sunday 20 March 'Sparred with Jackson again yesterday morning, and shall tomorrow'; Monday 28 March 'Got up earlier than usual – sparred with Jackson *ad sudorem* [until the sweat came]'; and 10 April 'I have not stirred out of these rooms for these four days past: but I have sparred for exercise (windows open) with Jackson an hour daily.'

On 28 March, the day that he mentions some virtuous sweating, Byron also records that he dined with Scrope Davies for six hours and they drank a bottle of champagne and six bottles of claret. At other times, he was more abstemious, as on 10 April, when he records eating only six biscuits and drinking four bottles of soda water.

In the same year as these records, London's Pugilistic Society was formed to try to bring some control into the sport and by 1838 the London Prize Ring rules, introducing a formal roped 'ring', were accepted throughout Britain and America. But the fights were still illegal, even though some of them were frequented by the Prince Regent and his courtiers at Regency London venues.

A fascinating account by a journalist writing in *Bell's Life in London*, on 14 September 1845, and recorded in Kellow Chesney's *Victorian Underworld*, reveals just how popular the big fights were. All the posturing and psyching up that surround today's professionals are there. The fight was between a 34 year-old called William Thompson, known as 'Bendingo', and John Caunt, the 30 year-old landlord of the Coach and Horses in St Martin's Lane. Bendingo, from Nottingham, was a great boxer and a thorough ruffian, who 'was as game and as active as a tarantula spider'. He was about 30 pounds lighter than Caunt, who had scaled down three stone for the fight, weighing in at about 14 stone. Both men had managers who were themselves ex-fighters.

Caunt's manager, Tom Spring and Bendingo's manager, Jem Ward, got together to decide on a venue for the fight that was a 'safe location', somewhere hidden from the 'maw-worms' (a popular term, meaning gut worm, for the magistrates and others who enforced prohibition). They settled on Newport Pagnall in Buckinghamshire, a point roughly halfway between Nottingham and London. Secrecy was difficult to keep. Supporters in a frenzy of excitement poured to the designated area from north and south, benefiting from the very new but already extensive railway system of Victorian Britain. A few wore the coloured handkerchiefs given personally by one or other of the contenders as 'favours'. If you received one of these you had to pay your man a guinea if he won, so you needed to make sure you stood to win more than that. The money piled on.

As well as catching trains to nearby Wolverton junction, people streamed out of London in their hundreds on foot. The locals made a few pennies selling their barn space for travellers needing somewhere to sleep; others provided food and drink to the gathering mob.

On the day of the fight, the Prize Ring commissary set off early in the morning in a cart carrying all the equipment to the ring. This was close to a village called Whaddon. The commissary's cart was a good marker for the crowds and some 5,000 people are reported to have followed the cart and horse as it trundled along byways and field lanes to the supposedly secret destination.

This was too much of a giveaway for the Buckinghamshire magistrates. They sent a very polite and apologetic officer to Caunt's party waiting at an inn at Stony Stratford to say that both fighters would be arrested if they proceeded with the fight. Bendingo's side did not want to move from Whaddon, but eventually had to concede that there was a problem and the fight was moved over the county border to another spot, at Lillington Lovel. The crowds duly traipsed or rode onwards.

It was not until three thirty on a very hot late summer afternoon that the fight officials were in place and a locally known sportsman had been co-opted from the crowd as reluctant referee. The money was six to four on Caunt, the bigger man, but there was nothing to distinguish the determination of the contestants once the fight was underway. More than two hours later, Bendigo won the day in the 93rd round, having punched Caunt well below the waistband in the 92nd. All through the fight the crowd had yelled and fought among themselves, sometimes spilling into the inner ring and occasionally threatening the referee with murder.

A great deal of money changed hands that day. But it was just one of many thousands of days when fortunes were lost or made in London.

✺ EXCESSIVE GAMBLING ✺

According to Cicero, gambling was forbidden under Roman law both during the Republic and the Empire. Gaming of most kinds was considered effeminate and unmanly. Horace complains that 'youths' in particular were taking up games of chance instead of riding and hunting. Nevertheless, as Martial, another Roman chronicler, reports, gambling was allowed during the feast of the Saturnalia, when the populace was given licence to indulge to the full in all kinds of merrymaking. Euripedes records that gambling was in fact allowed at other seasons but only among the older men, presumably past fighting age.

Whether they were licensed or not, the great Tacitus himself informs us that gambling games involving dice and board were enjoyed in Roman Britain, among other Germanic peoples. And we can be confident that wagers on gladiatorial combats and chariot races were a common activity among many of the population of Londinium. But there is no record of gambling of the extraordinary and excessive kind that later Londoners of all classes particularly enjoyed. So the spotlight will move rapidly forward to the time when the sporting wager is documented, inventive and excessive by comparison to anything we have seen since.

First to Henry VIII, whom we already know was an inveterate gambler. For similar reasons to those of the Roman authorities, Henry VIII banned gambling in an act of 1541. The act was devised with for the double purpose of 'maintaining artillery and debarring unlawful games'. The 'artillery' referred to meant archery and the preamble of the act noted that the skill of the people in this martial art 'is sore decayed, and daily is like to be more and more minished'. The reason for this degeneracy is said to have been the practice among the people of 'many and sundry new and crafty games'. These games not only diverted the popular attention from the more manly and patriotic art of shooting with the yew bow, but apparently gave rise to murder, robbery and other felonies.

The act goes on to make provisions for getting archery firmly back on the agenda, ordering that everyone between the ages of 11 and 60, except justices and clergymen, had to practise with the long bow and keep bows and arrows ready for use. Meanwhile 'crafty games' were prohibited: 'none articifer or handy craftsman, husbandman, apprentice, labourer, servant at husbandry, journeyman or servant of artificer, mariner, fisherman, waterman or serving man shall play at tables, tennis, dyce, cards, bowles, closh, coyting, logating.'

The working class of the period was thus barred and carding was specifically abolished in any common house. Again, as in the Roman law of so many centuries before, these various crafty games were all allowed during the 12 days of Christmas.

Meanwhile, Henry VIII's own living quarters and social milieu had nothing to do with common houses or the lower classes and he and his courtiers gamed on happily. Henry VIII had learned to gamble at his father's knee; one Christmas night Henry VII took with him 'thirty-five unicornis, eleven French crowns, a ducat, a ridare, and a leu', a wedge altogether valued at £42 in the money of the day according to Bartlett in *Past of Pastimes*.

Thus curtailed, common Londoners had to learn to be more careful but they did not stop carding or other forms of betting during the Tudor and Stuart periods. They loved to bet and some of them lost their family patrimony or their livelihoods, even their lives, in its pursuit. Subsequent monarchs continued to indulge freely too. Elizabeth I was a keen card player although a bad loser, so courtiers involved in a game had to be careful to watch her mood. James I gambled hugely but was said to have been so lazy that often he had someone else to hold his cards.

England's first national lottery, held in London over an extended period between 1568 and 1569, was intended to raise money for state coffers. It also promised very substantial prizes for individuals, livery companies and parishes taking part. According to John Richardson in *The Annals of London*, the state gave permission to Peter Grimaldi and George Gilpin to launch a lottery scheme in 1567. This early equivalent of Camelot devised a game that according to the publicity broadsheet was to be a 'very rich Lottery General, without any blanks, containing a great number of good prizes, as well as ready money as of plate'.

The intention was to raise the vast sum of £200,000, half of which would be for prizes. The first prize was to be £5,000 in cash, plate and furnishings; second was £3,500 and so on down to 9,418 prizes of 14 shillings in cash. As an additional lure that has no modern equivalent, ticket-holders were also granted freedom from arrest except for felonies, murder, piracy or treason. Tickets were priced at ten shillings each, precluding any but the wealthy from taking part. Unfortunately for the organizers, and the state coffers, the lottery was poorly subscribed.

Richardson reports that despite an extended subscription period and plenty of pressure applied to livery companies and the corporations of Elizabethan London, the eventual prize money was valued at only £9,000, just over 10 per cent of the amount the organizers had hoped to dole out. He writes:

> The method of funding the winners was incredibly complicated. Each ten shilling ticket-holder had his name put 12 times into the drawer. In one pile were 400,000 counterfoils naming purchasers and in another were 29,505 winning tickets with a value scaled down by one-twelfth, and also 370,495 blanks. The draw then began, matching one counterfoil against whatever came out of the other pile. Derisory prizes were received because of the scaling down. The mayor won 1/3d, as did towns such as Bexley and Cambridge.

This is rather like winning 1/360th of a pound for your single pound placed on today's lottery. The fate of Grimaldi and Gilpin is not on record.

We know already about Oliver Cromwell's attitude to sports and gambling, particularly where the most sinful game of tennis was concerned. But Commonwealth suppression was superficial and temporary, merely forcing a growing gambling endemic under the carpet until Charles II arrived. But even Charles II's government reinforced the former act of Henry VIII as far as the lower orders were concerned. And another act in Queen Anne's day declared that all bonds given for money 'at play' or money lent at the time with which to play, should be considered legally void. So gambling was officially illegal.

Unofficially of course, and with little regard to the law or any concern about excessive behaviour, gambling raged on in London, particularly among the wealthy. Apart from the gaming houses and clubs and visits to the turf or to the 'listing' or betting shops that later emerged, lotteries became very popular, despite their inauspicious start. By the time they were legalized, with the Lottery Act of 1778, there were already 400 lottery offices established in London alone. Upon legalization, another 50 were added in haste. Such was the scale of gambling in England that it was calculated that in 1796, there were 9,500 men employed in the lottery offices.

Gambling was such a phenomenon that it attracted plenty of latterday speculation as to its cause in cultural or sociological terms. Some have seen it as a kind of Baroque extravagance reflected in people's lives. Speaking more plainly, the early 20th-century cultural historian Johan Huizinga believed it fitted in with the 'general tendency to overdo things' in this period.

Excessive gambling must also be seen in the context of the rich mercantile society in London. This was a time when increasing affluence allowed more people, the growing middle class in particular, to play the big games that were once the domain of the very rich. This in turn caused a backlash. Members of the old feudal order became more clubbish and defensive, determined to show their standing by being the first to throw money about with excessive zeal, as if it did not matter. To do this showed one's style, bold heart and good breeding; therefore not to do it was pusillanimous, the reserve of hard-working merchants and traders still struggling to succeed. This was a simplistic position for the aristocracy to take because most of the merchants and others in the lower orders had already achieved wealth and respectability on the back of London's position in global and domestic trade. They had arrived, and were happily placing their bets.

Alongside gambling itself, and very closely equated with it, new notions about commercial money-making arose in the mid-17th century. This was the age which saw the birth, in London, of the concept and practice of insurance. Among the moneyed classes, insurance quickly became a favoured form of gambling. Insurance could be taken out on virtually anything – as it still can today in London. Life spans were very popular subjects for investment of this kind and to help customers make up their mind whom to 'back', daily quotations of the rates placed on the lives of eminent public people were issued by the early insurance houses, Garraways and Lloyds. In 1708, the Taylors' Friendly Society advertised insurance on the lives of adults and children with the slogan 'longest liver takes all'.

After the establishment of the Bank of England in 1695, another form of gambling presented itself in London, in the form of stocks and shares. Fortunes could be made, substantially increased, or lost, through dealings in shares and speculation on credit, both of which shared the same spirit as pure gambling. The 17th-century economy has been described as an 'enormous casino, where all were obliged to risk their fortunes on the winning combination'.

This is the economic context for the forms of gambling that Londoners have long loved best: the turf and the tables. Some of London's traditional gentlemen's clubs – White's, Almack's, Crockford's and Brooks' – were built on the proceeds of money that was itself made through gambling. Crockford's, built sumptuously in St James's, was the brainchild of William Crockford, who had started life as an illiterate but quick-witted fishmonger, for whom gambling became a crock of gold. He is said to have amassed a fortune worth more than a million pounds – eventually losing most of it on speculation.

Throughout his life, Crockford remained illiterate but quick-witted, the rich servant to the rich masters of the *bon ton* who came to his club to spend money and accomplished this in the fashion of the fabulously wealthy. These clubs were designed to be exclusive, requiring strict codes of dress and etiquette. Socially, Crockford's was controlled by gentlemen and noblemen such as the Earls of Sefton, Chesterfield and Lichfield. Membership was a means of confirming one's distinction in an increasingly mobile society. The very words White's, Brooks and Crockford's were synonymous with style and class. In his *Reminiscences*, Captain Rees Gronow, an intimate of Shelley, wrote that 'no man can describe the splendour and excitement' at Crockford's. 'The members of the club included all the celebrities of England, from the Duke of Wellington to the youngest Ensign of the Guards . . . soldiers, scholars, statesmen, poets and men of pleasure . . .'

Fortunes were made and lost at these clubs by both men and women; among the latter Georgiana, Duchess of Devonshire, is famous for all but bankrupting herself and her long-suffering husband. As Captain Gronow recorded, one of the most distinguished members of Crockford's was the Duke of Wellington, though he is said to have joined only to be able to blackball his son, Lord Douro, should he apply for membership.

Horace Walpole wrote in 1770 that, at Almack's, 'the young men of the age lose ten, fifteen, twenty thousand pounds in an evening . . . Lord Stavordale, not one and twenty, lost £11,000 there last Tuesday, but recovered in one great hand at hazard.' To put this in perspective, one-hundredth of this amount would pay the annual salary of the king's personal surgeon at the time. According to Christopher Hibbert in *A Social History of England*, the statesman Charles James Fox would leave the House of Commons after a debate and gamble all night before returning to the House for a debate the next day. He once lost £13,000 to the Earl of Carlisle in a single sitting and another time he gambled continuously for 24 hours losing money at the rate of £10 per minute.

Almost every visitor to England commented on the national fervour for gambling. In 1754, *The Connoisseur* noted that 'there is nothing however trivial, or ridiculous which is not capable of producing a bet'. The members of White's would even bet on the way a fly travelled on a window pane. There were bets as to whether Mr Cavendish would succeed in killing 'the bluebottle before he goes to bed' and, on a wet day, Lord Arlington bet £3,000 at White's on which of two raindrops would reach the bottom of the window-pane first.

Historians accord the account of one of the most grotesque of bets of the time to an anecdote related by Walpole. There are various versions of this story. A man, presumably a gaming man himself, collapsed in or near one of the gaming houses. Bets were immediately placed on whether he was dead or alive and those who had wagered that he was dead protested that attempts to revive him would affect the fairness of the bet. Consequently, he was left alone and he died, much to the satisfaction of those who had bet on that outcome.

Death was a factor in another way, too, because ruin brought about by excessive gambling drove people to suicide. In 1755, Sir John Bland, MP for Ludgershall, shot himself after being ruined at White's where he had squandered his entire fortune playing hazard; at one stage he had been £32,000 down. In the same year, Lord Mountford shot himself after losing substantial sums. A few years later Lord Milton's eldest son followed suit at the age of 23, shooting himself at the Bedford Arms in Covent Garden.

The sportsmen and noblemen who were members of the Fancy in late 18th-century and early 19th-century London were also present among the clubbers in the gaming houses. But their main pursuits, as previously mentioned, included the Prize Ring and horse-racing and dreaming up outrageous wagers of other kinds.

Notable among this group was a Scot called James Douglas, Earl of March and later the 4th Duke of Queensberry. As a young man he outwitted his contemporaries with a series of ingenious bets which established his lasting fame.

According to John Robinson in *Old Q: A Memoir of William Douglas, Fourth Duke of Queensberry, Kt*, the first of these bets involved a journey by carriage and four horses. In 1748, at the age of just 23, William Douglas wagered 1,000 guineas that he could produce a carriage drawn by four horses that would cover 19 miles in an hour. This was impossibly fast in those days on England's roads. The bet was taken up. William Douglas commissioned the London coachmaker, Wright, to build a very special carriage for the purpose at his premises on Long Acre. It took nearly two years to produce the carriage and four. The final, ingenious contraption amounted to little more than a seat strung on leather straps with oil cans poised over the wheels to drip continuously and reduce friction. The horses' harnesses were made of silk and the horses were specially selected and trained racehorses. Winning his wager, Lord March completed his 19-mile course at Newmarket in a time of 53 minutes 27 seconds, averaging just over 21 miles per hour.

Three years later, Douglas bet that he could convey a letter 50 miles in under an hour. This again was thought quite impossible. A master of lateral thinking, he had a ball made of the same size and weight as a cricket ball and placed a letter inside. He then arranged for 20 skilled cricketers to practise their throwing and catching skills. On the appointed day he placed the cricketers 45 yards apart in a circle that was more than half a mile in circumference and they threw the ball quickly and accurately round the circle; even under intense pressure it appears that no one dropped the ball once. One hundred laps of the circle equalled a little over 50 miles. There were arguments about the fairness of this and the despondent losers of the bet had the circle measured again. It turned out that the ball had in fact travelled several miles more than the required 50.

When sheer inventiveness of this kind failed him, Lord March was not averse to a bit of cheating to win a bet. Between the 'carriage' and 'letter' wagers, he had plotted with his jockey to shed his weights during a race and restore them before and after the weigh-in. When this was discovered he was challenged to a duel, which he accepted with reluctance. At dawn on the appointed day his opponent arrived with a small procession carrying a coffin draped in black and on it was a brass plate engraved: 'James Douglas, Earl of March, born November 5th 1725, died June 10th 1750'. Douglas decided to apologise.

In 1735, there is a record that Count de Buckeburg bet a considerable sum on being able to ride a horse from London to Edinburgh backwards. Even more extraordinary, on 11 May 1749, there was a wager that an 18-month old girl could not walk the distance of the Mall (half a mile) in half an hour. The crowds gathered in their hundreds to see this special event and a lot of money was staked. The girl finished the walk in a comfortable 23 minutes. Another wager involved a journeyman who rode three times between Stilton and Shoreditch – a total of 213 miles – in 11 hours 34 minutes using 14 different horses. Big money, some £20,000, was placed on a young Irishman who had bet that he could walk to Constantinople and back in a year, and did so.

The journeyman's and the Irishman's and indeed the little girl's achievements indicate the way in which physical sports and gambling had become such close partners. In many respects the money wagered by the rich was the prize money of its day. Gambling thus underpinned sporting achievements of many kinds and drove the development of sport. The 'celebrated Captain Barclay' was one sportsman and nobleman for whom the necessity to make very big money led to one of the most remarkable physical feats ever recorded.

Captain Barclay was a Scot for whom London, as the source of most betting money, was a second home. He kept rooms just behind Haymarket in a seedy area known as 'Porridge Island' but, as a member of the Fancy, he kept far from seedy company. Like Lord Byron and the Prince of Wales, he sparred in Jackson's Rooms at 13 Old Bond Street.

Born Robert Barclay Allardice and brought up in Ury, Aberdeenshire, he was a fine sportsman by the age of 17, when he won his first 100-guinea wager by walking six miles 'fair heel to toe' (meaning that the heel of the front foot should strike the ground before the rear foot left it) within an hour. This he achieved comfortably and started his career as England's greatest pedestrian. Pedestrianism, meaning walking races, was a major sport throughout the country and much of it was focused in London, where it attracted significant betting.

In *The Celebrated Captain Barclay*, Radford gives a thorough account of Barclay's graduation from his early wager to a number of others. On his father's death, Barclay, only 18, had to become head of the family, which comprized seven children. He was continually looking to escape the confines set by strict guardians that his father had seen fit to appoint before he died. The 12 guardians managed to get Barclay back in harness after he had succeeded in signing up as an officer in a local regiment, but his abilities as a pedestrian were a means of forging his own future direction.

Aged 20, Barclay won another sporting wager by beating a seasoned pedestrian called Ferguson over 70 miles. He then embarked on a series of bets with a fellow Scot known as the Daft Laird, who proved not so daft. Although Barclay was by then a skilled pedestrian, he lost all those bets – amounting to the huge sum of £6,175 – more than enough to ruin his family.

Barclay needed to win some very serious money to recover his losses. In 1801, he bet the Daft Laird that he could walk 90 miles in 21½ hours. The laird took up the bet for a stake of 5,000 guineas and also drew up stringent articles of agreement which, among other stipulations, contained the clause that the walk must take place in November. Having walked 300 miles to Oulston in Yorkshire from his home in Ury, Barclay was trained for the coming ordeal by Jackey Smith, a great English trainer of the day. Smith took him under his wing and put him through a campaign of preparation that makes training for a Royal Marines Commando green beret look reasonably pleasant by comparison.

The regime involved alternate walking and running in very heavy clothing through most of the morning, starting at 4 a.m. and spending the afternoon labouring around the farm. Smith was hard on his pupil, haranguing him continually, controlling his diet and improving his technique. Barclay responded by being a hard-working and avid trainee. The forthcoming contest caught the interest of the media and *The Times* reported that: 'Smith ordered him about just as if he had been a spaniel'. At a time trial in October, Barclay completed 90 miles in less than 20 hours. Then, in November, he won his wager by walking the full amount with 68 minutes to spare. Thus, he became known as the celebrated Captain Barclay.

In the years that followed, he accepted the occasional challenge and turned others down, but it was not until a rival threatened to outdo him that he came up with the most extraordinary wager ever known. Who would give him 1,000 guineas to walk 1,000 miles in 1,000 hours, never doing more than one mile in one hour?

Walking 1,000 miles in six weeks without stopping is difficult enough, but being deprived of sleep was another problem. The eyes of the gambling world were on Captain Barclay and his impossible task. Money poured in from every quarter. A man called Bold Webster took up the 1,000-guinea wager and with bets on the side, Captain Barclay stood to win about 16,000 guineas in all. *The Times* estimated that some £100,000 was tied up in the betting. This was the equivalent of £40 million today.

For safety and guidance, Captain Barclay set up gas lamps at Newmarket where the walking took place in the summer of 1809; some lamps were shot at or stoned in order to divert the Captain from his course. For protection he carried a pair of pistols and occasionally was accompanied at night by a heavyweight champion fighter. During the day, thousands of people would turn up to cheer him on. Despite strained ligaments, toothache and severe sleep deprivation, Captain Barclay succeeded and became a rich man.

Primarily known for this great feat, Captain Barclay was also famous as the trainer of other athletes. He trained bare-knuckle fighter Tom Crib, who was a coal-man from Seven Dials, and went on to defeat Tom Molineux, a freed slave from Virginia, for the championship of the Prize Ring in 1811. This was the first black versus white championship bout. Like the fight between Caunt and Bendingo, described above, this one had to be arranged in a location away from London. It was kept secret and was never advertised; nevertheless 20,000 people turned up. As so many fighters did, Crib went on to become a publican and ran a pub which remains today on the corner of Oxenden Street and Panton Street, just off Piccadilly. Molineux himself became an adopted Londoner and went to live with Bill Richmond, a black publican, cricketer, trainer and fighter. He also kept a pub called the Horse and Dolphin, just south of Leicester Square.

Barclay and Jackson were 'permanent' members of the Fancy; others came and went, representing every part of London society. There were politicians such as the Honourable William Wyndham and Lord Thurlow; poets such as Lord Byron; artists such as Sir Thomas Lawrence; and others whose lives must have been much like that of Mr JJ Brayfield whose obituary in *The Sporting Magazine* of March 1821 says it all:

> . . . almost from infancy attendant upon all the fairs, boxing matches, races, and diversions of every kind round London from the ring made by the first rate amateurs of the Fancy down to the weekly badger-baiting in Black Boy-alley. Also constant at Newgate executions.

But London never achieved quite this degree of abandoned gambling as a pleasure pursuit again, at least not without sanction, as the age of respectability drew its mantle over the gas lights and parties. Taking the moral high ground, the instructive writer of the entry under 'gambling' in *Chambers Encyclopaedia* of 1862, offers a comment that takes us full circle back to Horace:

> In general, it is resorted to as a refuge against the depressing sensations of languor and vacancy, which the want of active exertion causes in the minds of those who have no inner life; and the classes most addicted to it in all countries are the idle, and mere men of business in their idle hours.

He could just as easily be referring to the drug-taking – from cannabis and opium to gin and tobacco – that has been intimately linked with sinful behaviour in Sin City since the early Romans first slipped under their tables at a drunken symposium.

ALTERED STATES

∽ INTOXICATING EVIDENCE ∾

The majority of Londoners and their forebears have always preferred the state of intoxication to that of sobriety. A pale version of mead was consumed by people in the region of the Thames valley as long as 4,000 years ago, since which time oceans of ale have passed through the body of London, along with countless lakes of wine. But the gluttonous tale of wine and beer comes in the next chapter, appropriately washing down an account of the mountains of food that prosperous Londoners have had the pleasure of consuming over the centuries.

Our concern here is intoxication of another kind – narcotic magic, escape and adventure: the drowsy inspiration that comes from poppies, cannabis, henbane, mandrake, deadly nightshade and ergot; the transformations wrought by salves, herbal preparations and resins that both lift and deaden the senses, inducing excitement and torpor, bringing both temporary and permanent oblivion. Tobacco is included because Londoners are historically very keen on this mottled leaf and have worn its thick halo in the conduct of their business and pleasure in a way that makes a mockery of today's public distaste for smoking. Gin is also included because it occupied its very own altered state – a place of incredible degradation – in London's history.

As far as drug-taking in the capital is concerned, the modern population appears to outdo its forebears in excessiveness – unless we take the standard from gin-drinking in the first half of the 18th century, which was a desperate problem and a far more visible one than today.

Nowadays, whether we choose to take part or not, we live in a global drug culture and, as one of the world's richest nations, Britain is a notable consumer. As jet-setters, junkies, students, clubbers, rockers and grey-haired partizans we snort, inject, swallow and smoke tons of cannabis, thousands of kilograms of cocaine and heroin, volumes of ecstasy, amphetamines, barbiturates and other mind-bending substances. We use drugs to go up, down and sideways, to expand our minds, extend our sexual performance, lose weight, gain favour, remain in the in-crowd, or at least to show our ticket. We are ever keen to experiment and keep the party going. London is not surprisingly responsible for the biggest cut of the UK's estimated £2.3 billion annual spend on heroin alone.

By comparison, records show that drug-taking as a habitual or recreational exercise used to be generally rare in London, with the notable exception of opiates and gin. However, there are indications that our earliest antecedents used drugs that many Londoners use today; not to the same extent, yet for a similar spread of medical, recreational and pseudo-mystical purposes.

ꕔ BLOWING THE MIND; HEALING THE BODY ꕔ

One of the most important and mysterious items discovered in the ruins of the Temple of Mithras, built in third century Londinium, was a silver casket, the outer casing of which was covered with a rich iconography of wild and exotic beasts, lions and elephants. Within the casket was a small silver strainer, which was almost certainly used as an infuser of some kind. There was also a remnant of a silver bowl.

The purpose and meaning of these items is still the subject of scholarly debate, but there is a general consensus that they were used in cult rituals as a means of creating powerful drugs.

The late Roman London historian Ralph Merrifield believed that they were used for Mithraic cult initiation rites. He deduced that the triple bars on the strainer offered 'a precise measure . . . for a dry herbal preparation which would produce a drug of known strength and efficacy if the strainer were suspended in the correct volume of water'. It is understood that the primary initiation into the Mithraic society required the initiate to endure ordeals by heat and cold before being buried in the ground and later symbolically resurrected. Merrifield argues that the 'initiation was a painful and dangerous business, and oblivion by means of a powerful drug would not only produce the appearance of death, but also perhaps give the candidate a better chance of survival'.

Martin Henig, an expert in Bacchic cults of the period, agrees with Merrifield about the use of the strainer as an infusor, but believes that the imagery on the casket was more in keeping with the later third- and fourth-century period when the temple was taken over by worshippers of Bacchus. He suggests that the casket was more like a miniature *cista mystica*, a little box containing sacred things used specifically in the Dionysiac mysteries'. His conclusion is that the infuser 'was surely used for lacing wine with a measured quantity of narcotics', and 'offers another symbol of life very much at home in the Bacchic worship'. Citing other examples of these sacred containers and the imagery that they portrayed, Henig reflects that they may have evoked a similar state to 'the mind-blowing, drug-induced, mystical experiences of the 1960s'.

Taking this further, he suggests that the 'physical manifestations of Bacchic ecstasy, as shown in literature and art, agree with the symptoms of strychnine poisoning'. But what the Greeks and Romans understood by *strychnos* was not the tropical vines from which strychnine is derived, but a range of plants that could have included deadly nightshade and the highly poisonous thorn apple.

Whatever the truth, the purpose of these wonderful remnants from early Roman London must have been to blow the mind.

For centuries, the solenaceous family of plants, which includes deadly nightshade (*atropa belladonna*), henbane (*hyoscyamus niger*), and mandrake (*mandragora officiarum*), has played a distinctive role in medicine and has been used both for its anaesthetic and hallucinogenic properties. These properties derive from the three potent alkaloids found in these plants: hyoscyamine, scopolamine and atropine. The Romans used mandrake as a means of doping and as an anaesthetic. Dioscorides, who was Emperor Nero's personal surgeon, wrote in the first century AD that: 'a man sleeps in the same fashion as when he ate it, sensible to nothing for three or four hours . . . and physicians also use this when they are about to cut or cauterize.' The Romans were well aware of the fatal effects of large doses of belladonna, the prime-mover in deadly nightshade. A lethal injection of this substance finished the great Emperor Augustus himself at the hands of his murderous wife, Livia.

The narcotic as well as the poisonous properties of henbane were particularly famous in the ancient world. In Greece, it was believed that people who took appropriate doses of henbane became prophetic; thus the priestesses of the Delphic Oracle were thought to have inhaled the smoke of its seeds. Three hundred and fifty years of influence from the ancient world brought this knowledge to Londinium for sure, but its record remains largely buried, or perhaps the users of such mind-altering concoctions were too stoned to document their experiences. Nevertheless, some items have been found which suggest that the Roman Britons inhabitants made occasional use of weeds and seeds.

In the mid-1990s archaeologists excavating under Regis House at 43-46 King William Street in the City of London came upon a small leather pouch containing hemp seeds. This had been dropped in the rubble and mud infill between timbers used to construct the Roman waterfront that was built during 63 AD. It was Londinium's first find of hemp of the intoxicating variety known as *cannabis sativa*. This plant, like its cousin the common nettle, has always been easy to grow in Britain. There are records of the cultivation of cannabis at Old Buckenham Mere in Norfolk around 400 AD by which time the differing properties of the male and female genders of the hemp plant were well known to the Romans for their various medical and industrial uses. Again Dioscorides recorded *cannabis sativa*'s various soporific and anti-convulsive medicinal properties, while Pliny gave an account of the various industrial uses of hemp's highly fibrous stalks. All over the world and in England too, the non-smokeable and inedilbe form of hemp has been used to make paper, special forms of linen and other material. In the 21st century, it is seeing a resurgence as a raw material for these purposes.

The cannabis plant was clearly being grown by people in Anglo-Saxon households too. The plant is mentioned in an 11th-century Anglo-Saxon Herbarium. Here recorded as 'haenep', its use was recommended as a kind of analgesic for sore and swollen breasts. There are other records of its use against nodes and 'wennes' (lumps, cysts or warts) and other 'hard tumours'.

There is evidence to suggest that the solenaceous plants were generally used by Anglo-Saxons, as by their predecessors, in religious rituals. But why was cannabis apparently ignored as a psychoactive drug? It is puzzling that if some of cannabis' medicinal properties were understood by the Anglo-Saxons, there is no mention of its potential as a soporific or as a ritual drug. These people were great advocates and users of herbal remedies and adopted all kinds of plant seeds and materials for use as cures, or for their health-giving properties. We should bear in mind also that this was the age of herbal-based love-charms and potions, sometimes prepared by monks and clerics, at least until the penitentials of St Theobald, among other church laws, laid down sanctions against the practice. But someone somewhere would have surely found a socially acceptable psychotropic use for cannabis.

Current research indicates that *cannabis sativa* is a plant capable of psychoactive properties as a result of different growing conditions. The thinking goes that the plant's potential to act as a mind-altering drug may be affected by lack of sunlight, and that this might explain why the relatively sun-starved Anglo-Saxons did not enjoy their hemp to the same extent as their southern European cousins. Modern Londoners, who occasionally have curious plants growing indistinctly alongside their nettle cousins in a scratchy bit of ground behind their rose beds, may wonder at this interpretation. It is more probable that as the Christianization of the Anglo-Saxon community embedded the Church's authority, so authoritarian suspicion and distaste increased for any kind of drug-induced behaviour. Such behaviour represented paganism or even devil-worship.

References to pleasurable uses of cannabis continue to be thin throughout British history. They crop up in herbals and medical journals but always in a totally pragmatic light. For example 'water of hempe' is recommended as a cure for headaches and 'all hete whereso'er it be' in Andrew's *The Vertuous Book of Distillacioun* of 1527.

There is, however, one reference in Gerard's *The Herbal* of 1633 which does invest hemp with quite substantial psychotropic potential. In order to communicate with the dead, the writer suggests that hemp seeds and herbs (and he includes henbane here) are to be steeped in wine and strained through a cloth 'woven by a whore'.

Twenty-five years before Gerard's fascinating proposal saw print, Shakespeare's audiences would have understood the reference to other types of plant-based drugs in *Othello*:

> Not poppy, nor mandragora,
> Nor all the drowsy syrups of the world,
> Shall ever medicine thee to that sweet sleep
> Which thou owedst yesterday.

Nor would this avid audience have been perplexed by Cleopatra's poignant lament:

> Give me to drink mandragora . . .
> That I might sleep out this great gap in time.

However, in both cases the association in the minds of ordinary Londoners would probably have been with the exotic and the far eastern, as emblemized by the well-travelled Moor and the enigmatic Egyptian queen.

It took Londoners on the move during the Tudor and Stuart age of exploration – when spices and nutmeg were sought after as fervently as gold – to provide accounts that show up the tricks that modern cannabis-users might recognize. The sailors, soldiers and merchants of this age often had marvellous stories to tell on their return from the wondrous east.

One such voyager, in the 17th century, was the merchant seaman, Thomas Bowrey, who returned to London from a trading visit along the coast of Bengal. He provides a detailed report of his drug-sampling experiences in *A Geographical Account of Countries Round the Bay of Bengal, 1669 to 1679 by Thomas Bowrey*.

With a group of eight or ten fellow sailors, Bowrey spotted the locals enjoying a drink called 'bhang', which consisted of dried, crushed cannabis seeds mixed with water. The group went to the local bazaar and bought a pint of bhang for the equivalent of around sixpence. As Richard Davenport-Hines points out in his book *The Pursuit of Oblivion – A Global History of Narcotics*, these intrigued lads obviously thought there was something potentially demeaning or dodgy about their experiment, because they hired the services of a local fakir to attend their sampling of the substance so 'that none of us might run into the Street, or any person come in to behold any of our humours thereby to laugh at us'.

The results of Bowrey's foray into the mind-altering substance will evoke memories of evenings enjoyed by many a late 20th and early 21st-century student conducting similar experiments in halls of residence:

> It Soon tooke its Operation Upon most of us, but merrily, Save upon two of our Number, who I Suppose feared it might doe them harme not beinge accustomed thereto. One of them Sat himselfe downe Upon the floore, and wept bitterly all the Afternoone, the Other terrified with feare did runne his heade into a great Mortavan Jarre, and continued in that Posture 4 hours or more; 4 or 5 of the number lay upon the Carpets (that were Spreade in the roome) highly Complimentinge each Other in high termes, each men fancyinge himself noe lesse than an Emperour. One was quarrelsome and fought with one of the wooden Pillars of the Porch, until he had left himselfe little Skin upon the knuckles of his fingers. My selfe and one more Sat sweatinge for the Space of 3 hours in Exceedinge Measure.

The bhang described by Bowrey was one of the simplest possible mixtures of this drug. But there were various versions of this popular eastern concoction, often called 'bang'. Always ingested orally, it would often be made with milk, prime resin-laden cannabis flowers and leaves and was sometimes mixed with sugar, pepper, almonds, cardamom, poppy seeds, ginger and other herbs to make an exceptional kind of milkshake. In its simplest form it was the least powerful of the Indian cannabis preparations. Earlier than Bowrey, but with less anecdote, it is described in Robert Burton's *The Anatomy of Melancholy* of 1621 as 'like in effect to opium which makes its user gently to laugh'. Further up the scale of potency was 'ganja' prepared from the flowers of cultivated female cannabis plants, while 'charas' was the pure resin and more potent still.

As an initiation into the effects of cannabis, there were other English travellers who reported back the extraordinary effects of taking bhang. According to Sir John Chardin in *Travels in Persia*, two women, travelling in northern Bengal in 1678, noticed a beggar pounding up a 'charming Green' potion. They decided to try some and Chardin recounts: 'They began to be affected with that mad and comical Drunkeness, which is the infallible Effect of that Potion, then they were taken with a Laughing Fit and with a Humour of Dancing, and telling Stories, without either Head of Tail, till the Potion had perform'd its Operations.'

It is possible that British soldiers enjoyed some experience of cannabis as a result of contact with Napoleon's soldiers, who had discovered its stress-reducing properties during their invasion of Egypt. But it took Britain's imperial contact with India to ensure that psychoactive cannabis was embraced, to some extent at least, in London households from the 1830s onwards. Nevertheless, the medical rather than recreational properties of cannabis continued to be the subject of the greatest focus. Delivering a paper 'On the Preparation of the Indian Hemp or Ganja' in 1841, Dr WB O'Shaughnessy was notable for introducing to western science various well tried medical uses of cannabis. By the 1860s, cannabis was known to be beneficial in the treatment of many ailments: neuralgia, nervous rheumatism, mania, whooping cough, asthma, chronic bronchitis, muscular spasms, epilepsy, infantile convulsions, palsy, uterine haemorrhage, hysteria, alcohol withdrawal and loss of appetite.

Even Queen Victoria herself found Indian hemp very efficacious against her menstrual cramps and, as a result, many women in high society followed their sovereign's lead. But in the great age of respectability, decorum and self-control, there was concern about the less respectable mind-bending nature of this drug. It was duly avoided by many in favour of alcohol or the opiates, the better known devils. Nevertheless, cannabis could be self-prescribed and used as and how anyone wished until prohibition came with the Dangerous Drugs Act of 1928, an act which drove the weed underground and back into favour, starting with the early jazz clubs.

∽ FLYING SALVES ∾

The earlier suggestion that cannabis did not appear to be used as a psychoactive substance by the Anglo-Saxons because of moral or ecclesiastical prohibition is purely speculative. But the more general

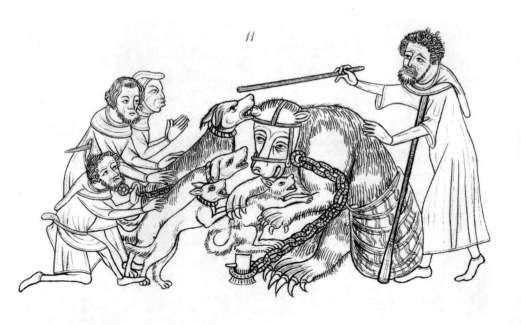

By the middle of the 16th century, as it approached its heyday in London after centuries of practice, bear-baiting was enjoyed by most Londoners from the monarch down. It was often provided as an entertainment for visiting foreign dignitaries.

WHIST.

Gambling became a national obsession and clubs such as White's and Crockford's developed as exclusive preserves for the wealthy, with some people losing or winning the equivalent of £1,000,000 and more in one sitting.

Hogarth's famous depiction of the 'Royal Cock Pit' in Tufton Street (1759). This was one of many cock-pits where Londoners pursued England's national sport before football.

Pall Mall, or 'Pell Mell', was a kind of croquet, golf and rudimentary form of billiards all in one. Charles II is alleged to have been a great player at this sport in St James's Park – although perhaps not. Samuel Pepys recorded his distaste when the king's fawning courtiers complimented the monarch's game.

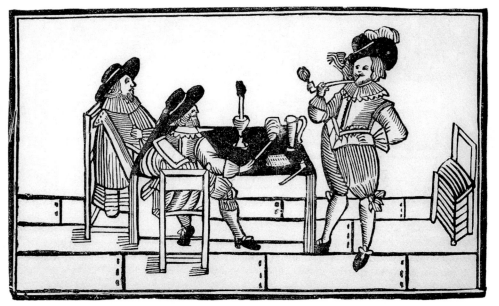

Elizabethan Londoners light up their pipes; men, women and even children took to smoking as if they had been designed for it.

THE UNION.

No attempts at ridiculing smoking, chewing and snuff-taking had any effect on London's flagrant affair with tobacco.

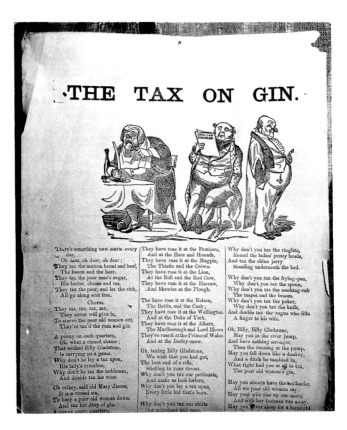

Ballads and broadsheets proliferated, both supporting and reviling the successive Gin Acts of the first half of the 18th century. These attempted to curtail gin-drinking, which had become a national disaster with London at its core.

Cruikshank's *Battle of A-gin-court*. Public disorder resulting from drunkenness was a common concern although the energy of the mob was frequently too depleted to do substantial damage.

CREAM OF THE VALLEY AND OLD TOM.

London, Published by J. L. Marks, 91, Long Lane, Smithfield.

Like so many of the capital's drunken vagrants today, gin-drunk Londoners of the 18th century tended to use their special booze to wipe out the world around them.

THE POOR CHILD'S NURSE.

An infant neglected because of a parent's gin habit; one famous case concerned a mother who murdered her child to sell her clothes to pay for her next gin fix.

LONDON SKETCHES—AN OPIUM DEN AT THE EAST END

One of Gustav Doré's dark-toned illustrations of London low-life. This one shows a visit made to an opium den in the East End. These were actually rare in London and became demonized more because of xenophobia concerning the Chinese who ran them than for their dissipating influence.

In this 1500 engraving by John Lydgate, *Assemble of Goddes*, the hooded figure between the nobleman and his lady appears to symbolise the ultimate provider – through the mediation of the church. The church is often remembered for taking most of the fare for itself; fat friars and drunken bishops were common.

London's cookshops and other takeaways have always, as they do now, had enormous fattening potential. But Londoners have always loved them.

Hogarth's *The Conversation*. Hogarth himself was a member of The Sublime Society of Beefsteaks, one of several clubs devoted to beef and conversation.

Scoffing and swallowing as much as you can for as long as you can was almost an unwritten maxim for Londoners. Here things get a little heated in a London Oyster Bar.

THE TOAST.

The 18th century was a time of monstrous excess in all things edible and quaffable, yet according to Samuel Johnson around 20 Londoners died every day from starvation.

use of mind and mood-altering drugs in the capital and elsewhere has and always will be viewed by some people as an act that has distinct moral implications. Particularly in post-Christianized Britain, the use of psychoactive substances was always accompanied by debates about morality. For the leading opinion-influencers of 15th, 16th, and 17th-century London there was no doubt – get yourself involved, and you were doing the devil's work. The connection in people's minds was so strong that if women used, in their recipes, any of the traditionally known mind-altering plants available in medieval, Tudor or Jacobean London, for medical use or any other purpose, they were assumed to be witches and in league with Satan.

Members of the solenaceous family of plants, continued to be the prime suspects among the native plants used, but there was also parsley, so innocent today. Within the canon of folk knowledge during the Middle Ages, it was known that oil extracted from parsley contains a property that behaves in a similar way to modern amphetamines.

As a result of the far wider influences on European folklore and superstition, the solenaceous plants were believed to have diabolic or magical properties. One European commentator, Emboden, reports of belladonna:

Known as the devil's herb, apples of Sodom and deadly nightshade, this solenaceous plant is said to be tended by the devil himself, who nightly looks after this plant except on Walpurgis night, when he retires to the mountains to prepare for the witches' Sabbath. At such a time the herb may metamorphose into an enchantress lovely to behold, but deadly in the viewing.

The psychoactive plants were mixed with others that were deemed to be potent symbolically or because they produced marginal physiological or psychological changes. Two 16th-century European sources list known recipes for 'flying ointments', those that took the person who applied them on an astonishing virtual voyage. The various recipes included, for example:

- Parsley, water of aconite, poplar leaves, and soot;
- Water parsnip, sweet flag, cinquefoil, bat's blood, deadly nightshade and oil;

- Baby's fat, juice of water parsnip, aconite, cinquefoil, deadly nightshade and soot.

To an ultimately God-fearing population, the use of baby's fat and bat's blood, soot and deadly nightshade would have been enough to send tremors down the communal spine. A little additional invention from the Bard leaves us with the three witches' own potent brew for upsetting the natural order of things, in *Macbeth* (1605):

> Double, double, toil and trouble;
> Fire burn and cauldron bubble.
> Fillet of a fenny snake,
> In the cauldron boil and bake;
> Eye of newt and toe of frog
> Wool of bat, and tongue of dog;
> Adder's fork and blind worm's sting,
> Lizard's leg and howlet's wing,
> For a charm of powerful trouble,
> Like a hell-broth boil and bubble . . .

This is the classic image of the cackling witch, stirring her disgusting brew. It is a fairy tale conception which is also closely related to the witch who takes off on her broomstick; and to the evil spirit who rides out, even in the early 21st century, after midnight on 31 October each year.

In fact the 'witches' of the Middle Ages were not evil sorcerers as often imagined. The view of British Egyptologist Margaret Murray, which predominated for most of the 20th century, was that witches were the lingering adherents of a once general pagan religion that was displaced by Christianity. More recently, historian Hugh Trevor-Roper theorized that the presence of so many 'witches' was the result of the way the medieval Church systematically 'demonized' the scattered folklore of peasant superstitions in the period between the Dark Ages and the Middle Ages. Neither of these views casts witches into the cauldron of myth and fairy tale in which they are still mostly perceived.

These pagan worshippers, or demonized adherents of old super-stitions, actually maintained much of the knowledge about the healing, harmful and hallucinogenic properties of a number of native plants. As practitioners they were certainly at work in London in the Middle Ages and later. From the 'flying' recipes quoted above it seems likely that they used deadly nightshade, henbane and mandrake and boiled these with fat in their cauldron. Evidence indicates extraordinary uses for some of the ensuing mixtures. Some of them were rubbed on the porous areas of the skin in the form of a salve. Records relate that the skin treated was often the mucous membrane of the vagina and that the mixture was applied – gently, one hopes – with a broomstick. The 'witch' would then fall into a deep sleep in which she would dream of flying, dancing and enjoying debauches with gods.

Modern-day researchers who have experimented with henbane (apparently by inhaling the smoke from burning seeds) report hallucinogenic experiences that would tie in perfectly with the accounts of witches flying to meet the devil at the Sabbat. One researcher reports:

> Each part of my body seemed to be going off on its own. My head was growing independently larger, and I was seized by the fear that I was falling apart. At the same time I experienced an intoxicating feeling of flying. The frightening certainty that my end was near through the dissolution of my body was counterbalanced by an animal joy in flight. I soared where my hallucinations – the clouds, the lowering sky, herds of beasts, falling leaves which were quite unlike ordinary leaves, billowing streamers of steam and rivers of molten metal – were swirling along.

These potions harnessed the active alkaloids in the plants but, by applying them in the form of salves rather than brews or potions, the 'witch' would avoid the harmful side effects of ingesting the plants. Most of the ingredients grew in Britain although *mandraga officianaris*, another species of mandrake from the same solenaceous family, is known to have been imported in fairly substantial quantities for occult use. Francis Bacon noted that the plant was used to make 'ugly images', but it also occurs as an ingredient in the witches' brews. A common saying in the 16th and 17th centuries, when referring to a sleepy or indolent man, was that he 'had eaten mandrake'.

Curiously, the women – and it generally was women – who prepared and used the potions and flying salves or 'witches' salves', did little to help their case when they were brought to trial accused of heresy and satanic practices. Many confessed both to flying, as described above, and to union with the devil both spiritually and carnally. But we have to remember that some pressure was more than gently applied when they made their confessions.

✒ TOBACCO ✒

As the world grew smaller, particularly under the dominion of the Tudors and Stuarts, the intoxicating possibilities for London and Londoners expanded. Stimulants and psychoactive substances slowly came to be available to the population as a commercial product and entirely secular products, rather than quasi-sacred substances, to be used in religious ritual or celebration. These exotic substances were often held in real awe. Although 16th century Londoners considered themselves sophisticated and knowledgeable compared to most of the surrounding rural population, they were only just getting to grips with the notion of just how enormous the no-longer-flat world was, with undiscovered or largely unexplored lands, strange peoples and other extraordinary creatures of land and sea. A narcotic introduced from the New World would have had the same kind of cachet as a similar unknown substance brought to earth today by a space probe from Mars or Venus, or found at the bottom of a Pacific Ocean trench. When Londoners first grew and cooked potatoes, tried bitter Mexican chocolate or coffee from the Far East, they would have been intrigued, judgemental and wary. Their very first taste or inhalation of tobacco would have been an act of some daring.

Apothecaries, the official drug-providers of their day, ensured a buoyant supply of these new foreign treats in London. The trade was a brisk one and it enabled the druggists to set up what was in effect their own guild, the Society of Apothecaries, in 1617. This was an important moment for them. Their powers and commercial strength were constantly under threat because the London apothecaries competed hotly with physicians as the most reliable preparers of drugs for curing the sick and preserving the healthy. At the same time physicians sought the moral and physical high ground and keenly promoted their own diagnostic skills over what they considered to be the more dubious offerings of the apothecaries. The Royal College of Physicians had been established since 1518 and its members watched their rivals keenly. Thus, the establishment of their own guild was a statement about the quality of the apothecaries' trade. They endeavoured to ensure this quality by keeping their own standards high and administrating a nationally recognized level of competence.

One of the 'herbs' passing through the apothecaries hands was tobacco. Originally classed as a medicinal herb and included in books such as Dodonaeus' *Cruydeboek, Book of Herbs* (1554), the plant gained a reputation as a panacea and an aphrodisiac. It was used as a kind of compress for injuries and as a cure for syphilis. Most enthusiastically, and quite fruitlessly, desperate Londoners put their faith in the plant as a form of disinfectant as plague blasted the city in 1665.

The properties of tobacco as an addictive substance were also noticed relatively early on. Appropriately enough – given France's continued determination not to renege on their love affair with cigarettes – it was a French ambassador, Jean Nicot, who alerted the European kingdoms to the potential recreational pleasures of tobacco, when he described its pleasing uses to the Portuguese court in 1560. Nicot's name is of course immortalized in tobacco's addictive constituent, nicotine.

Londoners were very quick to catch on. By the late 16th century tobacco was being openly smoked in the capital – in pipes inspired by American Indian models which were commercially produced throughout the city from around 1580. Elizabethan Londoners quickly realized that a well-packed pipe helped to ease away the cares and of the day. Introduced as a luxury, tobacco quickly became a mass-market addiction so that the streets of early Jacobean London steadily became engulfed in the Virginian aroma.

Pipes were on sale for men and women alike in the theatres. Communal pipes were also available in the alehouses for those who could not afford their own supplies. In the early days of tobacco smoking these pipes were often passed round, not unlike a joint of marijuana is today, with each man or woman in the group inhaling a few whiffs of the weed. The preferred method was to inhale through the mouth and exhale the smoke through the nostrils to gain maximum effect from the narcotic. Smoking plant substances in pipes was not in itself a new phenomenon in the 16th century, although many people would not have experienced it before the tobacco craze. Crude pipes made of hollowed elder stems with home-baked clay bowls had already been in use, perhaps for centuries before this, for smoking mixtures of various vegetables, weeds and herbs including colt's-foot, yarrow, mouse-ear and lettuce.

In response to the foul tobacco habit, a hardcore of Jacobean Londoners grouped together in an early prototype of our own anti-smoking lobby. The campaigners of the day were deeply concerned that the habit of smoking tobacco would lead to dissolution and intemperance among users and they took it upon themselves to smash pipes and literally stamp on stores of this terrible 'drug'. But with remarkable speed a habit had been formed in the capital and it took vicious hold, creating new business empires in its wake.

There was such a boom in pipe-making that London manufac-turers, who had enjoyed a monopoly in London since 1601, became a chartered body in 1619. Their coat of arms depicts a 'Moor' holding a pipe and a roll of tobacco. Types of pipe varied enormously. The antiquarian John Aubrey, writing in 1680, reported that the first tobacco-users used silver pipes 'but the ordinary sort made use of a walnut shell and a straw'. Elizabethan pipes were made principally of clay as they would be for centuries afterwards.

Shops specializing in different brands of tobacco became a fixture in the capital in the early 17th century. Their symbol was a carrot-shaped roll or leaf, an image that would evoke a 'splif' among a 21st century clientele.

British moralists were suspicious of the effects of tobacco on the native population, if for no better reason than that this was an imported and exotic substance. As with the herb-garden 'uppers' and flying salves produced by medieval women – and just as later with the uplifting effects of coffee and chocolate – the fact that a puff of tobacco could change a man's mood was, to suspicious critics, a sure indication that evil was at work. James I fuelled the anti-tobacco lobby's case by publishing his fulminating *Counterblaste to Tobacco* in 1604 on the advice of his private surgeon. Here he describes its use as: 'A custom loathsome to the eye, hateful to the nose, harmful to the brain, dangerous to the lungs, and in the black stinking fume thereof nearest resembling the horrible Stygian smoke of the pit that is bottomless.' His remark about tobacco's danger to the lungs was prescient.

James I's problem with tobacco was significant for another reason. Narcotics and stimulants of any kind were considered a threat only once they became fashionable with the masses as well as the elite. The king's concern was that instead of being taken by the 'better sort as a physic', tobacco was now being used by 'a number of righteous and disorderly persons of mean and base condition'. Central to his counterblasting strategy was the plan to hit smokers in their pockets. He decided to increase the tax levied on tobacco by some 4,000 per cent – such a move by today's Chancellor of the Exchequer would be unthinkable in its excess. Through excise duty, the Crown was to take six shillings and eight pence per pound, as against the tuppence per pound required during Elizabeth's reign. Home-grown production was also banned.

Later, in 1627, there was an attempt to channel the import of every tobacco leaf through the ports of London as a means of maintaining excise controls. For a brief period the capital became a unique Mecca for tobacco enthusiasts from all over the country. Annual imports reached around half a million pounds. But soon the demand grew just too great, and tobacco shipments started to arrive once more at other ports around the country. Such punitive taxation inevitably meant that tobacco also quickly became a favourite commodity for smugglers – just as it is today owing to the marked difference in price between the heavily taxed tobacco products bought in Britain, and their lightly taxed counterparts sold in continental Europe.

Smoking the tiny pipes that were common at this time – almost certainly because they were so inexpensive to fill – must have felt deliciously wicked. And smoking came to have the added allure of being considered absolutely evil in other countries and cultures during the 17th century. Stories came back to London, via travellers such as George Sandys, reporting that men were being paraded through the streets of 'Muscovy' with a pipe stuck through the cartilage of their nose; of merchants having their ears and noses cut off for importing tobacco to Persia in 1628. And from 1634, habitual tobacco use carried the death penalty in Moscow. This particular news, reported in London circles, must have engendered a frisson of guilty pleasure, since it was English traders who introduced tobacco to Russia in the late 1560s.

The 'tawney weed', so called by Ben Jonson, was always a magnet for controversy. To the Elizabethan playwright Christopher Marlowe is attributed the opinion that 'they who love not tobacco and boys are fools'. Jonson offers a very different perspective in *Bartholomew Fair* (1614): 'The lungs of the tobacconist are rotted, the liver spotted, the brain smoked like the back-side of the pig-woman's booth here, and the whole body within, black as her pan you saw e'en now without.'

Just the fact that men enjoyed smoking seemed enough reason for censure by some. Robert Burton, the author of *The Anatomy of Melancholy* (1621), thought that the English smoked more than any other nation in his experience. He writes that: 'It is commonly abused by most men, which take it as Tinkers do Ale, 'tis a plague, a mischief, a vicious purger of goods, lands, health, hellish, devilish, and damned Tobacco, the ruin and overthrow of body and soul.'

The bible could not be cited as a means of condemning the use of tobacco because there is no reference to the habit contained there. But this did not stop London parsons from berating parishioners from their pulpits about the evils of the weed, particularly with its use by many as a perceived aphrodisiac.

Others invested tobacco with a quasi-divine status. Despite their radical Puritanism, the Ranters, one of several break-away religious sects that sprang up in the 17th century, smoked during their religious services. They even used the narcotic as a means of attaining a state of millenarian ecstasy in which individuals were recorded to have witnessed or predicted the Second Coming of Christ.

Writing in 1667, Samuel Pepys noted that a consignment of troops dispatched to Gloucestershire, in theory to suppress an uprising in this western county, was in fact destroying fields of home-grown tobacco. In the libertarian atmosphere of the Restoration, all London's places of pleasure – the playhouses, brothels, alehouses and taverns – were thick with tobacco smoke, another sure indication to the temperate and well-behaved among London society that the narcotic was spawned by the devil. It is interesting to note that one of the venues for the two new theatre companies granted a licence to perform shortly after the Restoration of the monarchy in 1660, was the Apothecaries Hall.

Given the plague of smoking that engulfed the city, increasingly desperate countermeasures were attempted by campaigners who tried to promote the notion that the homeland of tobacco was itself a place of hell. They produced pictures of orgiastic American aborigines eating each other and then finishing off the evening with a quiet smoke of the dreaded tobacco; the inference being that this could happen to you.

Once tobacco had arrived in London, though, it never left. Its bluish haze came to be synonymous with a good time. Lawyer and orientalist John Seldon's comment about tobacco has a general resonance about the habit-forming potential of many pleasures: '. . . that which is the great pleasure of some men, tobacco; at first they could not abide it, and now they cannot be without it'.

The shores of the river Thames remain a clear testimony to the comment that Londoners could not 'be without it'. Take a walk along the river at low tide and there is a high chance that you will find at least one broken section of clay pipe amid the shale, or cosseted in the Thames mud. On the South Bank hundreds of these broken pipes remain, dropped from the overworked wherries or tossed into the river by the capital's pleasure seekers after a night of passion and enjoyment in the whorehouses, theatres and bear yards of Bankside and Paris Garden.

The use of tobacco, and the way it was administered, came to reflect one's class or one's aspirations to class, and this remains the case today. Charles II popularized snuff-taking in England, borrowing the habit from France, almost certainly as a means of distinguishing himself from the hoi polloi. Pipe-smoking came to be a symbol of the working classes as did chewing tobacco, which was a habit enjoyed mostly by sailors who were prohibited from smoking because of the danger of fire.

The satirical journalist Ned Ward provides a wonderful account of the habit of snuff-taking, taken up by the periwigged swells of London, witnessed by him on a visit to Man's, a fashionable coffee-house near Scotland Yard on the river. Man's was unique in its day for forbidding smoking entirely. Ward describes how he and his companions 'squeezed through the fluttering assembly of snufflers'; he remarks that he found that no one was interested in taking any coffee at all – what he calls the 'Politician's porridge'. He continues: 'Their whole exercise was to charge and discharge their nostrils, and keep the curls of their periwigs in their proper order. The clashing of their snuff-box lids, in opening and shutting, made more noise than their tongues, and sounded as terrible in my ears as the melancholy ticks of so many death-watches.'

Back in the more typical land of the smokers, Ned Ward visited a tobacconist and made some wry observations about the devotion to the weed shown by the assembled smokers.

They behaved themselves like such true lovers of the prevailing weed, that I dare engage custom had made their bodies incapable of supporting life by any other breath than smoke. There was no talking amongst 'em, but puff was the period of every sentence, and what they said was as short as possible, for fear of losing the pleasure of a whiff, as 'How d'ye-do?' *Puff*. 'Thank ye.' *Puff*. 'Is the weed good?' *Puff*. 'Excellent.' *Puff*. 'It's fine weather.' *Puff*. 'G-d be thanked.' *Puff*.

Added to smoking, chewing and snuffing, there was also a method known as 'plugging', which involved stuffing the nostrils with quids of tobacco; but this never quite caught on.

Nevertheless, the tobacco habit in various forms crossed all social boundaries. Whatever your chosen form of administration, whether you were George III's wife known unkindly as 'snuffy Charlotte', a cigar-smoking parson or an alehouse urchin puffing on the communal pipe to stave off the pangs of hunger, Londoners embraced the vice, a handy tranquilliser for the hectic demands of the capital. In 1867, *Chambers Encyclopaedia* noted of tobacco that: 'All opposition . . . was in vain. The use of tobacco increased and has continued to increase to the present day, when it is more prevalent than at any former time, the luxury of rich and poor, of civilized nations and savage tribes.'

So for almost 450 years, London has been a city of tobacco smokers. Only now, at the beginning of the 21st century, does public opinion seem to be set implacably against recreational tobacco use. Our forebears in the city of the past would have been amazed. The same year that Pepys saw troops going out to destroy home-grown tobacco, he was on his way to Islington in a carriage with his wife when their horse collapsed. When bleeding did not revive the poor creature, the coachman blew tobacco up its nose. The horse was back on its way within minutes. The amazed diarist comments, 'One of the strangest things of horse I ever observed, but he says it is usual.'

✍ OPIUM ✍

Opium is probably the oldest narcotic known to mankind and there is evidence of its use in prehistoric times. Since it occurs naturally, it is even possible that it predates the discovery of alcohol although that is arguable. Nevertheless, this world-renowned narcotic, occurring naturally in a gummy resin that oozes from the head of the opium poppy (*papaver somniferum*), has been documented since ancient Greek times, both for its use as an analgesic providing pain relief and for producing euphoria.

For the Greeks, opium was commonplace. When Homer refers to Helen of Troy and how 'she slipped a drug [into a bowl of wine] that had the power of robbing grief and anger of their sting and banishing all painful memories', he was doubtless referring to opium; as he was when he mentions a substance called 'nepanthe', the drug of forgetfulness. It is a soporific also described by Virgil in the *Aeneid* and *Georgics*. The Greeks used opium medicinally, but it also had a spiritual and occult role; their priests regarded it as a metaphysical substance, until the philosopher and physician, Hippocrates overturned what he considered to be a superstitious attitude.

For the Romans, the poppy was a powerful symbol of sleep and death. Somnus, god of sleep, was often portrayed as a small boy or sprite carrying a bunch of poppies and an opium horn, the tool used by growers to collect the juice. Ceres, goddess of fertility, used the drug to relieve pain; the poppy image was even found as a symbol on Roman coins.

Like tobacco, opium entered the London and then the England scene during the age of exploration and came predominantly from trade with Persia, Smyrna, Egypt and other parts of the Levant. With the establishment of the Levant Company in 1581, travellers to and from the Ottoman Empire heard reports of the Turkish people's recreational use of the drug. William Biddulph remarked how in the coffee-houses which were 'more common than Alehouses in England, men would take 'Opium, which maketh them forget themselves, and talk idle of castles in the air, as though they saw visions, and heard revelations'. Such reports intrigued their audiences and the London market for opium grew steadily.

Most commonly, opium was sold in London as a tincture known as laudanum, which derived its name from the Latin word *laudare*, meaning to praise. Laudanum was made by macerating the sliced or sometimes powdered form of the resin in spirit or in strong red wine or port. The eventual tincture was a deep reddish-brown colour with a distinctive opium smell. As an anodyne and soporific it was regarded by Londoners between the 16th and 19th centuries almost as a universal panacea. It was a bathroom cabinet anodyne much like paracetamol or aspirin is today, but had many further uses. Some people used it cautiously because of its notoriously addictive properties; many were simply addicted to it.

Opium soon became the old wives' cure *par excellence*. In the cities, both medical men and quacks became enchanted by laudanum. A physician called Thomas Willis complained in 1660: 'There was a Swarm of Pretenders to Physick; whereof each brags of his own particular laudanum, which they give in every Distemper.' One possible 'pretender to physick' was a capuchin monk called Rousseau, whose own version of the tincture included pearls, coral and amber, Lancaster 'Black Drop', opium, fermented crab-apple juice, nutmeg, saffron and yeast.

Another physician, Thomas Sydenham, developed a possibly more scientific recipe for an alcoholic based-opium, not so much a tincture as a punch with kick. This contained two ounces of opium and one ounce of saffron dissolved in a pint of Canary or sherry wine, and mixed with a drachm of powdered cinnamon and cloves. The resultant brew was then left in a vapour bath for two to three days. Sydenham was convinced that he had stumbled upon a miracle wonder cure. He eulogized its benefits so forcefully that he became known as 'Opiophilos'.

We can see how such a sobriquet came about. Printed in London in 1676, Sydenham's medical observations, *Concerning the History and the Cure of Acute Diseases*, included a rush of devotional thanks to the God: 'Who hath granted to the human race, as a comfort in the afflictions, no medicine of the value of opium, either in regard to the number of diseases it can control, or its efficiency in extirpating them.' The doctor nevertheless warned against opium's immoderate or indiscriminate use, although it was Thomas Willis who provides the most vigorous caveat. He writes that opium might have an 'Angelical face . . . but if you look upon the other side of it . . . it will appear altogether a Devil'.

But Londoners desperately needed both cures for their disease ridden city and fillips for their darker days. Laudanum supplied both and, according to its greatest advocates, it had many benefits. The Welsh physician John Jones wrote in probably the earliest book to deal specifically with opium, *The Mysteries of Opium Reveal'd* (1700) that 'it prevents and takes away grief, fear, anxieties, peevishness, fretfulness' and causes a 'Promptitude, Serenity, Alacrity and Expediteness in Dispatching and managing Business . . . assurance, ovations of the spirits, courage, contempt of danger and magnanimity . . . euphory, or easie undergoing of all Labour, journeys . . . satisfaction, acquiescence, contention, equanimity . . .'

We can assume that Jones was almost certainly an addict himself, not just because of the detail in his account of the pleasures of opium but because of the poignancy of the negative effects that he records. He witnessed that withdrawal caused 'great, and even intolerable Distresses, Anxieties and Depression of Spirits, which in a few days commonly end in most miserable Death, attended with strange Agonies'.

Readers of Jones's book may have been put off from trying opium themselves by such a caveat, although the more numerous benefits may still have proved attractive. But if anything would sway first-timers, particularly men, to try a drop or two of the dark stuff it would have been Jones's coy suggestion that: 'It has been compared (not without good cause) to a permanent gentle degree of that pleasure which modesty forbids the name of . . .' by which he means orgasm. Less bashfully he adds that opium causes 'great promptitude to Venery, Erections etc . . .'

Laudanum soon came to be used for many recreational and medicinal purposes. It was frequently prescribed for children to alleviate most common ailments, from coughs to stomach upsets.

Women took opium pellets or laudanum to cure or alleviate period pains and were prescribed it to counter the effects of morning sickness in pregnancy.

Whether for medicinal or habitual use, determining the dosage of laudanum that one should take was often a hit and miss affair. Users found it difficult to buy the tincture in a consistent strength. This is not surprising considering it could be bought in the market, at the apothecary, at the grocers, and at just about every other retail outfit imaginable in London until the middle of the 19th century. The variety of its strength probably explains the reports of hardened laudanum drinkers quaffing as much as three pints of the stuff in one day, while other accounts reveal that the equivalent of one 'minim' of laudanum – about 120th of a single grain of morphine, the later refinement of opium – could prove fatal when administered to a child. Much depended on where you purchased the mixture and who prepared it. There was no regulation.

Even as late as the 1850s a Dr Christison wrote complainingly about these inconsistencies: 'Laudanum is made by all the colleges with such proportions of the opium and spirit that about thirteen minims and a half, or about twenty-five drops, contain the entire part of one grain of opium. But the London tincture may be sometimes sixteen per cent stronger than the others, as dry opium is directed to be used.' Adding to this difficulty, laudanum – like so many drugs today – was frequently adulterated.

From the early days of its use, plenty of experimentation was carried out to see just how much of the drug was efficacious and how much it might tax the body's system. Christopher Wren and Samuel Pepys both attended experiments which, in Pepys's words, involved 'killing a dog by letting opium into his hind leg'.

Clearly this powerful substance was the talk of the town in the 17th century. Apart from tobacco – used largely for pleasure and rarely for medical purposes – and with the notable exception of gin, London was virtually a drugless city. The idea of stumbling on a wonder-drug must have been irresistible. Aphra Benn, the female playwright, wrote a satire sending up the population she knew so well, who were hoping to find a panacea for human existence.

Opium was a drug taken across the classes. Horace Walpole thought that a speech given by Sir Robert Godschall – then Lord Mayor of

London – to the House of Commons was 'so dull, one would think he chewed opium'. And if Godschall had not taken a fix himself, it was more than likely that many of the audience had prepared themselves for his speech in their own way. Drug-taking was a daily event among the exalted of the land, including many in the House of Commons in the 18th and 19th centuries. Lord Liverpool, Prime minister in the 1820s was not so much partial to opium as to ether, which he used to sniff before making speeches in public; his Foreign Secretary, Lord Castlereagh did so too. Prime Minister William Gladstone dropped a measure of laudanum in his coffee before addressing the Commons and his sister became an addict also, allegedly because she wished to dull the pain of a thwarted love affair. Lord Rosebury, Prime Minister in the 1890s, is believed to have used the new synthetic drug, cocaine, before getting up to address fellow peers in the House of Lords. Another MP, who was solicitor-general in Rosebury's government was heavily addicted to morphine. His doctors left a detailed description of his method of injecting himself in the thigh and biceps through his morning suit on the benches of the House of Commons.

As with other narcotics, the chosen dependency of a few wealthy Londoners was a matter of occasional private embarrassment, although these 'eminent Victorians' considered that opiates were useful as a means of continuing throughout their hard-working days. Doctors and other professionals used it as a stimulant for this reason. However, the notion that opium use might become a mass-market phenomenon was threatening to this very same group. In 1742, Prime Minister Robert Walpole complained of the spread of 'a universal opium over the whole nation'. The establishment increasingly perceived that, generally taken, opium might cause problems for the health of British society, causing dissipation among the workforce at the time they were most needed. And the anxiety of these prominent Londoners was not without its foundations.

As industrialization began to take a firm hold throughout the country in the second half of the 18th century, factory workers found that their local grocers and chemists were the perfect place to pick up phials and tabs of laudanum and opium on a Saturday night. Opiates were cheaper than spirits.

Writing about habitual opium use, the poet Samuel Taylor Coleridge assures readers that its spread was very broad indeed, across all classes of society and throughout the whole of the realm. He advises his readers to: 'Talk with any eminent druggist or medical practitioner, especially at the West End of the town, concerning the frequency of this calamity among men and women of eminence.' He also described how: 'Throughout Lancashire & Yorkshire it is the common Dram of the lower orders of people – in the small Town of Thorpe the Druggist informed me, that he commonly sold on market days two or three Pound of Opium, & a Gallon of Laudanum – all among the labouring Classes.'

For poor Londoners, their few drops of weekly or nightly laudanum must have provided inordinate comfort in a life so tough it is scarcely imaginable today. The drug was sold cheaply and readily over the counter as a cure for 'fatigue or depression'. It continued to be sold unregulated so there was no drug subculture involved. The overt reason for buying it was for medicinal use, but it gave individuals all kinds of comfort. Opium users today attest to the drugs capability of increasing one's own sense of self and self-esteem, both factors that were largely missing in the lives of the London poor who were an excluded majority, abused and denigrated by wealthier classes. The kick from the drug must have suited the urban poor perfectly, allowing individuals to feel pleasantly isolated and yet elevated from the mass around them. As the foppish opium-smoker Sir Edward Bulwer-Lytton put it in 1827: 'He who lives surrounded by the millions never thinks of any but the one individual – himself.'

The habitual opium-eaters of the day could not help eulogizing the effects of the drug, particularly the literary members of London society, some of whom dressed opium in a veil of aesthetic fancy. One of the artistic group of opium-eaters was Arthur Symes, a 19th-century sometime poet whose lines are reminiscent of some of Coleridge's, although more overblown. Symes wrote:

> I am engulfed and drown deliciously
> Soft music like a perfume, and sweet light
> Golden with audible odours exquisite,
> Swathe me with cerements for eternity.
>
> Time is no more, I pause and yet I flee.
> A million ages wrap me round with night.

I drain a million ages of delight.
I hold the future in my memory.

A Saturday fix of cheaply bought laudanum, offering a little of such careless and timeless bliss as Symes describes here, must have provided temporary respite in the lives of the dockers and labourers of London's East End.

But poignantly, laudanum could be put to a far more sinister use. One form of Victorian 'child-care' was known as the 'baby farm'. Ostensibly, these 'farms' provided cheap, nursery-style, full-time care for children of working-class or lower-middle class families. But some of them came to be the means of disposing of unwanted children rather than protecting them. In the 1870s, two Brixton sisters called Sarah Ellis and Margaret Waters were convicted of drugging, starving and then disposing of more than a dozen babies in the period of just a few weeks. There was a similar scandal in Greenwich. In 1867, John Brendon and Ernest Hart (the latter was editor of the *British Medical Journal*) wrote a paper, *The Waste of Infant Life*, recommending state intervention in child-care. Eventually, another case, in 1896, when a Mrs Dyer was caught dumping bodies in the Thames at Reading, sparked sufficient outcry to motivate council intervention in the case of abused children.

Among all the users of opium the attitude towards addiction or overuse was mixed, very much in the way that so many people in today's society have an ambivalent and often dismissive attitude to their own sometimes inordinate drinking habits: 'I can take it. It doesn't affect me.' The poets and politicians of the period could 'take opium' too and if they privately knew they took too much, they tended to remain quiet about it. Because the tentacles of opium abuse had ensnaring effects at the highest echelons of society, outright denigration was rare, even during the late 18th and early 19th centuries, when its addictive effects were well known.

Not surprisingly, opium had a profound effect across Europe as a whole on the literature, and inspiration, of the romantic revival. Coleridge was a notorious addict, but was in denial about his habit, which he tried to play down – a response common among opium-eaters. In 1802, he was taking in the region of 100 drops of laudanum a day. Once he was able to admit to himself that he had a problem, Coleridge made various attempts to wrest back control over the drug. In April 1804 he made a journey to Malta to try to break his habit, but this failed. In 1812 and 1814 he sought medical help but this was no use either. He even employed a man to stand between him and the door of any chemist he might approach and to forcibly prevent him from going in. By 1816, Coleridge was drinking a minimum of two pints of laudanum a week and sometimes this much in a single day. This is the equivalent of 20,000 drops of laudanum, approximately 20 times the amount that could kill a first-time user. In *Dejection: an Ode* (1802), Coleridge refers to 'my shaping spirit of imagination'; one wonders to what degree his imagination was shaped by opium.

When Thomas De Quincey published *Confessions of an English Opium Eater*, first in the *London Magazine* in 1821, and then as a book in 1822, he was exposing a common form of vulnerability. This was a brave personal memoir which others in De Quincey's social class would have found difficult or embarrassing to read.

The book tells how De Quincey exiled himself from the power of his guardians after leaving Eton and became temporarily destitute in Wales and in London. In the capital he spent some time living as a down-and-out on Oxford Street, which he called a 'stony-hearted stepmother'. De Quincey explains how his addiction to opium started later, at Oxford University. He was introduced to the analgesic effects of laudanum by a fellow student who suggested it would be useful to counter the violent pains of facial neuralgia he regularly suffered. Subsequently, over a period of eight years, his addiction grew steadily, until he records taking 8,000 drops of laudanum in one day.

In describing his addiction and his determination to reduce his enslavement to the drug, De Quincey – much like the physician John Jones, mentioned above – is typical of the addict who is still too close to his forbidden friend; one who cannot properly distinguish the pains from the pleasures of the drug. He writes: 'Thou hast the keys of Paradise, O just, subtle and mighty opium.' He becomes philosophically and spiritually embroiled in his attempts to communicate his 'burden' to readers and, at the heart of the book, he describes opium as almost a 'master key' to the universe, sharpening his senses, increasing his amazement and wonder. He relates how he used to take an appropriate dose before an outing to the opera so that the full glory of the music and atmosphere of the assembly would harmonize with his exulting mind.

Even to modern readers, *Confessions* is as likely to lure as it is to repel. Despite the therapy of this public confession, including descriptions of how he reduced his dosage and suffered numerous attendant nightmares and 'dream fugues', De Quincey continued for many more years of life with a decanter of laudanum at his elbow.

De Quincey's dubious success at positing the evils of opium ties in with a mood that prevailed among other writers and thinkers whose reports of the drug were becoming less favourable during the late 18th and early 19th centuries. Travellers' tales of opium-eaters in Turkey at this period became openly censorious rather than warily fascinated. And the drug was clearly becoming a bane in the lives of men and women of great political vision as well as of poets and writers. Even the great anti-slave campaigner William Wilberforce was a victim of addiction, having first taken laudanum with some reluctance on the advice of his physician as a cure for a debilitating digestive problem in 1788.

Among a procession of critics of opium was the author, Anna Seward (1742–1809) who wrote a *Sonnet to the Poppy* including the lines:

> So stands in the long grass a love-crazed maid,
> Smiling aghast; while stream to every wind
> Her garish ribbons, smeared with dust and rain;
> But brain-sick visions cheat her tortured mind,
> And bring false peace. Thus, lulling grief and pain,
> Kind dreams oblivious from thy juice proceed,
> Thou flimsy, showy, melancholy weed.

As Richard Davenport-Hines makes clear in *The Pursuit of Oblivion: A Global History of Drugs*, it was the abuse of laudanum by the monarch George IV himself that helped to demonize opium in a nation that was by then yearning towards respectability. Two months before George IV's death in 1830, the Duke of Wellington visited him and having recorded the vast amount the gluttonous king had eaten and drunk, added that: 'He had taken laudanum the night before, again before this breakfast, again last night and again this Morning!'

George IV died a deeply unpopular man as *The Times* makes singularly clear following his demise: 'There was never an individual less regretted by his fellow creatures than this deceased king.'

Respectable Victorians were determined to distance themselves from the vicious self-indulgence of this former monarch. Britain was fast becoming the world's first and greatest industrialized nation with a growing empire. The British were patrons and leaders in the world, openly proud of their exploitation and rule in foreign dominions. Excessive recreational use of laudanum did not fit into this picture. But it was only through the establishment of the Pharmaceutical Society of Great Britain in 1841 that regulation of any kind was attempted; and subsequently through the provisions of the Pharmacy and Poisons Act of 1868.

While pressing for some degree of control at home, the growing export of opium during this period was hugely important to British coffers. Under the agency of the East India Company in India, there was an ever more fervent push to increase cultivation of what became a vital export, the vast proportion of which went to China.

The Chinese rulers attempted to ban these imports because of the effects of opium-eating on such a scale. The British retaliated through military might, achieving victory in the two Opium Wars of 1840–42 and 1856–60 and thereby forcing the Chinese to sign up to continued imports of the drug. In 1861, the East India Company reported that 63,490 chests packed full of gobbets of opium, weighing 4,251 tons, were produced in India to a value of £10,184,713. China's share of this was 59,405 chests, costing the country £9,428,887 in that year alone. At the same time, opium used for laudanum and its derivative medical preparations in Britain was imported from Turkey because it was deemed to be of far better quality.

In *Opium, A History* by Simon Booth, there is a fascinating account of the way that opium was bought and traded in London. He records that Liverpool, Dover and Bristol were all opium ports although the main centre for the trade in the whole of Europe was London. Initially, the trade here was run by a cartel but this disintegrated in 1825, leaving opium open to free trade. At this point the wholesale importers took over, buying opium in private deal and also at auction – opium was just one more commodity.

The centre of the opium business was in Mincing Lane, where some 90 per cent of trade was conducted. This had been an important market-place since the 16th century but by the 18th century, the dealing in the coffee houses was specifically in opium. At Garraway's Coffee-House near the Royal Exchange opium transactions were sealed in a system known as 'buying the candle'. A small candle was lit at the start of an auction and bids were accepted until the wick burnt away, at which point the highest bid 'under the candle' was accepted. Bidding went on throughout the day at the fortnightly auctions, each attended by about 100 bidders.

Further down the line of consumption, opium products bought from the grocer were common items in a London housewife's shopping basket. Yet it is one of those quirks of history that despite the ubiquity of opium in domestic use, it was the 'opium den' that gained most notoriety in Victorian London. Mathew Sweet in his book, *Inventing Victorians* points out that these dens were actually very rare and became so notorious and demonized only because of their association with the Chinese immigrants who typically ran them.

Davenport-Hines confirms this and adds that these dens began to appear only with the start of the major Chinese immigration into the docklands area around the 1870s. They have remained part of the myth of opium abuse primarily as a result of the publicity accorded them by the 'tourist' visits of Charles Dickens, among others, who provided a sensationalized account of an East End den in his last novel, *The Mystery of Edwin Drood*. The opium dens were not in fact secret or clandestine; they were even visited by the Prince of Wales, who went on a very public tour of them. Members of the unseated French royal family visited them too, accompanied by an inspector from Scotland Yard and the illustrator Gustave Doré, who made sketches that have subsequently become famous.

Davenport-Hines believes that the sensational reputation of the dens owed significantly to their equivalents in the United States during the same late 19th-century period. There they became identified with minor hoodlums, young male delinquents and prostitutes.

The popular tide might have been turning against the wonder drug at the end of the 19th century, but by then a more potent opium derivative had already taken its place. Morphine was the new medical panacea of the age. It was a young German chemist called Sertürner who first isolated this important opium alkaloid in 1804. According to Davenport-Hines, Sertürner was a disagreeable man who spent much of his life trying to prove that sunlight was cold. Nevertheless, in medical terms, he did the world a huge favour. Following its popular reception on the continent, morphine was readily adopted by the British medical establishment in London and elsewhere.

Morphine is even more addictive than its parent because it is a distillation of the most effective alkaloid of the parent drug and is therefore much stronger. It is surprising therefore that it was prescribed so promiscuously, mainly to treat nervous diseases of any description. It was also used, much like valium in the 1960s and 1970s, to sedate and pacify neurotic or unhappy middle class women.

The invention of the hypodermic syringe in 1853 ensured that morphine could be self-administered and enabled it to be taken to excess without fear of sanction. Initially doctors were delighted with the new syringe. They could advise their patients to go to specialist shops such as Ferguson's of Giltspur Street which sold small elegant syringes to the gentility, thus saving themselves the trouble of endless visits to their patients to administer morphine. At this time, morphine was injected directly into the muscle. Injection into the veins was a distinctly 20th-century approach. It seems incredible to the drug-savvy population of today, but physicians also believed that injecting morphine was one way to counteract the addictive effects of laudanum taken orally.

In his interview for the *Sin City* series, Richard Davenport-Hines gives a particularly jaundiced view of the way in which Victorian doctors – all men during this period – treated their female patients:

> They had an extraordinarily patronizing and contemptuous atti-
> tude to many of their female patients. They had, what seem to
> us, disgusting views about the emotional fragility of women and
> they were sedating them very heavily with morphine, or other
> opiate drugs as a way of making them less troublesome at home
> and better, more compliant wives and daughters. Elizabeth
> Barratt, the poet, was a lifelong laudanum user; she couldn't

give it up even when she was pregnant. It was prescribed by her physician, Dr Chambers. Her father said that it was Dr Chambers's job to make foolish women face up to their folly. There was a lot of medical use of opium, morphine and laudanum for this kind of reason.

Opiates were taken for all sorts of other reasons too. Throughout the 18th and 19th centuries, the search for aphrodisiacs was a preoccupation among the male population. Anything that was said to be able to make the sexual act last longer was sought out and tried. The early 18th-century medical texts extolled this quality among other virtues of opium. But Victorian gentlemen did not stop at opium. There were some who borrowed the idea – from France mostly – of taking arsenic, also an addictive drug, because it was touted as yet another early Viagra. Astonishing amounts of arsenic could be tolerated by the habitual user, but there were plenty of fatalities too.

German scientists were very much at the forefront of pharmacological development during this period. They prepared another drug, animal nitrate, for use in a vast range of medical treatments. Victorian Londoners seized on this, too, as a means of achieving and maintaining their erections. Then, in 1898, the Bayer Company added acetyl groups to the morphine molecule and synthesized an even more potent opiate – the dreaded heroin. Other synthetic drugs were produced during the last decade of the 20th century, including cocaine from coca. Meanwhile, experimentation with ancient plant-based drugs continued. The essayist and physician Havelock Ellis recorded his scientific experiment of taking three buttons of mescal – a derivative of peyote used by the North American Indians – during the afternoon of Good Friday in 1876. He published his results in the *Contemporary Review, Mescal: The New Artifical Paradise* (1898).

But in the artificial paradise of drug-taking, heroin was the most seductive. By 1903, heroin's addictive properties had already been observed: an article in a medical journal from Alabama bewailed 'The heroin habit: Another Curse'. But those who took it were not yet 'junkies'. This term emerged from the USA, when New York addicts in the 1920s tried to raise the money for their next hit by collecting discarded metal from industrial scrap-heaps.

The history of heroin abuse is a continuing tragedy of global dimensions; altogether another story from this one. But heroin's capacity to propel its abusers into a downward cycle of hopelessness and even premature death can only be equalled in the London of former years by the advent of gin.

৶ THE SPIRIT OF DEGRADATION ৶

Around 1600, a professor of medicine at the University of Leiden in the Netherlands, called Franciscus Sylvius de La Boe, embarked on a course of medical research to find a cure for the tropical fever attacking Dutch settlers in the East Indies. He was the first to distil a mixture of alcohol and juniper berries. Further experimentation and trials on patients demonstrated that this potential medicine had distinct pleasure-giving properties if taken orally. Those trying out the putative medicine tended to forget about their complaints even if they were not cured of their ailments. Thus, the Dutch 'genever' arrived in Europe. Holland's merchants seized the day and over the course of the 17th century they distilled and exported increasing amounts of the new drink throughout Europe. Initially, 'geneva' was used for medical purposes, but the spirit became a particular favourite for other reasons with soldiers and sailors; the seaports of continental Europe and England became a hive of gin drinking activity. Londoners took up, popularized and made this spirit their own, calling it 'gin'.

Londoners had long had a taste for spirits of various kinds. While beer and ale were the most popular drinks during the 17th century, the wealthy had also been enjoying French brandies and Irish or Scotch whiskies for some time. And the use of starchy grains for the distillation of spirits was certainly practised in England during the Middle Ages, well before the advent of gin. Some of the earliest English distillers, usually the alchemists, heated wine and prepared 'strong waters' from the condensed vapours. They experimented by adding various spices and herbs, even minerals and gem stones to the new elixir that seemed to offer boundless possibilities. According to one contemporary chronicler, even dead animals were added to the brew to make the most visceral of concoctions, with wide-ranging medical applications:

Waters of capons [castrated chickens], as men call them, are given to drinke to restore the strength of women in childbed or cold sickmen in diseases of great weaknesse, or through too much evacuation. They are want to seeth the capon very long in water, that all the flesh may fall from the bones and be distilled together with the liquor, either by itself or other precious waters put unto it, and spices, gold, silver and precious stones. Some allow the capon the more the elder he is, neither do they cut his throat, but strangle and choke him; and [when] he is cut up in small pieces they distill him.

In its way, the 'capon' tradition has its equivalent even today in that the strong 'natural cider' made in England's West Country is alleged to derive its pungency, taste and character from the addition of the occasional dead rat or other animal during fermentation.

In 1559, the medicinal and other properties of the spirit known as 'aqua vitae' were roundly promoted:

It helpeth red and duskish eyes. It is good for them that have the falling sickness [epilepsy] . . . It cureth the palsy if they be anointed therewith. It sharpeneth the wit, it restoreth memory. It maketh men merry and preserves youth. It putteth away fracins, ring worms and all spots of the face. It is merveylous profitable for frantic men and such as be melancholy. It expelleth poison. The smell thereof burnt killeth flies and cold creeping beasts. It restoreth wine that is turned or putrified. It is most wholesome for the stomach, the hart and the liver, it nouresheth blood, it agreeth merveylously and most with men's nature.

As French brandy and Irish whiskey poured into London alongside other wines and ports from France, Spain and Portugal, Londoners had great choice of very high-quality European produce. They took their drink seriously and the London-made preparations of spirit had to be good quality and accessibly priced to compete with the incoming products. By 1637, the London distillers had incorporated themselves into a distinct distillers company. In 1638 – apparently following advice given to King Charles I by his physician – the distillers received their Royal Charter and became the Worshipful Company of Distillers. This secured their monopoly by ensuring that all distillers within a 21-mile radius operated within the regulations of the new company. Importantly, it also prevented the use of inferior raw ingredients such as sour wine, returned ale, dregs – or even the occasional capon. The company's monopoly was comprehensive and covered the distillation of all 'strong waters' as well as 'beeregar' and 'alegar' and the manufacture of vinegar. The idealizing motto that the company chose for its new coat of arms was 'Droppe as Raine – distill as Dewe'.

William of Orange, Charles II's Dutch nephew arrived on the throne following the Glorious Revolution of 1688, which ousted James II. No sooner was William ensconced than he set about dismantling the hard-won monopoly of the Distillers Company dissolved it entirely in 1690. A good number of distillers who were already operating illicitly, were now able to make and sell their produce. William II effectively ensured that anything or everything could be distilled by anyone, without a licence. His main reason for doing this was both political and religious; principally, as a fierce Protestant, he wanted to counter the burgeoning imports of French brandy from that unspeakable Roman Catholic country.

Gin was the distillers' choice of cheap home brew. Following a reasonable harvest, surplus from the grain crops grown on the English grass lands went into gin production in London and elsewhere. The landowning ruling class saw gin as particularly beneficial because it helped to keep up the price of their grain.

The London method of production was to distil the grain twice in order to achieve a more potent proof. Each maker would include a variety of botanical additions alongside juniper berries, the more scrupulous makers attempting to attract an early form of brand loyalty by adding fruits or fragrant plants to develop unique flavours.

With the regulatory authority of the Distillers' Company so thoroughly weakened, the cowboy makers were quick to the fore. Their gin was cut with an extraordinary range of other liquids and dubious chemicals: beer dregs, water, young and old wine – it is even recorded that sulphuric acid was added into the stills of the most unscrupulous producers. One recipe for fake gin was 'oil of vitriol, oil of almond, oil of turpentine, spirits of wine, lump sugar, lime water, rose water, alum and salt of tartar'.

The British navy was already a keen promoter of the virtues of gin as a reward for its sailors. Compared to beer or ale, the spirit was more potent, had a longer shelf-life and, importantly, was lighter to carry on board in sufficient quantity to provide solace and recreation. Gin was subsequently drunk by both soldiers and sailors before they went into battle and their resulting enthusiasm and bravery became known as 'Dutch courage'. Gin had found a true home in its adopted country.

Naturally, in the recklessly libertine years of the post-Restoration period, a cheaply produced, potent drink was bound to be a winner in London. A new drinking habit had been born and the consumption of gin quickly soared. By 1684, distillers were selling around 530,000 gallons of gin. By 1721, one in four houses in Westminster was selling gin. By 1739, London had 8,659 premises retailing spirits, as well as 5,975 alehouses; and by 1751 close to one in four houses across the whole of London was a dram-shop of some kind, and the capital was consuming more than 11,300,000 gallons of gin. Throughout this period the supply of home-produced gin was never interrupted by any of the intermittent wars in Europe, as was the supply of wine, port and sack (a form of white wine imported mostly from Spain).

According to David Kerr-Cameron in *London's Pleasures From Restoration to Regency*: 'As well as in inns, gin was reckoned, conservatively, to be obtainable in back rooms, dram-shops, barber shops, tailors', haberdashers', shoemakers', off street barrows, in bordellos and even in prisons, including the courtyard trading area within the King's Bench Prison. When a tax was levied on French brandy imports, the home-distilled varieties of gin were even more sought out and the quick hit came cheaply, considering that labourers and middling artisans of this period earned between five shillings and one pound per week. A quarter-pint would cost only a penny and for the same price you could drink a two-pint mixture of gin and water in a quart-pot. An apocryphal saying of the time (also depicted on a dram-shop sign in Hogarth's famous illustration, *Gin Lane*) goes:

Drunk for a penny
Dead drunk for two,
Clean straw for free.

By 1720, with its increased quantity and reduced quality, gin was a poison drunk by virtually all the poor people of London, young children included. The quick fix of cheap gin became a national obsession and a national disaster and its effects in the capital, where the majority of the teeming and fast-growing population were already living in squalid conditions, started to cause serious concern. In the blind alleys and grand public places of the city alike, a London mob had always had an insistent energy all of its own; a gin-drunk London mob was a far more terrifying threat.

Attempts were made to diffuse the situation. Parliament introduced the 1729 Gin Act, which raised duty on gin and charged retailers for a license to sell; but this proved so unpopular that it was repealed in 1733. It had also been ineffective as retailers continued to sell gin under various new pseudonyms such as 'Old Tom' and 'Parliament Brandy'.

Matters worsened and the scene described by an assiduous anti-gin campaigner, Thomas Wilson, who visited East Smithfield in 1736, was evidently typical. Wilson was concerned to provide a clear and forceful account of the conditions in the back-alleys of London. He reported that:

In one place not far from East Smithfield, a trade has all large empty room backwards, where as his wretched guests get intoxicated, they are laid together in heaps promiscuously, men, women and children, till they recover their sense, when they proceed to drink on, or, having spent all they had, go out to find the wherewithal to return to the same drunken pursuits; and howe they acquire more money the sessions papers too often acquaint us.

Thomas Wilson had by this time already assembled a range of social, economic and moral arguments against the terrible scourge of gin on the population. As Patrick Dillon writes, in his thorough account of the gin-craze in the 18th century in *The Much Lamented Death of*

Madam Geneva, Wilson produced tracts that 'invoked his readers' worst demons: high wages, shortage of cheap labour, beggars, street-robbers and housebreakers. He played on the country mistrust of London, which sucked in honest countrymen and turned them into gin addicts. Gin was the cause of crime. Gine debilitated the army and left the nation defenceless. Gin added to the burden of social security.' Wilson even likened the effects of the gin craze on the population at large to the way the Romans lost their Empire because of dissipation, effeminacy and luxury.

Recognizing that drinking as excessively as this was making a large section of the population unfit for work, Parliament introduced another Gin Act in 1736. But, by this time, the hook of gin was firmly embedded among the London poor. The new Act, passed in April 1736, was intended to reduce severely and to control the number of distillers while increasing the penalties for infringements of the new law. The London populace waited fretfully for 29 September that year when the statute actually came into force. The gin-drinking population was wrought to fever pitch, their anxiety fuelled by street broadsheets, provided by pro and anti factions, that gave the impression that their precious gin would be virtually unobtainable by the end of the month of September. Anxiety turned to frenzy and frenzy to riot; mobs broke into the house of Sir Thomas de Veil, the Westminster magistrate living in Soho, because they believed he was hiding informers. These were typically paid a handsome £5 for each tip-off about illicit stills or other infringements. The riot continued all over central London. Five informers were killed; three stoned to death and two murdered in other ways by the crowd.

Right up to 'D-Day' on 29 September, the preoccupation of Londoners was to make sure they got their last fix of 'Mother's Ruin'. *The Daily Gazette* of 30 September reported, 'It was observed that Monday, Tuesday and Wednesday [27 to 29 September] several retailer shops were well crowded, some tippling on the spot, whilst others were carrying it off from pint to gallon, and one of these shops had such a good trade that it put every cask they had upon the stoop, and the owner, with sorrowful sighs said, "Is this not a barbarous and cruel thing, that I must not be permitted to fill them again!"'

The same paper reported another extraordinary event. In several London parishes gin-worshippers gathered together on the final

Wednesday night of each month to perform formal funeral obsequies to lay Mother Gin to rest. The report notes that 'some of the votaries appeared in ragged clothes, some without and others with one stocking . . . We hear from Bath that Mother Gin has been lamented in that city in much the same manner.'

Despite the hysterical reaction to the event, the 1736 Act did little to staunch the flow of gin, nor did it change the drinking habits of the London poor. More gin was smuggled into the country and more illicit stills were quickly and profitably established in the many hiding places supplied by London's cornucopian back alleys and wharf-side tenements. Grocers, barber-shops and other retailers maintained some element of their former trades by selling gin in different forms and under a number of new aliases, often with delightful names, such as 'Cuckold's Comfort', 'Lost Shift', 'Ladies' Delight', 'King Theodore of Corsica', or simply as 'Colic Waters'. Possibly the most thinly disguised brand was a potion called 'Madame Geneva'. Some enterprising merchants took on the guise of apothecaries selling a coloured version of gin. This would carry labels with instructions such as 'Take 2 or 3 spoonfuls of this 4 or 5 times a day, or as often as the fit takes you.'

So the gin craze raged on. It is tempting to imagine that the availability and quantity of gin consumed eased the wretched lives of the drinkers. Certainly the fact that men, women and children all beat a path to the dram-shop's door would suggest that their experience was at least pleasurable in some respects. But from contemporary accounts it seems clear that the aim of this drinking was not to enhance their pleasure so much as to wipe out the world around them. Another observer emphasises this desire for obliteration:

It charms the unactive desperate and crafty of either sex, and makes the starving sot behold his rags and nakedness with stupid indulgence, or banter both in senseless laughter and more insipid jests. It is a fiery lake that sets the brain in flames, burns up the entrails and scorches every part within, and at the same time a getter of oblivion, in which the wretch immersed, drowns his most pinching cares, and with his reason all anxious reflection on children that for food, hard winter, frost and horrid empty hours.

Just five years after the 1736 Act, Lord Lonsdale provided the House of Commons with his own eye-witness description of the London epidemic, as seen from his carriage window. Lonsdale's account is notably devoid of compassion. Apart from being an exaggerated but nevertheless shocking account of the degree of drunkenness affecting the capital, it is an insight into the attitude of many of London's ruling classes during most of the 18th and much of the 19th centuries. The poor and labouring people of London are here reviewed as chattel and fodder:

In every part of this great metropolis whoever shall pass along the streets will find wretchedness stretched along the pavement, insensible and motionless, and only removed by the charity of passengers from the danger of being crushed by carriages or trampled by horses, or strangled by filth in the common sewers, and others, less helpless perhaps, but more dangerous, who have drunk too much to fear punishment but not enough to hinder them provoking it . . . These liquors not only infatuate the mind, but poison the body, they not only fill our streets with madmen and our prisons with criminals, but our hospitals with cripples . . . The use of distilled liquors impairs the fecundity of the human race, and hinders that increase which providence has ordained for the support of the world. Those women who riot in this poisonous debauchery are quickly disabled from bearing children, or, what is more destructive to general happiness, produce children diseased from bearing children, and, who, therefore, are an additional burden, and must be supported through a miserable life by that labour which they cannot share, and must be protected by the community to which they cannot contribute to the defence.

As we can see contemporary alarm at the situation was not based on moral outrage. Illustrations such as 'Gin Lane' and 'Beer Street' by Hogarth carried an important message. Gin-drinking was killing off London's population at a time when its economy was growing; a time when the workforce should ideally have been growing to meet the demands of an expanding empire and escalating consumerism. In the worst period of its grip between 1730 and 1751, not only was gin making sure that the workforce was not expanding but it was ensuring that, in some years, the population actually shrank – as the hospital admissions and mortality rates for the period clearly suggest.

In 1750, a presentation about the significant rise in hospital admissions in the first half of the 18th century was made to a select committee of the House of Commons. Overall, the rise recorded in this period was disproportionate to the growth in London's population. Between 1704 and 1731 total admissions went up from 5,612 to 8,819 which was above a third; but the increase from 1734 to 1749 was from 12,710 to 28,147. When a physician involved in the presentation was asked what he thought the cause was, he answered: 'From the melancholy consequences of gin drinking principally.'

Remarkably, the patients in these hospitals were allowed to mitigate the effects of the terrible hospital food they were given during their stay by swallowing as much gin as they liked, purchased for them or by them at the nearby dram-shops. And if the hospitalized were unfortunate enough to catch what was known as 'hospital fever' – probably typhus – they were encouraged to drink through it. A leading authority, Dr Pringle, was a hearty advocate of the restorative effects of wine, in particular, for those who could afford it: 'There's nothing compared to wine,' he wrote, 'whereof the common men had an allowance of half a pint a day of a strong kind . . . Wine was the best antiseptic and . . . cordial.'

As a testament to soaring mortality rates, Peter Haydon in his book *Beer and Brittannia* estimates that in the period between 1749 and 1751 the population of London actually fell by over 9,300; and gin was to blame.

Anyone who has walked through Soho or the West End after midnight on a Saturday night will know how pungent the smell of second-hand alcohol can be – whether it is coming from drinkers' breath or wafting up off the beer-soaked carpets of the pubs and clubs and bars. The experience must have been a hundred times more intense for the capital's 18th-century inhabitants, as Henry Fielding, satirical playwright, journalist and author of *Tom Jones* (at that point a Westminster magistrate) describes the predicament in 1751 in his paper *An Enquiry into the Causes of the Late Increase in Robbers*:

Gin is the principal sustenance (if it may be so called) for more than 100,000 people in this metropolis. Many of those wretches there are who swallow pints of this poison within 24 hours, the dreadful effects of which I have the misfortune every day to see, and to smell too.

Sir John Fielding, the novelist-magistrate's younger half-brother and a magistrate himself, was equally descriptive in his condemnation, referring to gin as 'this liquid fire by which men drink their hell beforehand'.

The dreadful effects of drunkenness were frequently brought home to those of the population who were appalled by the problem. A record taken from the *Gentleman's Magazine* 1748 reports:

At a christening in Beddington Surrey, the nurse was so intoxicated that after she had undressed the child, instead of laying it in the cradle, she put it behind a large fire, which burnt it to death in a few minutes. She was examined before a magistrate and said she was quite stupid and senseless, so she took the child for a log of wood . . . on which she was discharged.

Another woman, called Judith Defour, did not get away with her gin-driven crime. She took her two year-old daughter from the workhouse, strangled her to remove her new clothes and sold them for gin money amounting to one shilling and fourpence.

With accruing problems of crime, disorder and intemperance of this kind, the gin phenomenon the government had unleashed in the first half of the 18th century was eventually subdued by government itself in 1751. The most intelligent of all the acts that dealt with gin consumption finally recognized among other things that the gin craze relied on licensees (and of course the landlords of illegal drinking houses) selling much of their liquor on credit. In the Tippling Act of 1751 drinking debts under the amount of one pound became unrecoverable by law. This was a lot of money in the 18th century and the fizz went out of the gin-pushers' trade. It also became illegal for distillers to sell to retailers who did not have a licence so the legions of unofficial dram-houses lost their *bona fide* supplies.

Gin drinking did carry on in significant quantities throughout the

18th century with a continuation of attendant crime, health and mortality problems, but by 1760, records show a substantial reduction in the annual gin quota in the capital, down from well over 11,000,000 gallons in 1751, to a figure much nearer 2,000,000. The first figure equates to every man, woman, child and baby in London consuming nearly 16 gallons of gin each year.

By the end of the Regency period, in 1830, gin had brushed up its image. In some of London's least salubrious enclaves at this time – areas such as Drury Lane, Holborn, St Giles, Covent Garden and Clare Market – gin was offered in the dazzling glass and brass venues known as gin palaces. According to David Kerr-Cameron in *London's Pleasures From Restoration to Regency*: 'They boomed, paradoxically, these garish palaces in the parishes of the deprived, nirvanas for the crushed and defeated, with their customers now including the better-off.' Kerr-Cameron records that these palaces were a 'one-room, usually one-floor structure, utterly commercially functional. Its barmaids were "showily-dressed damsels with large necklaces", dispensing spirits and "compounds".'

Charles Dickens's eye was always acute in documenting the social ills of the 19th century, particularly when these ills occurred in the the prison that London had become for the poor people drawn into its maelstrom. As a young reporter working on the *Morning Chronicle*, he wrote in 1835:

> Gin drinking is a great vice in England, but poverty is a greater; and until you can cure it, or persuade a half-famished wretch not to seek relief in the temporary oblivion of his own misery, with the pittance which, divided among his family, would just furnish a morsel of bread for each, gin-shops will increase in number and splendour.

Dickens's prediction was accurate. Gin-palaces grew in number and continued to present themselves smartly and attractively to their mostly poor customers. They were a haven of polished bars, brass and bright lights; they even presented their customers with plates of free cakes and biscuits as they tippled. The poor were being treated like the rich. Historian Mark Girouard places this in context: 'The 1830s saw the beginning of one of the major 19th-century marketing discoveries – that, if the turnover is big enough, there is money to be made out of the poor and they can be given something approaching the amenities of the rich. The rich found this very upsetting.'

Nevertheless the rich among those in power saw economic benefit in repealing the Tippling Law of 1751 concerning the non-recoverability of debt, except for off-licence purchases or purchases amounting to less than a quart bought on the premises. With some degree of credit restored to regular customers, the gin palaces flourished until the end of the Victorian period. As Kerr-Cameron shrewdly points out, these outlets for London drinking set an example to the beer and alehouses, who brushed up their own image considerably. A great many splendidly decorated Victorian and Edwardian pubs, complete with their original stained glass, brass and panelling remain throughout London today. And many still have their own versions of the 'shewily-dressed damsels' of the former gin palace, providing a buxom and warm welcome to their customers.

The taverns, alehouses and also the cook-shops of London are an intrinsic part of the other side of the coin of pleasure-seeking through the ages. The capital's long history of gluttony – including alcoholic inebriation of a more general kind than gin-drinking – is packed with incident and misadventure.

GLUTTONY

⫸ LONDON FATTIES ⫷

London has always adored its food and drink. It made the biggest meat pie in the world which was wolfed in its entirety by hungry London crowds even before it arrived at its destination. It fed the most gluttonous, performance-eating fatties of all time, including men who were surely the early prototypes for Mr Creosote – the *Monty Python* mega-glutton. Its fountains and conduits have literally flowed with wine on days of national celebration. It drank itself not just to merriness or wobbliness but to suffocation and death. There are comparisons with modern excesses, but only in some respects.

London's children today, in common with the children of much of Europe, most of North America and other developed nations of the world, are fatter than they should be. In a recent piece of ephemera put out to promote a healthy diet for the nation, we learn that our children are being made 'pre-ill' because of the amount of fatty, additive-laden, non-fibrous and non-vegetable food they eat, packed with copious amounts of salt and refined sugar. They are 'pre-ill' because, although they may appear perfectly healthy on this diet if somewhat obese, they are storing up problems for later when real illness will manifest itself in such lifelong diseases as diabetes and heart conditions. The belief is that fat children with unbalanced diets are encouraged into this pre-ill condition by fat parents with unbalanced diets.

Such is the concern, that government-sponsored nutritionists have warned that we could be heading towards a North American scale of fatness; which is very fat indeed. Indications are that, unless we mend our ways, we will all be waddling, podgy, squashy people if we do not look out, squeezing ourselves and our enormous arses into ever larger amounts of denim as we plish-plosh along our very own London sidewalks. In effect, we are all pre-ill, if not virtually pre-dead. No amount of occasional tummy-tightening as we walk to the tube, or buttock-clenching as we rattle on to work, will be exercise enough to stop the tide of fatness from engulfing us.

This rising concern is the result of the policy of successive governments since at least the 18th century to try to ensure that we all get sufficient food to eat to be strong and healthy. The cost of food today is a far smaller part of our disposable income than it ever has been, while mass production, food-processing, industrial farming and a European-based agricultural policy have ensured that the entire population of London and every other conurbation in the UK can happily waste more than it eats and still grow fat on it. In the post-war years of the welfare state the policy has worked almost to its own detriment. Not only is food cheap and plentiful but literally everyone is entitled access to it, courtesy of the state. And because food is only a relatively small part of people's material or pleasure-seeking needs in an inveterately consumer society, those supported by relatively meagre state allowances tend to buy the cheaper, usually more fattening and unhealthier foodstuffs in order to leave something aside for other material needs. And despite the marvellous range and quality of food available across the whole country, a significant proportion of Londoners continue to prefer the processed pies and pasties, cakes, bread and confectionery that they have always enjoyed.

The point here is perhaps a little stretched but it concerns a historical predisposition in London to eat and drink more than enough. Yet, given the capital's history of piggery, it is extraordinary that Londoners today are not uniformly obese rather than just moving in that direction. A great many of our forebears made themselves exceptionally pre-ill because of the amounts that they ate and drank, and they found encouragement to do this at every quarter because eating and drinking like hogs was the expected behaviour. Scoffing and swallowing as much as you could for as long as you could was almost an unwritten maxim for the wealthy and – importantly – for those who wished to demonstrate their respectability and station in life. From the medieval period until well into the 20th century, a groaning table was the equivalent of a new BMW to the upwardly mobile – the merchant and aspiring middle classes – of London. The bigger the plate, the greater the belch, the bigger the man. In some respects this has not changed. London's rich young City traders, whose annual bonuses are sometimes as much as their fathers could earn in a lifetime, will show their power and kudos by spending vast sums on expensive champagne and meals at top restaurants.

The consumption of food and drink in London presents us with one of very few simple social dynamics. If you were wealthy, or even if you were just about able to feed your family and have a little more beside, you could eat in London somewhere between sumptuously and very well indeed. If you were poor, you and your family could well die of starvation. Provender in London has mostly been plentiful, varied and accessibly priced – but you have always had to pay for it or rely on begging. There was plenty of benevolence towards the poor and needy at the bottom of the scale, but the gulf between the haves and the have-nots was a sheer drop.

During the 18th century, a time of monstrous excess in all things edible and quaffable, Dr Johnson reflected to his friend and sidekick James Boswell that every day in his reckoning at least 20 Londoners died of starvation. If he was anywhere near correct that would amount to some 7,500 Londoners dying from hunger each year at a time when the growing capital had a population of about 800,000. It is the equivalent of 75,000 Londoners dying of starvation each year in today's capital. Johnson's remark would have doubtless been made, with genuine concern, after yet another fine meal at the Turk's Head Club or at another of the three clubs that he founded.

Londoner's love affair with food has to be set against the backdrop of the starving for two reasons. Firstly, it places the seriously groaning table of the prosperous in its social context; secondly it may explain just how and why Londoners of all people developed such enormous appetites. We do not – in London at least – fear starvation. For the most part we do not have the vaguest idea what true hunger feels like, although we see images of desperate malnutrition often enough on our television screens. But, even for the wealthy, life in London between the Roman occupation and the end of the 19th century, was lived far closer to death and poverty. Food and drink gave vigour and sustenance, enabling Londoners to look over the parapets of their own lot. But more than just nourishment, food and drink were emotionally and socially important; they were the means of communal celebration and also of affirming one's survival, success, and place in society. When it was feast time, the feasts were inordinately splendid; when it was a time of dearth from poor harvests, famine or plague everyone made do as best they could. And in London, the rich and poor lived in close proximity in times of plenty and in times of want.

This last section of *Sin City* is not a history of food and drink in London but more a series of spotlights on traditions of eating and drinking peculiar to London, often but not always involving gluttony. There is huge fatness here and a strong emphasis on beef. But at times there is also a preoccupation with sampling new, subtle and exotic foodstuffs and beverages and with new culinary skills – a preoccupation which has great resonance in the London of the 21st century. Londoners enjoyed over-eating and great drunkenness with the same gusto that they enjoyed fornication. Like the sin of fornication, that of gluttony was well understood by the highly Christianized population of post-Roman London, particularly by those wealthy enough to eat excessively, including numerous members of the clergy. Though understood, this particular sin was widely ignored or excused as a lesser evil by those who indulged in it, especially when the leftovers from a thundering good feast could be passed on to the poor, thus alleviating one's conscience.

So here we offer a series of tableaux unveiling the enormous amount that could be consumed by individuals and feasters alike. We start with the feast and the occasion for it, recorded meticulously by the clerks of royal and noble households and by the secretaries of livery companies. We include some spectacular drinking, the kind equalled today only by really serious bingeing after an away game, preferably on the continent; and the kind once practised by a far wider cross-section of London society who did not need a football match as an excuse to get legless. Alongside the beer and ale, wines and spirits, we take in Londoners' consuming passion for coffee houses and clubs and the shaping role of these institutions in London's commercial, literary and political society. Finally, we acknowledge the enormously fattening potential of the thousands of London cookshops and other takeaways that have had a major part in feeding Londoners on the move since records began in the capital, and doubtless before.

◈ ROMAN BELLIES ◈

The Romano-British population of Londinium ate and drank in plenty. Wine – the so-called 'red infuriator' – was imported in large quantities and distributed from London throughout the provinces. The Romans were past masters at viticulture and vines were soon grown in the south, and parts of the midlands and north of England to feed Romano-British taste for wine. However, Emperor Domitian, in power between AD 81 and AD 96, was so concerned about the reports of drunkenness in the British population that he ordered half of Britain's vineyards to be destroyed. Beer, ale and mead were also brewed and drunk regularly. And, because the city was surrounded by forests and fields in which game was abundant and regularly hunted, Londinium had plentiful meat supplies – and so it remained.

In the Museum of London a reconstructed second-century Londinium kitchen is displayed showing cooked portions of beef, pork, deer, chicken, duck and goose, placed on and around a large stove. Alongside domestic produce of these kinds, Londoners also had a highly varied and probably largely balanced diet because of the extensive range of food and drink products coming through the port from other Roman provinces in an Empire that at one point stretched as far as India. According to Peter Ackroyd in *London the Biography*, excavation at deep levels under the City of London has turned up remnants of oyster shells, the stones of cherries and plums and the remains of lentils and cucumbers, peas and walnuts. 'One surviving beaker or *amphora* from Southwark bears the advertisement: "Lucius Tettius Aficanus supplier of the finest fish sauce from Antipolis".'

Even the poorest plebeians of Londinium were ensured a basic diet of millet bread, polenta and drinking water, while members of the Roman hierarchy from slaves upwards ate enough – or as much as they wanted and more depending on their rank – of figs and olives, oysters, fish, cheeses, honey, melons, oranges and other fruits in season and sauced their dishes with delicate imported spices. But the very richest in Londinium, including the praetors, senior government officials and visiting generals, enjoyed food and craved after new tastes and experiences as guiltlessly as they enjoyed and explored sexual indulgence. In both cases, Rome ransacked the world for its delicacies and imported them to the villas of the rich in Londinium and other provincial headquarters in Britain. Even under the comparatively austere Roman Republic, wealthy Romans would feast lavishly on dainties such as a whole boar, goose, *foie gras*, peacock and Trojan pig – stuffed with all kinds of sausages, vegetables and other surprises.

With plenty of good food and the luxury to enjoy their fill, the upper classes and Roman patricians regularly convened 'symposia', a combination of all-male Roman dinner party and philosophical discussion group. In some respects, the symposium was not unlike the modern book club that has grown in popularity across the UK in the 21st century. In a similar way to book clubs, the symposia often proved to be social rather than intellectual evenings, the main purpose being good eating and drinking. The Romans went a little further by occasionally adding illicit gambling to their pleasures; and for these all-male events, women were sometimes introduced for other entertainments – if the food and drink still allowed movement within the toga.

Other Roman feasts, at times of the Saturnalia and other festivals, involved many courses and huge amounts of wine punctuated by entertainments that could include buffoonery, acrobats, dancing prostitutes, sometimes copulation or grotesque mimicry performed by clowns, and occasionally gladiatorial combat. It all depended on the guest list, the taste of the host, and who was endeavouring to impress whom. But, as a rule, in times of relative stability and ease Roman London witnessed highly creative feasting centred around eating and drinking but including just about every excess imaginable, the more novel and surprising the better. A host, might for example, arrange for realistic fights to break out between his servants and might even intervene heroically to prove his valour, or perhaps let some genuine blood mix with the wine to enliven the show. Fruits and exotic foodstuffs would be lowered from the ceiling in panniers. Always the wine would flow and the feast would be prolonged as long as invention, capacity and jaded appetites allowed.

✧ ANGLO-SAXON FEASTS AND MEDIEVAL TIPPLING ✧

Feasting with one's lord during the Anglo-Saxon period of Lundenwic was less hedonistic and luxurious but was nevertheless a centrally important community occasion. In Old English the term for the hall, *sele*, denotes the feast hall – the central point in the Anglo-Saxon warrior's life. It was there that the lord and 'ring-giver' held sway; as chief, he was the provider of food, honour and position in society. For this reason *sele* is the basis of several compound words that concern 'the people of the hall' (*selesecg*), or 'the joy of the hall' (*seledream*), or 'the sad loss of the hall' (*seledreorig*). Feasting and drinking, sometimes for days on end, is described in detail or carries symbolic emphasis in some of the great Anglo-Saxon poems such as *Beowulf, The Battle of Maldon*, and even in the highly elegiac, transcendental pieces such as *The Ruin*.

Indications are that the menu at one of these feasts would include meat in the form of pigs and oxen and may also have included dishes of vegetables and root crops such as leeks, onions, garlic, radishes and turnips. Later, Anglo-Saxon Londoners of the first millennium would increasingly demand eels. Ackroyd points out that there is evidence for eel fisheries dating back at least as far back as the 11th century at various spots along the banks of the Thames near London.

Alongside the symbolic position of the feast hall and the lord, the occasion of the feast itself was important in this culture, reflecting the hierarchy of society in the arrangements of guests and the food they ate. The feast was about affirmation, comradeship, the sense of belonging and duty among the warrior peasants in each community.

Despite its apparent order, Anglo-Saxon feasting was often a time for bragging, brawling, buffoonery and general exuberance. Prodigious drunkenness occurred as the cups were continually filled and passed round by the women. This often led to serious fights, blood-letting and feuding between factions. But taking aside this sinister addition, the Anglo-Saxon feast is an early forerunner of the rugby club piss-up, the stag party and the regimental dinner. Just as the yard of ale is still drunk at any of these, the Anglo-Saxons would tip down the mead and ale in proof of their manliness and the capacity of their legs. They ate to stuff themselves utterly full and they drank to get drunk. Drinking at feast time was not understood in any other way.

On the other hand, a pint or quart of ale or beer with breakfast in the morning carried the more straightforward purpose of quenching thirst while providing slightly more nutrition than water. Ale was also generally safer to drink than water, so everyone in the family would drink it including very young children; any alcoholic after effects were not a consideration.

After the Christianization of the community in the Anglo-Saxon period, records show that the greatest abusers of drink were not members of the secular community but clergymen. The touring missionary Boniface was not best pleased with the drunkenness he encountered at the very doors of the church when he toured England in about 800. He wrote to Cuthbert, Archbishop of Canterbury, that he was deeply concerned to discover that even the bishops were frequently drunk on strong beer and ales. The result was a general tightening of regulations concerning drunkenness, as applied both to members of the Church and to their parish flocks.

Along with land acquisition, the early Church employed penances to develop its hold over Anglo-Saxon society, gradually gaining a more central position in society as an arbiter, teacher and enforcer of moral behaviour. The penitential devised by the Irish clergyman St Cumian were widely used as the definitive list of ordinances stipulating how different sins should be punished according to the rank of the offender. If a bishop was drunk, he would be deposed, whereas a minor clergyman would receive 30 days' penance and a drunken layman would have to do only 15 days' penance.

The Church was principally concerned about drunkenness because of its potentially violent consequences and tendency to promote disorder. Carrying weapons, particularly daggers of all kinds was common, and drunkenness often resulted in brawling that led to stabbings. Drunkenness also involved shouting and screaming, blasphemy and the taking of God's name in vain, among other forms of sinful behaviour. However, drinking alcohol itself was never deemed a problem. Many monasteries serving the London community were places that brewed beers and ale and produced wines for their own tables and sometimes for the local communities. It was drunkenness that was abhorrent.

Rules, however, always depended on adequate implementation or good example, as well as some degree of willingness to obey them. In London, few of these pertained. While religious doctrine had increasing hold on the capital's morality, commerce was always the driving force in London. Where drinking was concerned, Londoners were role models and carried on regardless within the clergy and laity alike. In the later 10th century, King Edgar, who reigned between 959 and 975, tried to restrain the drunkenness that he was alarmed to note among his subjects. He decreed that pegs should be put in tankards to mark the limit of what should be quaffed at a given feast. Ever inventive and dismissive, the revellers were quick to use these markers as a means of scoring who could drink the most.

There is a rumour – probably an unfair one – that when Harald II's army came to do battle with William the Conqueror's at Hastings, far from arriving late and exhausted after his last-minute march from the north, he actually arrived in plenty of time. The malicious story goes that the English army rested up and drunk extremely heavily in preparation for the battle to come. On the day, William and his men, by contrast to the defending army, were fit and ready for battle and made slight work of the opposition. This is anecdote only, and probably the result of a northern ruse to discredit Harald's best efforts. But the drinking element of the story appeals because Anglo-Saxon armies would have been rewarded with food and drink whenever the opportunity arose – for sustenance and good cheer.

In medieval London, excessive drinking was commonplace. Londoners mostly drank ale and beer, although wine was imported from the European continent and consumed at the tables of the wealthy. English wine-making did occur during the Middle Ages, but it was generally small-scale and often the grapes were used for making verjuice (the juice of unripe grapes for use in cooking) and vinegar. In the London suburb of Holborn, for example, the Earl of

Lincoln's gardens produced only verjuice from its vines in 1295–6, but both verjuice and wine in 1304–5.

As a daily and regular beverage during this period Londoners would drink beer and ale – usually made from barley and sometimes from barley mixed with oats known as dredge. Oats on their own would be used occasionally for a lower grade of ale, while high-grade ale would sometimes be made from wheat, usually reserved for bread-making. By the 14th century, ale was brewed all over London, not just in commercial breweries but also in households. James Galloway in *Food and Eating in Medieval Europe* believes that London in 1300, with a population of some 80,000, would have supported between 1,000 and 2,500 small-scale brewers. One chronicle, *Annales Londonienses*, reports that 1,334 brewers and 354 taverners responded to a summons to appear at the Guildhall in 1309. This number would not have included the brewers and taverners who lived outside the city's jurisdiction. Galloway believes that there is no truth in the statement that medieval ale was universally weak and watery; his research into some of the household ingredients and quantities produced indicates that these ales were at least as strong as modern beers.

Langland's 14th-century character Glutton, in *Piers Plowman*, seems to need about the same as a modern Londoner before becoming legless. He drinks 'a gallon and a gill' in a London alehouse before finding he cannot stand or walk without his staff. He stumbles about like a bird-catcher or a minstrel's dog before falling flat on his face at the alehouse door.

Glutton's drinking was by no means exceptional in medieval London where inebriation was often the cause of accidents, suicides and murders, as it is today. The court records of 12th and 13th-century London are full of accounts of men and women toppling off ladders, steps, wharf-sides and out of windows. We can readily compare this to a Saturday night visit to any of London's Accident and Emergency hospital departments.

There are many accounts of drink-fuelled fights and of savage violence such as when a group of strangers entered a tavern, one of whom immediately killed the person who dared to ask who they were. A document which provides some insight into drunkenness is *The London Eyre* of 1244; among various cases it records a quarrel between three men in a tavern that led to a fatality when one was attacked by an 'Irish knife' and a 'misericord' – a savagely effective knife meant to guarantee quick and merciful death. Peter Ackroyd in *London the Biography* gives a vivid account of the sense of violence on the streets of medieval London recounting that there were 'continual fights in the street, ambushes and arguments over nothing – or over a 'goat's wool' as it was known'. He also notes that the trade guilds, so central to this community which depended on trade, were always fighting one another in the streets. 'A group of goldsmiths, for example, fell upon a saddler and proceeded to lay open his head with a sword, chop off his leg with an axe and generally belabour him with a staff; he died five days later.'

But it was these very tradespeople who formed the backbone of the livery companies of medieval London; and it is the livery company records that offer the most vivid illustration of sumptuous eating during the Middle Ages and later periods.

✧ LIVERY COMPANY FEASTS ✧

In medieval London the dinners of the livery companies, unlike the feasts of the former Anglo-Saxon communities, were highly formalized and generally well-behaved affairs. The livery company dinners played an extremely important role both in projecting the status of the particular trades represented by the companies within the London commercial community, and in reflecting the status of the individual tradespeople – the 'freemen' – within the companies themselves. The livery companies developed from the earlier medieval religious and craft guilds of London. No one could practise a trade within the city unless they belonged to a company which gave them the 'freedom' to do so. (The 'livery' itself refers to the suit of clothes that each member of the guild received annually.) And within London society, the livery companies not only regulated and administered their particular trade, often carrying out inspections of ware bought and sold within the company halls, but they also provided a basis for charitable work within the city.

Livery company dining for members took place on set days in the year and, notably, on the company's patron saint day. Special feasts were reserved for the appointment of a new Master of the livery company. According to *London Eats Out: 500 years of dining in the capital*, edited by Moira Johnston, the appointment of the new Masters merited three dinners on three consecutive days. The first two would be relatively modest; for example, they involved roast mutton, goose and capon, with codlings (stewed apples flavoured with rose-water), spiced biscuits, cakes and comfits (whole spices such as fennel, coriander, caraway and nuts coated with sugar). After a church service on the third day, the assembly of all the members and their wives started the main feast at about 2 p.m. Here the food would be handed out in graded portions according to status and even those unable to attend because of illness or infirmity would be catered for by means of food dispatched to their homes. On the following day, the remaining food was taken for distribution to the poor. In times of national crisis, plague, or financial shortages, these feasts were reduced or cancelled, although charitable activities remained a dominant concern.

If the Master also happened to be the Lord Mayor, the feast would extend to senior members of other companies, visiting dignitaries and distinguished guests, including the sovereign and courtiers. On these occasions the total bill could amount to more than £100, or about £15,000 today.

Livery company archives offer a marvellous insight into the formal and status-conscious arrangements for these feasts, involving several menus, most of which were for those at the top three tables. The court guests sat at the top table and the two side tables were occupied by other guests, wives and senior livery. Guests sat close to the cupboard or buffet where the silver and silver-plate were displayed as a sign of wealth and status. In a separate room sat the wardens and other officials, with their ladies occupying another parlour.

Most of the livery halls were not large and catering was difficult with much of the cooking prepared by caterers as it is today for corporate or other functions. The newly joined and younger members of the companies, the 'batchelors', served the seniors and when they had had their fill, would seek a place for themselves. This sometimes caused tensions when the seniors refused to budge or ate more than their share. In 1588 batchelors of the Drapers 'contemptuouslie departed' without their dinner, 'using some harde speeche and apparent shews of discontent'.

Meat predominated at the livery dinners and its range would astonish the most jaded modern banquet-goer. There was beef, pork, brawn, lamb, chicken, rabbit, venison, goose, duck (both mallard and teal), woodcock, 'greenplover' (lapwing), lark, snipe, pigeon, quail, swan, heron, crane, partridge and turkey. On an exceptional feast for James I, the Merchant Taylor's added to this list by eating pheasant, peacock, ruff (a type of wader), doves, godwits, martins, owls and cuckoos. In medieval feasts the feathered bird would often be perched above the pies to indicate their contents and to add flamboyance.

The turkey had been introduced in Europe from Mexico and Central America in about 1524 by the Strickland family of Boynton in the East Riding. In 1541 Archbishop Cranmer recommended this bird as one of the greater fouls; it offered medical as well as aphrodisiac benefits, being 'very good nourishment; [it] restoreth bodily forces; [is] passing good for such as are in recovery; maketh store of seede; enflameth Venus'. Aphrodisiac foodstuffs were much more openly recommended and flaunted on the tables than they are today. For the Elizabethans, the stimulation of food came as much from wordplay or even from the shape and arrangement of food, whether or not it had any attributed aphrodisiac properties. Thus Elizabethans would find the 'a-*pric*-ot' suggestive, while the asparagus left its own impression on their minds. In the season, this vegetable was grown in 'neathouses' (used at other times for cattle) to the west of modern Vauxhall bridge.

Foreigners were often astounded by the variety and the quantity of meat eaten at the livery company feasts. The Italian merchant Alessandro Magno remarks in his journal dating from 1562. 'It is almost impossible to believe that they could eat so much meat in one city alone'. A 16th-century attempt to introduce fashionable Flemish food to the capital was short-lived. People complained that the portions were far too small; a response similar to the general reaction to *nouvelle cuisine* in the 1980s.

Even to contemporary Englishmen, the livery feasts were occasions of exceptional and exotic indulgence. One countryman, a certain William Harrison, thought that the livery company members were demonstrating pretensions beyond their station by indulging in so many strange foods and were behaving as if they were the nobility themselves. His 1576 account says that they would 'seldom regard anything that the butcher usually killeth, but reject the same as not worthy'. But whatever the excesses of the merchant classes, the nobility to whom they were accused of aspiring, were clearly over-doing the meat according to a later record by Harrison in his *Description of England* (1586). Here he comments that the nobility ate so much meat that for 'a man to dine with them . . . is rather to yield unto a conspiracy with a great deal of meat for the speedy suppression of natural health . . . than to sustain his body withal'.

The livery company dinner was not a place for vegetarians; very few vegetables were ever presented on the table, not because they were not in good supply, but probably because they were considered too lowly for the table. A bowl of carrots or peas did not have the same presen-tational appeal as a stuffed swan. However in the more affluent of the houses in the city, roast beef started to be exchanged for boiled beef which had been well salted a few days beforehand and this was 'besieged' with heaps of cabbage, carrots, turnips and other roots or herbs. A delicate addition in some households was roasted slices of buttered bread, cooked on a gridiron, which they called 'toast'.

Naturally, seasonal fluctuations in the supply of birds and beasts for these feasts meant that the livery companies had sometimes to make do with more standard fare. Nevertheless, they tried to counter this by making payments to suppliers to obtain migratory species in advance, or to fatten up cygnets and quails specially for the big day. This seasonal variation was reflected in the general London diet of the period. There were fresh herrings at Christmas time; pork and sprats at All Saints; veal and bacon at Easter.

Fish was the second most important feast food, although it always topped the bill if the dinners occurred on fish days or during Lent, when meat was entirely avoided. The staples were sturgeon and pike but many other varieties were enjoyed, mostly taken from the Thames. John Stow's description of the bounty of the river in his day would have most modern anglers and conservationists weeping: 'What should I speak of the fat and sweet salmon daily taken in this stream, and that in such plenty . . . as no river in Europe is able to exceed it? But what store also of barbells, troute, chevens, perches, smelts, breams, roaches, daces, gudgeons, flounders, shrimps, eels, etc are commonly to be had therein.'

From the nearby sea, Londoners added lampreys, cod, ling, crab, oysters, mullet, sole, plaice, whiting, haddock, turbot and a lot of 'britts' – young herrings or sprats. The accounts of the companies show the use of fish that were 'green', 'fresh' or 'olde', the latter being in preserved form, usually powdered or salted. The Drapers even ate carp, an imported rarity in 1567. The Company of Grocers did not stop at fish, but have a record of 'freshe sele' (seal) on their menu. Testifying to this taste for sea mammals, archaeologists have discovered the bones of whales, dolphins and porpoises in medieval sites in the city.

Swans, as royal birds, were great favourites at the livery feasts. At one sitting there were no fewer than 150 swans which would have been a true reflection of the company's importance. Other traditional fare included capon and 'hernshoe' (heron). Edward Hale wrote a poem in 1579 which includes an account of such a feast and lists bitterns, larks, lapwings, stonechats, bustards (like short-legged ostriches, these sizeable birds were once indigenous to England in such areas as Salisbury Plain), blackbirds, cranes, followed by:

Straunge kinds of fysh at second course to come in their degree,
As Porpesse, Seale and Samond good, with Sturgeon of the best.

His observation that this was 'straunge' reflects that the far more usual daily fare was a mess of potage followed by 'plain roast and boiled'. According to William Salmon in *The New London Dispensatory* (1690), eating such generally unpalatable birds as cranes and blackbirds was not always for the purpose of taste. They were 'not of a very pleasant taste and smell, but with a certain kind of Acrimony'. Nevertheless they were thought to 'stop Looseness, heal the Dysentaria and Cholick and resist infection of the Plague'. In plague-ridden London, such Renaissance medieval theories would have been most attractive.

Where fat, protein and medicinal properties were concerned, the merchants of medieval, Tudor and the later periods were truly well catered for. But these numerous forms of meat, fish and fowl were only the middle part of the dinner. There was pudding to come. The many thousands of diners who ate at these livery company feasts during the course of the 15th and 16th centuries were treated to a remarkable range of confections and sweetmeats, with sweet alcoholic cordials to wash it all down.

The accounts in the archives of the Drapers' Company between 1564 and 1602 include 139 different products. Among the basics were 'marchpanes' – baked almond confections made with rosewater, sugar, wafers and eggs. According to *Day's Glossary*, the marchpane was a disc of almond paste dried slowly in an oven and decorated with various standards or heraldic motifs, including animals and other emblems of the livery, made from sugar paste and marzipan. There were also comfits enjoyed for their digestive benefits. These were usually eaten at the end of the meal in the dessert course. Liveries tended to buy their comfits directly from the London confectioners, ordering coating and colours to suit the occasion.

Added to the list of 'basics' were cakes, buns, spice bread and decorative wafers, dyed yellow and red, which were swallowed with the 'hippocras', another regular item on the livery feast menus. The hippocras was a sweet, spiced wine which derived its name from *manicum hippocraticum* (the sleeve of Hippocrates), a woollen filter used to strain out the spice particles from the 'gyle' which was a mixture of wine and spice. The spices recorded include cinnamon; long pepper; an aromatic version of the peppercorn hailing from Java, called 'cubeb'; and 'grains of paradise', which were aromatic seeds from tropical West Africa. The livery feast records are therefore a testament to London's dominance in the European spice trade, alongside Antwerp.

The dessert courses at important meals derive from an old medieval ceremony, which, according to Day, was called *voidée* or void. After grace, the sovereign or Master offered the hippocras and wafers as part of a thanksgiving which has echoes of the Eucharist. But the main purpose of the void was medicinal. The spices of the hippocras were supposed to settle the stomach and prevent indigestion, while the comfits were given for both their digestive and carminative (anti-flatulent) properties. As the Tudors became influenced by the culture of the Italian courts in the late 15th and 16th centuries, so we find that some marvellous and exotic additions were offered to guests. These include boxes of quince paste and other preserves; also a range of sugared seeds, candied roots and flowers. And to these were added fresh fruits and cream cheeses. Much fruit was eaten, in season, and not just for dessert. There were plums, prunes, raisins, currants, quince, gooseberries, mulberries, barberries, figs and apples cooked in tarts, boiled and made into purées and sauces. The expanded version of the void was a 'banquet', from the Italian *banchetto*, and in time the event itself came to be known as a banquet.

Inevitably, refined sugar was an essential ingredient in these confections. Tudor Britain developed a taste for this very expensive commodity, although it was not refined in London until 1551. By 1585, London replaced Antwerp as the leading sugar refining centre in Europe. The Tudor taste for sweet things included marmalades initially imported from Portugal and then reproduced using homegrown quinces, or various other fruits such as warden pears, damsons, apricots, peaches, oranges and lemons.

All this fare was the province of London eaters alone because the capital became a storehouse of infinite variety, particularly during the second half of the 16th century. As a dweller in the provinces you had to rely on traders or peddlers to bring food and other products your way.

After the fall of Constantinople to the Turks in 1453 and the subsequent tilting of trade from the Mediterranean towards the Atlantic, Antwerp had become the great trading centre in Europe, with London as its satellite. Antwerp shipped all kinds of necessities and luxuries up the Thames, which had been deepened and widened in the 1540s. There was silver, bullion, silks, sugar, cotton, linen, tapestry, glass, swords, firearms, furniture, perfumes and spices from the Orient. Spices, almonds and dried fruit were among the major food imports. There were also Greek olives from Flanders and live quail from France; these arrived in specially made wicker baskets complete with hempseed and water to keep the birds healthy for the London market. Elizabethan explorers brought in yet more delicacies for the London table. There were yams or sweet potatoes from Virginia as well as rhubarb from China.

During the 16th century, London increasingly benefited from the channel that divided it from its rivals on the European mainland. Antwerp was closed to the English in 1568 and then sacked by the Spanish. Meanwhile, religious wars raged across the Netherlands and France; Elizabethan England was both peaceful and stable by comparison. The capital was well placed to profit as the new 'international' trade centre, almost set to rival Venice, Naples and Paris. The Thames bristled with the ships that loaded the exports of successful English merchants as well as with foreign ships visiting to disgorge their goods. William Camden of the Pool of London boasted in 1586 that: 'A man would say, that seeth the shipping here, that it is, as it were, a very wood of trees disbranched to make glades to let in light, so shaded is it with masts and sails.'

We should leave the livery feast with a summary from William Harrison, whose implicit grumbles, noted above, about merchant pretensions and the nobility's over-consumption of meat are overtaken in the following description by a sense of awe and wonder:

> . . . it is a world to see what great provision is made in all manner of delicate meats from every quarter of the country. In such cases also geliffes [probably jellies] of all colours, mixed with a variety in the representation of sundry flowers, herbs, trees, forms of beasts, fish, fowls, and fruites, and thereunto marchpane wrought with no curiosity, tarts of divers hues and sundry denominations, conserves of old fruits, foreign and home-bred, suckets, codiniacs, marmalades, marchpane, sugarbread, gingerbread, Florentines, wild fowl, venison of all sorts, and sundry outlandish confections, altogether seasoned with sugar . . . do generally bear the sway.

✎ A RIGHT ROYAL EXAMPLE ✎

We have already noted contemporary reaction to the pretensions of London's merchant community, as evidenced by the splendour and status-driven ceremony of the livery company feasts. Plenty of noblemen of this period and much later did not feel they needed to demonstrate their wealth or position in the same way. A nobleman's feast was certainly a show of power and wealth, but in a way that reflected the confidence of the established, as against the social chess of mercantile empire-building. At a nobleman's feast, guests were treated to gargantuan amounts of food and drink for the day, or many days, of the feast. Gluttony was a prerequisite, while buffooning and stupefying drunkenness were usually expected too.

In 1470, the Duke of Warwick's tables groaned under the weight of 104 tuns of wine, 300 tuns of ale, 6 bulls, 1,004 wethers (rams), 3,000 calves, 10 fat oxen, 300 pigs, 4,000 deer, 2,000 chickens, 340 capons, 4,000 ducks, 1,000 game birds, 100 peacocks, 4,000 rabbits. Pudding consisted of 1,000 jellies, 400 tarts and 2,000 custards. The preparations involved 62 cooks and 515 assistants. There is no record of how many guests took part in this fantastic orgy of food and drink, but a poet wrote that 'each man shall have six men's share'. (A 'tun' in the above list is a reference to a large barrel or cask used for wine, beer or ale; it does not refer to a set volume or weight of liquid although it does denote a substantial amount.)

The example of hospitality on this scale had been set by earlier kings. On his coronation in 1377, King Richard II celebrated by ensuring that the city conduits ran with wine for three hours. Quite apart from the amount of wine involved, this was no mean technical feat. The king also provided food for up to 10,000 people daily at court. In the last year of his reign, during Christmas 1398, Richard II's court got through 200 tuns of wine and slaughtered and ate 2,000 oxen. This was a major feast, particularly for people who, according to later chronicler John Stow, had endured severe hunger in 1392 and 1393. In these years, and in many others when the harvest was bad, or when plague or war reduced the amounts of food available, the poor of London were forced to make do with a diet of apples and nuts.

In 1429, the coronation feast of the eight-year-old Henry VI, King of England and France, took place at Westminster Hall. This was a more decorous affair in keeping with the king's young age. Placed in front of him was a two-foot high confection of marzipan and sugar depicting the Madonna and child and the patron saints of both nations, with the young king shown kneeling in front.

Even in the good times it is doubtful that the poor fared well during the 14th and early 15th centuries. A scullery assistant in a household earned eight pence a day and, although some of this servant's food came from leftovers from the household table, this wage was the same as the cost of just one capon pasty. Labourers earned sixpence a day, which would just about cover the cost of a hen pasty with a penny to spare for the family.

Meanwhile, the rich and powerful always enjoyed themselves at the table. Henry VIII was another monarch who knew how to throw a good party. At one feast he kept 1,000 guests at Greenwich entertained at the table for a seven-hour sitting. When he celebrated his wedding to Anne Boleyn, both the fountains of the court and the conduits of the city ran with wine for all to enjoy. It is recorded that for a royal feast of this kind Henry VIII would pay his cook 15 shillings and his preacher 6 shillings.

Royal coronations and wedding celebrations continued to be an excuse for excessive eating on an astonishing scale. According to Francis Sondford in his 1687 *Account of the Coronation Feast of James II*, the feast in Westminster Hall included several courses each with no fewer than 145 dishes. When it came to frequent swallowing, the personal excesses of some former monarchs were often noted even by courtiers and gentlefolk for whom eating heartily and well was natural.

Visiting royalty were among those celebrated at feasts in the capital and records show how they were quite accustomed to eating and drinking on a vast scale even before they arrived. En route to London from Portsmouth in 1698, the formidable Russian Tsar, Peter the Great, appeared to be very much at ease with a big feast. There is a record of what he and his party of 21 attendants consumed at an inn in Godalming, where they stayed on their journey to the capital. First they rested and then ordered seven dozen eggs with salad. For supper they ate five ribs of beef weighing three stone, a sheep weighing four stone, three-quarters of a lamb, a roasted shoulder and a loin of veal, eight pullets and eight rabbits, and they drank 'two dozen of sack, one dozen of claret', bread and beer and then had six more quarts of sack before retiring for the night. For breakfast they had half a sheep, 19 lbs of lamb, ten pullets, a dozen chickens and drank four quarts of brandy. The entire bill for this stupendous amount of food and drink was just £1 – although one suspects a certain amount of grace and favour was part of the bargain. The £1 bill remains at the Bodleian Library as testimony to this eating feast.

Queen Anne (who was crowned in 1702 and reigned until 1714) became so fat from over-eating that she hunted stag in a chaise that had been specially reinforced. When she was older she could not climb the stairs of her palace, but had to be hoisted from floor to floor in a chair attached to ropes and pulleys. Notably, her statue is placed with its back to St Paul's, facing her favourite vintners.

George IV was another infamous glutton. By 1818, when he was still Regent, it was reported that his 'belly now reaches his knees'. On his coronation on 19 July 1821, he held a banquet in Westminster Hall where the food comprised 7,442 lbs of beef, 7,133 lbs of mutton and 2,474 lbs of lamb among the meat dishes. There were also 160 geese, 720 pullets, 1,610 chickens, 520 other fowls for stock, 1,730 lbs of bacon and 8,400 eggs. There were 1,000 dozen bottles of wine, port and sack and the total extravaganza cost £238,000, which seems reasonable but is probably more than £7,000,000 in today's money.

The extravagance often involved the table decorations too. In 1811, the younger Prince Regent, or 'Prinny', attended a banquet at Carlton House for which the goldsmith Paul Store had made a special dinner service, part of which involved a plateau with running water and live goldfish. One of the Regent's favourite dishes was turtle soup and this was widely popular among the *bon ton* of London. The turtles were brought live for the table in special ships from the Caribbean and, like lobsters today, they could be selected by the diners as they swam. There are tiles from a 'turtlepool' of a London pub on display in the Museum of London.

The Regent's punch – or at least one of his favourites – combined alcohol and invention in a potent mix. It consisted of three bottles of champagne, two of Madeira, one of hock, curacao, a quart of brandy, a pint of rum and bottles of seltzer-water flavoured with raisins, oranges, lemons and sugar candy – all this diluted with iced green tea.

Even as a very frail man, George IV's appetite did not diminish. The Duke of Wellington reported, with some incredulity, what the monarch was eating just two months before he died: 'What do you think of His breakfast yesterday for an Invalid? A Pigeon and beef Steak Pye of which he ate two Pigeons and three beef-Steaks, three parts of a bottle of Mozelle, a Glass of Dry champagne, two Glasses of Port [and] a Glass of Brandy!'

Even in the early 20th century, it was typical for Edward VII to have 14 courses for lunch and the same at dinner and he most enjoyed the turkey stuffed with a chicken, stuffed with a pheasant, stuffed with a woodcock, which was filled with truffles. He is alleged to have kept little stashes of food all over the palace.

✍ INDIVIDUAL AND GENERAL INDULGENCE ✍

The totally dedicated glutton was actually a rare beast in former London and as such was treated with special awe. There was one such called Nicholas Wood, whose story is recorded by John Taylor in a monograph entitled *The Great Eater of Kent* (1630). Wood is reported to have eaten an entire raw sheep at one sitting, including all internal organs and offal, and only leaving behind the skin, wool, bones and horns. Taylor records that 'two loins of mutton and one of veal were but as three sprats to him'. Once, at Sir Warham St Ledger's house, he 'ate enough for 30 men', a feat that he performed again in the household of Sir William Sydleye.

Nicholas Wood was clearly a performance eater and an early prototype of *Monty Python*'s Mr Creosote, the fictional character whose exceptional greed led him to explode in the middle of a restaurant. But Nicholas Wood's eating was real, although his art had a fairground quality to it that was much beloved by London audiences and would be accompanied by the laying of wagers. But Wood was a few notches above even the 'fat boys' – reported by Jonson and Pepys – who demonstrated their pie-eating skills at Bartholomew or Southwark fairs. Taylor reports that Wood anointed his paunch with grease and butter in front of the fire to stretch it sufficiently to enable further intake – or perhaps it was to prevent explosion.

As to more general feeding of the gut, the distilled 'spirituous liquors' that started to become popular during the Tudor period were initially prepared by alchemists for medicinal purposes but were typically taken up by the population for their intoxicating qualities. These 'strong waters' were the precursors of gin, which is dealt with in some detail in the last chapter. For the most part, ales, beer and wine were the staples, depending on one's purse.

Alehouses and taverns continued to be the focus of public roistering, whoring and merry-making and they grew with the population in Elizabethan London. The playwrights of the day made frequent reference to drinking, which was also at the heart of the largely slapstick performances at the tavern playhouses. Excessive drinking is omnipresent in much of the finer work of Shakespeare, from the low-comedy episodes to the addled tomfoolery of Sir Toby Belch in *Twelfth Night* to gripping moments in the tragedies. In *Othello*, 'the demon drink', as manipulated by arch-fiend Iago, plays an abetting part in the tragedy. Iago, offering a comic aside about the English capacity for putting away the booze plays straight into the hands of the macho drinking fraternity of Elizabethan London: 'In England they are most potent at potting: your Dane, your German and your swag-bellied Hollander . . . are nothing to your English.'

Drunkenness was growing as fast as the population in the second half of the 16th century and the threat of social disorder was such that, in 1574, 200 alehouses in London were closed down. By this time brewers had amalgamated their operations to form larger premises and they would use brand names such as Huffe Cup, Mad Dog, Angel's Food, Lift Leg and Stride Wide, to sell their beers. Some of the beers were heavily spiced or distinguished by various flavours. One such, 'cock-ale', was a speciality in the Elizabethan brothels and it was a drink that continued in popularity as a form of special brew, well into the 18th century. It was a potent concoction, incorporating raisins, dates, nutmeg and a freshly killed cockerel, and was sold for both its rich taste and its aphrodisiac qualities; it was also said to promote fecundity.

In her book *1700 Scenes from London Life*, Margaret Waller offers a recipe for cock-ale which includes ten gallons of ale to which is added 'a large cock, the older the better'. This is parboiled, crawed and gutted, after the fleas had been removed, and then stamped in a stone mortar until the bones are broken. Next:

> . . . put the cock into two quarts of sack, and put it into three pounds of raisins of the sun stoned, some blades of mace, and a few cloves: put all into a canvas bag, and a little before you find the ale has done working, put the ale and bag together into a vessel. In a week or nine days' time bottle it up, fill the bottles to just above the neck, and give it the same time to ripen as other ale.

Peter Haydon in his book *Beer and Britannia* estimates that walking through the London of James I from Charing Cross to the Tower of London, you would pass a tavern approximately every 80 yards. The sheer number of places in London that were solely devoted to eating and drinking suggests that the city's culture was to ingest and imbibe almost as a competitive sport.

A Stuart contemporary called Thomas Young wrote in *England's Bane* (1617):

There are in London drinking schools: so that drunkenesse is professed with us as a liberal arte and science . . . I have seen a company among the very woods and forests drinking for a muggle. Six determined to try their strengths who could drink the most glasses for the muggle. The first drinks a glass of a pint, the second two, the next three, and so every one multiplieth till the last taketh six. The first beginneth again and taketh seven and in this manner they drink thrice a piece round, every man taking a glass more than the last.

What is meant by a muggle, incidentally remains a mystery (a second reference to a muggle in the *Old English Dictionary* throws no further light but suggests the muggle is highly prized by the owner). Robert Burton, in *Anatomy of Melancholy* (1621), writes of 'immoderate drinking in every place – how people flock to taverns as if they were born to no other end but to eat and drink – it was no disparagement for a man to stagger in the streets, reel, rave etc – but much to his renown'. The Reeve in *Plea for Ninevah* (1657) observes: 'We seem to be steeped in liquors, or to be a dizzy island . . . we drink as if we were sponges, or had tunnels in our mouths.'

This last comment might have been made to catch the puritan vote, given that it was made during the period of the Commonwealth, when drinking was common enough but drunkenness was prohibited and less overt. As always, there were punishments for being drunk and disorderly but these were variously applied and were similar in style to the punishment meted out to bawds, whores and linkmen: they involved public ridicule more than the deprivation of freedom, corporal punishment or heavy fines. Thus, in the puritanical 1640s '. . . men were drove up and down the streets with a great

Tubb or Barrell, open in the Sides and with a Hole one end with their Heads put through so covering their bodies down to the small of their Leggs: and then close the same calling it the New-Fashion'd cloak . . . The Punishment for Drunkards and the like . . .'

Such admonishment never much bothered regulars of the Everlasting Club – which enjoyed party after party for a period of about 50 years between the end of the English Civil Wars and the close of the 17th century. During this half-century party, revellers are alleged to have smoked 50 tons of tobacco and drunk 30,000 butts of ale, 1,000 hogs heads of port and 200 barrels of brandy.

Peter Ackroyd in *London the Biography* notes that even the Great Fire of London in 1666 was a direct reflection of Londoners' preoccupation with excessive eating and drinking. 'The Great Fire started at Pudding Lane and ended at Pie Corner, where the golden figure of a fat boy still marks the site; he was once accompanied by an inscription noting, "This boy is in memory put up of the late fire of London, occasioned by the sin of gluttony, 1666." '

A contemporary note made by Samuel Pepys during the year of the Great Fire concerns his surprise at the way that women could drink. He wrote that 'women would scold for drink and become as drunk as devels'. At the home of a friend he also records his astonishment when he sees a woman knock back almost a quart of wine in one go.

With the Restoration came a new fashion for drinking the King's Health, so that the clubs, alehouses, taverns and coffee-houses often rang with the name 'King Charles', or 'His Majesty'. Even the King, who loved his drink as much as he loved his mistresses and masked balls, became uncomfortable with the amount of toasting that was done in his name. As witnessed in his Proclamation Against Drunkeness: 'There are likewise a set of men of whom we have heard much, who spend their times in taverns and tippling houses and debauches, giving no other evidence of affection for us but in drinking our health, and in inveigling against all others who are not of their dissolute temper.' But toasting the King's Health remained an excuse for a good drinking bout and after the King had made his discomfort about it public, the drinkers would toast just about anything else that they could think of, including each other. Frenchman Henri Misson thought the custom of toasting quaint –

had long gone out of fashion in France. As recorded by Waller in *1700 Scenes from London Life*, Misson noted:

There are two principal grimaces [attitudes] which are universally observ'd, upon this occasion, among persons of all degrees and conditions: The first is, that the person whose health is drunk, if an inferior or even an equal, must remain as still as a statue while the drinker is drinking. If, for instance, you are about to help yourself to something out of a dish, you must stop suddenly, lat aside your fork or spoon, and wait without stirring any more than a stone till the other has drunk: After which, the second grimace is to make him a low bow, to the great hazard of dipping your peruke in your sauce.

Londoners had an increasing array of places in which to come and drink or eat, and also to converse about matters of the age, to do business, to prepare for other pleasures. Drinking and eating was a double lubricant in this respect. You can picture the scene with the half-drunk and the merry sitting at a loaded table with various drinks to hand. Some would have cock-ale, or ordinary ale or beer – which by now was in rampant demand. There was also 'Mum', a favourite of Pepys at one period, which was very strong beer brewed from wheat and oats. Pepys and Evelyn both drank Mum at The Fleece Tavern in Leadenhall, Pepys recording what a powerful effect it had on him, so that he was quite frolicksome with his housemaids when he returned home.

The combinations of ale and spice, or beer and spice multiplied during the later 17th century so that ales were enlivened by cardamom, ginger, sassafras, walnut rinds, madder (a red dye from *rubia tinctorum*), red sanders (another red dye, from sandalwood) and elecampane (a bitter aromatic root of *inula Helenium*). Others would drink sack from Spain and in one of the more salubrious taverns they could enjoy one of the rare newfangled bottled beers.

Although so many recipes abounded, there was never any hard and fast rule about what you might find in your beer, ale of wine; the latter in particular, like the mixtures that went into gin in the 18th century, was often adulterated. There is a record that the cider-makers in Exeter sent 50,000 hogsheads of cider to London in 1725, much of it used to adulterate wine. Earlier on, Pepys had put down his ability to get through so much wine at one sitting (about three pints of it) without feeling the worse for wear, to the fact that it had been watered down. He may well have been right. There is evidence that more wine was drunk in London than was imported from the continental vineyards. And just how did that happen?

Then there was French brandy, enjoyed plentifully and very happily exported by the French. Brandy was mistrusted by the London brewers who, in 1673, felt it their duty to point out to Parliament just how ruinous a tipple it was compared to their own brews:

> Before Brandy, which has now become common and sold in every little alehouse, came to England in such quantities as now it doth, we drunk good strong Beer and Ale and all laborious peoples, their bodies requiring after hard labour, some strong drink to refurbish them, did therefore every morning and every evening used to drink a pot of ale or a flagon of strong beer, which greatly helped the promotion of our own grains and is to them no great prejudice. It hindreth not their work, neither do it take away their senses nor cost them much money, whereas the prohibition of brandy would . . . prevent the destruction of his majesty's subjects, many of whom have been killed by drinking thereof, it not agreeing with their constitution.

The records of 18th-century feasting and drunken behaviour are in keeping with the general excessiveness of that era. One foreign visitor described Londoners as 'entirely carnivores'. Their love affair with meat, particularly with beef was constantly requited. Several clubs (as detailed below) were devoted to beef, alone and the English were actually proud of their French nickname, 'le rosbif', much preferring to be associated with this solid and sturdy meat, the 'roast beef of old England', than with what they considered to be the dandified sauces, thin soups and effeminate ways of the French.

In May 1718 a gargantuan meat pudding was made more than 18 feet in length and 4 feet wide. It was dragged through the streets by six asses on its way to the Swan Tavern in Fish Street Hill. Unfortunately, the delicious smell of the pie drove the curious

London crowd to a frenzy of hunger; eventually they overpowered the attendants at the procession and devoured the entire pie before it reached its destination.

Habitually, the prosperous in the growing city would settle down to fine dinners, or they would eat out in one of the many excellent city clubs or taverns. Elizabeth Raffald, author of *The Experienced English Housekeeper* (1769), suggests a first course in January should include small dishes of bottled peas, broccoli and salad, accompanying dishes of meat and poultry, with a Mock Turtle (calf's head) as a centrepiece. The second course should be pheasant, hare and collared pig, crayfish and snipe and with this should be elaborate puddings such as 'transparent pudding covered with a silver web [spun sugar]'. After this there would be dessert, which should have as many dishes as the first two courses, perhaps including candied and preserved fruits and ices. At smart dinner parties, the hosts might hire constructions of spun sugar from some of the better known confectioners; these sculptures were more for admiring than eating. The Earl of Northumberland's confectioner created a 'baby Vauxhall' for the amusement of the Earl's guests. It was the custom for women to leave the table to let the men get on with their drinking and conversation after dessert. Often the servants would also put out chamber pots, one for each male guest, who could relieve themselves where they sat.

Whether or not Elizabeth Raffald's culinary advice was followed to the letter, there is no doubt that prosperous Londoners ate very well. Parson Woodfordes's diaries in 1774 have a reference to a dinner of an average 'elegant'. This, he reports, consisted of part of a large cod, a chine of mutton, chicken pie, pigeons and asparagus, fillet of veal with mushrooms, roasted sweetbreads, hot lobster, apricot tart, syllabubs and jellies, Madeira, white wine and ports.

One contemporary 'elegant' who gave public notice that all this over-eating was not healthy was Dr George Fordyce. He declared that he would have only one meal a day. Closer inspection shows that this meal comprised a quarter of a bottle of brandy, a bottle of port and a tankard of strong ale to accompany a pound and a half of rump steak, broiled fowl or fish. After his meal he would have a brandy in each of three taverns on his way home. Fordyce died in 1802, a martyr to gout and 'acute rumbling pains in stomach and bowels'.

Other individuals were not so fastidious as Fordyce, the more extravagant examples being offered by London's *bon viveur* aristocracy. Lord Torrington would drink three pints of port and a half pint of brandy 'without any ill effects'. He also found alcohol useful to apply generally as well as down the throat. If he got wet in a downpour, his habit was to strip off and rub himself down with brandy or gin. Another nobleman, John Wilmot, Earl of Rochester, was continuously drunk for five years: 'his blood so inflamed that he was not in all that time cool enough to be perfectly master of himself'. At the Cock in Bow Street, by Covent Garden, Sir Charles Sedley got so drunk that he afterwards exposed himself naked to passers-by. Abetted by his drinking companions, the Earl of Dorset and Sir Thomas Ogle, he 'acted all the postures of lust and buggery' before urinating from a balcony on to the evening crowd. This nearly caused a riot as the offended assembly threw whatever they could lay their hands on at the noble entourage. Sedley and his cohorts each received a £2,000 fine for setting such an example.

This kind of behaviour still remains in isolated pockets of modern society and is still the preserve of the wealthy. Until recently Oxford University's Bullingdon Club demanded only two things of its members: excessively riotous behaviour and the creditworthiness to pay immediately for the damage and mess after a night's debauch.

James Boswell was often drunk and like his mentor, Dr Johnson, felt very much at ease in social groups where there was plenty to eat and drink. But Boswell's personal excesses never matched the truly boorish behaviour of Sedley and his companions, although it did sometimes lead to trouble, of a 'Toad of Toad Hall' type. Adam Sisman in *Boswell's Presumptuous Task* (about the writing of Boswell's *Life of Dr Johnson*), offers various insights into Boswell's carousing:

Boswell relaxed into the bottle; after a dinner at Sir Joshua Reynolds's, where he had stayed late, he was arrested and taken to the watch-house for calling the hour in the streets after midnight. The next morning he appears before the magistrate charged with creating a disturbance; Boswell's defence was that he 'did it to put the watchman right, as they never laid emphasis on the *hour* but on *past* and *o'clock*'. The magistrate's reprimand had little effect, because later that same day Boswell was again to be found wandering around London intoxicated.

Boswell's main concern, as a gentleman among gentlemen and the son of a highly respected Scottish laird, was to keep up with the cost of his continual dining, or even to repay some small part of the hospitality of his far richer friends, including Lord Eglinton. Money was a reasonably constant preoccupation. To provide dinner often meant furnishing a table at which men could drink four or five bottles of port apiece. In 1777, Boswell lamented that he had to sell his house because of drinking too much brandy punch.

Far from such domestic concerns, banqueting on a grand scale continued happily. When George III was invited to the Lord Mayor's dinner in November 1761, the city bought an entire new set of silver and the evening cost £6,898 5s 4d; it included six 'necessary women' and a dish of duck's tongues. Some years later, the report of the Lord Mayor's inaugural banquet on 9 November 1780 reflects a distinct move away from the relative calm and propriety of the city's livery company feasts of previous times. On this occasion the tables were entirely cleared of their offerings within five minutes, 'twenty hands seizing the same joint or bird and literally tearing it to pieces . . . the roaring and noise were deafening and hideous . . . which increased as the liquor operated'.

The tempo of such events continued high for some time after this. At another Lord Mayor's banquet in November 1828, the feast included 200 tureens of turtle, 60 dishes of fowls, 10 sirloins of beef, 50 roasted turkeys and more than 1,000 desserts. Table manners were not always as they should be. At the Lord Mayor's dinner in November 1883, a diner called Frank Harris observed an alderman gulping his soup 'like an ogre', while he kept a jeroboam of champagne beside him on the floor. On another occasion, Harris was also disturbed by the farting that he witnessed at a dinner party given by Sir William Marriott, MP for Brighton and where Sir Robert Fowler, who had twice been Lord Mayor of London, was also a guest. Harris refers to a 'loud unmistakable noise and then an overpowering odour.' It got worse: 'When the savoury of the soft herring roes on toast came on board, the orgy degenerated into a frenzy.'

⨭ CLUBS AND COFFEE-HOUSES ⨪

London is the global centre for clubs, societies, associations and non-governmental organizations. Whatever your specialist interest – the sex life of the Brazilian fig wasp, the shape of quantum space, Japanese flower arranging – you will find a club to share your enthusiasm in London. London's and subsequently the whole of Britain's devotion to this kind of clubbing started in the mid-17th century. But it is of little surprise that the earliest clubs were either totally devoted to food and drink, or were centred around it to such an extent, that other intellectual or business purposes would evaporate as the waiters brought yet more wine, port, sack, brandy and beefsteak to the table.

Before clubs became a major fad, coffee-houses had drawn the devotion of Londoners. Not only did they become enormously popular meeting places for men during the day, but they were highly influential in commercial developments that led eventually to London's dominance in international finance markets. Insurance and reinsurance, life assurance, commodities trading, stocks and shares, investment banking, bullion, shipping and transport – all these and more sprang from the coffee-houses of 17th-century London. The coffee-houses served both an economic and social functions. Even hardened port and brandy drinkers of the mid-17th century were tempted to palliate their excesses by taking coffee during the mid-morning and early afternoon, and reserving their indulgence for the evening in their clubs, ordinaries (dining houses, where the communal dinner called the 'ordinary' was taken), chop-houses or taverns among myriad London venues.

Not only was the exotic coffee-berry brought in from the east and enjoyed excessively – in the manner of the tobacco that generally and profusely accompanied it – but tea and chocolate were coming into favour at this period. Tea arrived almost at the same time as coffee in the 1650s and was sold at the Sultanness Head, near the Royal Exchange. Thomas Garraway, the owner, brewed it in an urn for customers to drink from cups, or servants took it for warming up at customers' houses. It was very expensive – at an initial cost of 95 shillings for 2lbs and 2oz. It was also very 'London' because when it was sent to a friend in the country, she boiled it and strained off the leaves which she served to friends with salt and butter. Chocolate was also quick to intrigue. An early advertisement for it is dated 12 June 1657: 'In Bishopsgate Street in Queen's Head Alley at a Frenchman's House is an excellent West Indian drink called chocolate to be sold.'

The coffee-houses also offered sherbets and ices, punches, cordials and alcoholic drinks, the more so as they began to vie for custom with the taverns, which in turn started to broaden their appeal. The functional distinctions between the tippling places, social watering holes, coffee-houses and clubs merged, but their general importance in the culture of London during the 17th and 18th centuries cannot be overstated.

The first coffee-house opened in 1652 in St Michael's Alley, Cornhill, and the owner was a man called Pasqua Rosie who helped to build custom by advertising the positive benefits of coffee-drinking in a published broadsheet of around 1655 called *The Vertue of the Coffee Drink, first publicly made and sold in England by Pasqua Rosie*. Rosie writes:

> The quality of this drink is cold and Dry and though it be a Dryer, yet it neither heats, not inflames more than hot posset . . . It is very good to prevent mis-carryings in child-bearing women . . . it is good against sore eyes, and the better if you hold your head over it, and take in the steem that way.

He also proposes that coffee will 'prevent Drowsiness, and make one fit for business'. It quickly came to be believed that men could be made fit for all kinds of business by coffee, and also by chocolate. It is a benchmark of London aspirations that every newfangled drug, spirit or beverage, no matter its origins in the exciting and exotic world beyond the Thames, was believed to be an aphrodisiac. There was no easier way of introducing these products to the male population and of establishing their desirability. It was even bandied about that a coating of chocolate powder on one's testicles would do wonders for the strength and mobility of the sperm and for maintaining an erection. Chocolate was also said to be a similar stimulant for women, as this verse from *A curious history of the Nature and Quality and Chocolate* suggests:

Twill make old women Young and Fresh;
Create new notions of the flesh
And cause them long for you know what,
If they but taste of chocolate.

Women served in, managed and even owned coffee-houses, but they were absent from the clientele. As the new drinking fad caught on and the men of London skipped from their beds to their coffee-houses, the women were steadily sidelined to the status of 'coffee-widows'; many were deeply outraged by the hold that the black substance was having on their husbands. One anonymous writer took the bull by the horns in 1674 and wrote a scathing diatribe on coffee-drinking and its effects on the male of the species in a pamphlet called *Women's Petition against Coffee by a Well-Wisher* (1674). Far from hailing the aphrodisiac qualities of coffee, the writer sees it as the cause of:

... The Decay of true old English vigour; our Gallants being in every way so Frenchified that they are become meer cock-sparrows ... Never did men wear greater breeches or carry less in them in any mettle whatsoever. There was a glorious dispensation (twas surely in the golden age) when lusty lads of seven or eight hundred years old, got sons and daughters; and we have read how a prince of Spain was forced to make a law that men should not repeat the Grand Kindness to their wives above nine times a night. But alas! Alas! Those days are gone, the dull lubbers want a spur now, rather than a bridle; being so far from doing any works of superrogation that we find them not capable of performing those Devoirs which their duty and our expectations exact ... we can attitude to nothing more than the excessive use of that new-fangled, abominable, heathenish liquor called COFFEE ...

The writer continues venomously in this vein for a further six pages. Exactly who the writer was remains contentious. The construction of the wit and use of imagery suggests a spoof by a playwright, and Aphra Benn was the only female contender of the period. Others believe that the tract was written by the London vintners who felt deeply threatened by the popularity of coffee. Maureen Waller in *1700 Scenes from London Life* is convinced the writer was a woman called Mary Astell.

Whoever it was, the broadsheet hit home and the men countered with their own anonymous pamphlet in the same year. This is attributed to John Locke, a famous coffee-house patron. He quickly gets to the point:

> It is base adulterous wine that makes a man as salacious as a goat and yet as impotent as Age, whereas coffee collects and settles the spirits, makes an erection more vigorous, the ejaculation more full, adds a spirtualescency to the sperme, and renders it more firm to the gusto of the womb, and proportionate to the ardours of expectation too of the female paramour.

So the battle was on. In the same year Charles II was petitioned to have all the coffee-houses closed down because of the 'base, black, thick, nasty, bitter, stinking, nauseous puddle water'. In 1675, the monarch issued a royal proclamation closing down all London coffee-houses – some 250 by this time – though his decision owed more to his own concerns that coffee-houses were centres of too much free-thinking and potential sedition. The shriek of foul play was so shrill that the ban was dropped after only 11 days.

There are various estimates of the number of all-male coffee-houses in London by Queen Anne's death in 1714, but there were probably well over 500, serving a population of around 800,000. By then, many of them were catering for specialised clienteles. Merchants went to those near to the Royal Exchange; book-sellers to those in Paternoster Row. The Cocoa Tree in Pall Mall was a meeting place for Tories (and was denounced as a Jacobite headquarters following the 1745 rebellion); nearby St James's was a rendezvous for Whigs. Man's Coffee-House behind Charing Cross was at one point a stronghold for snuff-takers with little else on their minds, and later served a city clientele of stockjobbers. London's many self-appointed wits would assemble at Will's Coffee-House on the corner of Bow Street and Russell Street in Covent Garden; lawyers met at Grecian by Temple; clergymen at Child's in St Paul's Churchyard;

artists at Old Slaughter's in St Martin's Lane; writers at Button's in Bow Street; military men at the Little Devil in Goodman's Fields; fops at Ozinda's in Pall Mall. Not least, the marine insurers met at Lloyd's in Lombard Street.

Where particular coffee-houses did not have such a tribal clientele they would often introduce other attractions to ensure a flow of customers. Some became famous as places of curios or entertainment, rivalling the taverns in displaying exotic beasts or freaks at the time of the Bartholomew and Southwark Fairs; others held print auctions. Londoners ate a great deal of home-grown fruit after the meat was cleared and they had an appetite for exotic fruit too, satisfied in one instance at least by a coffee-house sale: 'A parcel of choice mangoes lately come from the Indies, are to be sold by retale,' declaimed the advertisement, 'at 4s a dozen at Walsalls Coffee-house in Naggs-head Court, in Bartholomew Lane, behind the Royal Exchange.'

The aptly named Virginia Coffee House seems to have introduced rattlesnakes from the New World:

We have had these animals brought over to England alive,' writes N. Salmon in *A compleat Description of the several Nations of the World* (1752). 'I saw some of them at the Virginia Coffee house behind the Royal Exchange, they were kept up 2 pairs of Stairs, they had then lived upwards of 1/2 a Yr without meat, and yet struck at us with great Force, and the Wiers of their Cage only prevented them doing Execution on the Co.

Virginia Coffee House also offered a more sinister service. A 'Black Boy, aged 11' was advertised for sale there in the *Daily Journal* of 28 September 1728. This was one of many London venues for the traffic in slaves, a trade that continued until the end of the 18th century in the capital and other major cities.

For the most part, however, coffee-houses were London's heart of gossip, news and educated comment. 'No coffee-house no comment' could well have been their 18th-century slogan. Roy Porter refers to the coffee-house as a crucible of early modernity 'in a city of writing for money, doubting religion, reading newspapers, arguing about scientific experiments and constitutional principles'.

Not every Englishman was busy at this crucible, which seems to have been the place for men of letters, scholars, poets and men of affairs rather than for the greatest aristocrats or the labouring poor. But some men in the upper echelons of London society went to the coffee-houses too, primarily because they were there to be visited and offered another appointment in the generally vacant day. The 18th century traveller John Macky gives an account of the day in the life of an Englishman of this type:

> If you would know our manner of Living, it is thus: . . . About Twelve the Beau-Monde assembles in several Chocolate and Coffee-houses, St James's, the Smyrna, and the British Coffee-Houses; and all these so near one another, that in less than an Hour you see the Company of them all. We are carried to these Places in Chairs (or Sedans), which are here very cheap, a Guinea a Week, or a Shilling per Hour, and your Chairman serve you for Porters to run on Errands as your Gondoliers do at Venice.
>
> If it be fine Weather, we take a Turn in the Park till two, when we go to Dinner, and if it be dirty, you are entertain'd at Picket or Basset at White's, or you may talk Politicks at the Smyrna and St James's.

There is a sense of mental vacancy here that fits nicely with Dr Johnson's contemporary character sketch of Tom Restless, 'an acquaintance':

> When he rises he goes to a coffee-house, where he creeps so near to men whom he takes to be reasoners as to hear their discourse, and endeavours to hear something which, when it has been strained through Tom's head, is so near to nothing, that what it once was cannot be discovered. This he carries round from friend to friend through a circle of visits, till, hearing what each says upon the question, he becomes able at dinner to say a little himself.

It was because the coffee-houses were thought to be becoming too inclusive, admitting idlers and vacuous gossips, that men sought more privacy in their own clubs, many of which required either formal or semi-formal election to maintain exclusivity. These were usually established in the private rooms of favourite taverns.

One of the most famous was the Kit Cat Club, founded by the almost eponymous Christopher Cat, mutton pie-maker and owner of the Cat and Fiddle in Gray's Inn Lane. Among the members were eminent playwrights, wits and artists including William Congreve, John Dryden, Sir Godfrey Kneller, Thomas Addison, Horace Walpole and Sir John Vanbrugh who immortalized no fewer than 48 members in a series of portraits. The Kit Cat duly established a reputation for cultured discourse, but the meetings also involved heavy eating and drinking. At one assembly in 1689, the members drank '20 gallons of claret, 6 of canary [sherry] and 4 of white wine'.

It was at these clubs that the serious Restoration habit of toasting took wing. The Victoria & Albert Museum in London has glasses from the period with 'God Save the King' engraved on them. Another common receptacle was the 'firing' glass, made with a reinforced bottom so that when it was rammed down on the table following the toast, it made a noise like gunfire. Glasses were even made to hold deceptively small amounts for the more cautious toast-masters.

Johnson himself founded no fewer than three London clubs, including the Literary Club at the Turk's Head Tavern, which counted among its patrons Reynolds, Gainsborough, Charles James Fox, James Boswell and Joseph Nollekens along with other famous painters and writers of the day. In John Hawkins *Life of Johnson* (1787), the great man is quoted as saying that as soon as he entered the door of a tavern, he experienced 'an oblivion of care, and a freedom from solicitude; when I am seated . . . wine there exhilarates my spirits and prompts me to free conversation . . . I dogmatise and am contradicted; and in this conflict of opinions and sentiments I find delight.' This sentiment surely echoes through time to resonate with everyone who has enjoyed a snug London pub and a taste for banter in the company of good friends.

The Sublime Society of Beefsteaks was one of several clubs devoted to beef and conversation. It was founded in 1735 by John Rich, manager of the Covent Garden Theatre, which was initially its venue. It was attended by a society of actors and artists, including William Hogarth and George Lambert, who met weekly to exchange witticisms, play practical jokes and indulge their love of best beef, affectionately dubbed 'Sir Loin'. This was the only meat allowed and it was ritually grilled at the fireplace.

The Sublime Society had its forerunner and competitors. First of all there was the more simply named Beefsteak Club, founded around 1705, with a membership of gentlemen and wits who, according to some accounts, wore gold and silver gridirons and who gained a reputation for virility, attributed to the food they ate. Then there was the Patriots Club, another beefsteak club, founded around 1730 and attended predominantly by Whig politicians. Their bacchanalian revels were celebrated in a collection of verses called *The Toasts of the Patriots Club at London* (1734).

According to Kerr-Cameron in *London's Pleasures*, the president of the Sublime Society sat under a canopy, above which were emblazoned, in golden letters, the words 'Beef and Liberty'. The statement is evocative. Beef played an important part in bolstering national confidence in times of war. Hogarth's famous illustration, *O the Roast Beef of Old England* (1748), set at Calais Gate shortly before the Peace of Aix-la Chapelle, condemns the Catholic French and their Jacobite sympathies after the 1745 rebellion. In the picture a foppish French chef struggles under a haunch of beef towards a fat friar, obviously destined to receive the lithesome joint. By contrast, two soldiers carry a watery cauldron of *soupe maigre*, which image is intended to allay English fears of invasion by the French, suggesting their malnutrition, low morale and general corruption.

A letter to *The Connoisseur*, on 6 July 1764, would have equally stirred feelings of national pride. It describes thus the sensory pleasures of roast beef: 'juicy scallops of fat and lean, that come swimming in gravy, and smoking most deliciously under our nostrils'.

Alongside the clubs established to satisfy the higher pursuits of art, literature and politics – and beef – there were many others that accommodated more peculiar and sometimes more basic urges. No club connected with the Whig Party, as many were, caused more speculation and comment than the strange society of the Calves-Head Club. Set up as an anti-monarchical club to celebrate the beheading of Charles I, it flourished in London for nearly half a century. Then there was the Hell-Fire Club, which was so notoriously badly behaved that it was banned from London entirely and took up residence in the estate of its founder, Sir Francis Dashwood, near High Wycombe. Hell-fire clubs of many other types abounded and, in time, these were degraded, becoming more evocatively known as 'hells' by the 19th century. There was no exclusivity there; those dives were the watering holes of London low-life and the criminal fraternity.

In the early 18th century the more bizarre clubs included the molly houses, the Roaring Boys and the rakish Mohawks, or Mohocks. Apparently the latter were causing deep concern in London in 1712 when, between 1 February and the end of March, exceptional violence occurred on the streets of London late at night, most of which did not appear to originate in criminal motives. The Mohawks were like Sir Charles Sedley but with knives. They were aristocratic roisterers, sometimes referred to as Hawkubites, dubiously celebrated by John Gay in the farce *A Wonderful Prophecy taken from the mouth of the spirit of a person who was barbarously slain by the Mohocks* (1712). In this piece, a tortured and dying victim of Mohock cruelty sings:

> From MOHOCK and from Hawkubite,
>   Good Lord deliver me,
> Who wandering through the Street by Night,
>   Committing Cruelty.
>
> They slash our Sons with bloody Knives,
>   And on our Daughters fall,
> And if they ravish not our Wives,
>   We have good luck withal.

But with the Mohawks fact and fiction merge. Both the coffee houses and the clubs of this period were the butt of wit, satire and exaggerated record. Historical reference is more a reflection of inventive than real excess.

As a prime example of this, the satirical journalist Ned Ward describes the antics of the Farting Club of Cripplegate. We must only hope his description of their japes was true. According to Ward, the members of this club were: 'so vain in their ambition to out-fart each other – that they used to diet themselves . . . with cabbage, onions and Pease-Porridge, that everyone's Bum-fiddle might be better qualify'd to sound forth its emulation'. Judges were appointed to discern sound quality and members drank new ale and juniper water until 'everyone was swelled out like a blown bag-pipe, and then they began to Thunder out whole Volleys like a regiment of Trainbands in a vigorous attack'. The ground-skimming satire of *Private Eye* owes much to the exuberance of former exponents such as Ned Ward and his fellow writers in the Augustan era.

ᕷ WHAT GOES IN . . . ᕬ

Must come out. Ward's scatological jibes are a handy reminder that London had a perennial problem with waste management. Centuries before, there were plenty of medieval complaints about the stench of shit and piss. A number of streets were designated for calls of nature, although Londoners were neither obliged or inclined to keep to them. Near St Paul's was Pissing Lane, sometimes known as Pissing Alley. There were Dunghill Lanes near Puddle Dock and Whitefriars and at Queenhithe, and a Dunghill Stairs was located at the front of Three Cranes Wharf. The various Rose Lanes of old London were usually so called because men relieved themselves there by 'plucking the rose'.

The first public lavatories were constructed in the 13th century, usually on the wharfside and consisting of rows of planks with holes above trenches that would be sluiced by the waters of the Thames. The largest of the public 'conveniences' was the House of Easement or Long House, over the Thames, the 15th-century brainchild of the Lord Mayor, Richard Whittington. This contained two rows of 64 seats, one for men and one for women, who could drop their matter into the Thames at the end of Friar Lane. According to Peter Ackroyd, public exposure in these early privies was often dangerous. He records how a quarrel in a privy by the wall of Ironmonger Lane ended in murder. One of the earliest accounts of trouble came from the monks of White Friars who were close to the privy situated above The Fleet. They complained to Edward I in 1275 that the 'putrid exhalations therefrom overcame even the frankincense used in their Services and had caused the death of many Brethren'.

Soon after this there was a regulation that 'no one shall place dung or other filth in the streets or lanes, but cause the same to be taken by the rakers to the places ordained'. These 'places' were a form of rubbish tip outside the conurbation where garbage could be carted or boated, to be used later as manure. Sometimes pigs were allowed to roam through the streets to eat the excrement and other filth that lay there but they were a nuisance, blocking alleyways or snuffling their way into houses. Kites and ravens took over from pigs after a culling and according to Ackroyd 'they became so tame that they would snatch a piece of bread and butter from a child's hands'.

Excrement was an abiding problem. In 1349, Edward III wrote to the Mayor complaining that the streets were 'foul with human faeces, and the air of the city poisoned'. The response of the civic authorities was to ensure that four people – 'scavangers' – were responsible for collecting rubbish in each ward.

It was not just faeces that caused problems in the streets. There was also the mess that overflowed from the slaughterhouses, which were known formerly as 'shambles' and in which many beasts were killed and gutted in inadequately small premises close to people's homes. The odour of putrid animal entrails added another foul note to the noisome aromas of the city.

According to Reay Tannahill in *Food in History*, 'Edward by the Grace of God' complained to the dignitaries of the City of London in 1369, saying that he had received 'grievous complaint' from some of his subjects who were unfortunate enough to live near the 'shambles' of St Nicholas, where the butchers often killed their beasts in the streets. The complainants had also spoken of 'the carrying of the entrails and offal of the said beasts through the streets, lanes and places aforesaid to the said banks of the river . . . where the same entrails and offal are thrown into the water aforesaid'. This was the cause of 'grievous corruption and filth . . . so that no one, by reason of such corruption and filth, could hardly venture to abide in his house there'. The king gave warning that the city aldermen and sheriffs should get something done about this problem by no later than the Feast of St Peter's Chains (1st August), and when that date passed with no change, the king advised that they should clear up the mess by the Feast of the Assumption of the Blessed Virgin Mary (15th August). But two years later the St Nicholas shambles was still causing 'corruption and grievous stenches and abominable sights' and Edward continued to complain and threaten retribution, in vain.

Visitors to London were often amazed by the smell in the streets and the complacent manner with which Londoners added to it by urinating and defecating in the open. Almost 400 years after Edward III's complaints to the civic authorities, Casanova reported how he was taken aback by the sight of the 'hinder parts of persons relieving nature in the bushes' of St James's Park. Why could they not turn round and hide their bottoms? Casanova conjectures:

> Not at all . . . for then they might be recognized whereas in exposing their posteriors they run no such risk . . . you may have noticed that when an Englishman wants to ease his sluices in the streets he doesn't turn up an alley or turn to the wall . . . Yes, I've noticed them turning towards the middle of the street where they are seen by everybody who is driving in a carriage.

And it appears that the habit was still going on in 1810, according to *Anecdotes of London*, a memoir written by James Pellar Malcolm. Malcolm noticed that – just as today – the streets outside public houses were 'extremely unpleasant in summer. Delicacy forbids my adding more on the subject. Would that equal decency in the keepers would turn their customers backwards.'

৵ COOKSHOPS AND TAKEAWAYS ৶

While Londoners are no longer wined, dined and given a three-day party by kings and queens on their coronation, nor eat as much as some Lord Mayors of London, livery company feasters or sublime societies were wont to, we all rely on the takeaway, from fish and chip to sushi house and a great deal more besides. Takeaways are intrinsic to modern life in London where their number and cosmopolitan variety are unique. This is an unbroken tradition and a worthy one.

William FitzStephen's *Description of London*, circa 1174, offers a very clear picture of the importance of London's cookshops to the lives of Londoners and travellers to the city:

> Moreover there is in London upon the river's bank, amid the wine that is sold from ships, and wine-cellars, a public cook-

shop. There daily, according to the season, you may find viands, dishes roast, fried and boiled, fish great and small, the coarser flesh for the poor, the more delicate for the rich, such as venison, and birds both big and little.

FitzStephen even records how weary travellers who arrived at a friend's house and were impatient for food, would nip down to the riverbank to the public cookshop, 'and there all things desirable are ready to hand'. Moreover, the service offered by the cookshop seemed almost to be 24 hours a day. This was London's very own motorway service station: 'However great the infinitude of knights or foreigners that enter the city or are about to leave it, at whatever hour of day or night, that the former may not fast too long nor the latter depart without their dinner, they turn aside thither, so it please them, and refresh themselves each after his own manner.' But unlike the motorway service station of today, the food on offer appears to have been customized to suit the tastes of individuals. 'Those who desire to fare delicately, need not search to find sturgeon, or "Guinea-fowl" or "Ionian francolin" [partridge], since all the dainties that are to be found there are set forth before their eyes. Now this is a public cook-shop, appropriate to a city and pertaining to the art of civic life.'

Three later references suggest that FitzStephen's *publica coquina* was not a single establishment as this description suggests but a number of cookshops on the Thames: at Vintry where the wine wharves served the boats coming in from Rouen; between Queenhithe, where the main fishing docks were placed; and at Dowgate. These cookshops served travellers, sailors, fishermen, river boatmen and dockworkers at the time that FitzStephen mentions them, but they moved away from the docklands into the town itself by the end of the 13th century, because their dishes were demanded by many others too. They moved in clusters through the 14th century from Friday Street near St Paul's to Bread Street and to Ironmonger's Lane; poll tax records find six cookshops and four pie-makers in Southwark in 1381.

Langland's *Piers Plowman* describes cooks and their knaves in the 14th century shouting to the passing population in the London streets. There are cries of 'Good piglets and geese, go dine go!' and 'Hot pies hot', a shout that Henry Mayhew records in London in the

19th century some 500 years later; the tradition of shouting out wares and food for sale is age-old in the city. The taverners are there too offering their 'white wine of Alsace and red wine of Gascony, of the Rhine and Rochelle', to go with the food. The mid-15th century poem *London Lyckpenny* also offers an insight to the street-cries of the food-sellers and the variety of food available in various areas of London. At Westminster Gate the narrator, a poor countryman from Kent, is urged by a cookshop-owner to sit down and indulge himself in bread, ale, wine and ribs of beef. Street peddlers hawk hot peas-cods and fresh strawberries and cherries in Cheapside; hot sheep's feet in Candlewick Street and beef ribs and meat pies in Eastcheap. These descriptions present the cookshop as a vital public service, which it must have been, and not just because it was a form of fast food to suit the lifestyle of the travellers and hard-working artisans.

Hot food was a strong selling point in the street-cries of the London food-sellers: there were hot pies, pasties, peascod, flans, tarts, cakes, sheep's feet, roasted meat and poultry. For centuries, these cookshops offered hot food to the majority of Londoners and their families, who had no means, or few means, of cooking for themselves. As Martha Carlin states in *Food and Eating in Medieval Europe*, this suggests that the food was for eating immediately. This was genuine, original fast food. Customers would also bring their meat to the cookshops for the cooks to bake into pies and pasties on their behalf. This was a cheaper means of providing food than buying it cooked and, to some extent, it was a way of keeping meat fresh or at least edible for longer in the absence of ice or salt. Customers would also bring kneaded dough for baking by the cooks for a small charge.

The concept of a proper kitchen in every house does not occur until much later. Even in the late 18th century, many Londoners lived in overcrowded houses and tenements where cooking facilities would have been rudimentary, sparse or negligible. On the other hand, the wealthy of medieval London had large kitchens and pantries, gardens for growing vegetables and a superabundance of cooking hardware. When the house and chattels of a notorious London vintner, Richard Lyons, were seized and inventoried in 1376, his kitchen utensils, pots and pans were weighed at four and a half hundredweight. Carlin conjectures that families like the Lyons ate well and mostly cooked for themselves.

Clearly the cookshops and hot food peddlers played an important role in feeding the population of London. This was recognized by the city authorities who set price limits in 1350 forbidding cooks to take more than 1d for putting a capon or rabbit in a pasty, on pain of imprisonment. The aldermen and Mayor laid down specific price limits for a whole range of food in 1378. The list reflects not only the cost but the variety of fast food provided by the cooks: roast bittern at 20d; roast heron, 18d; roast pheasant, 13d; pork, 8d; lamb; 7d; goose, 7d; curlew 61/2d; capon 6d; capon in pasty 8d – and so on, including ten eggs or a finch for the equal price of 1d.

There is no evidence of what poor travellers spent at the hot food shops, but there are records from wealthy travellers that suggest they used the street cookshops only when they were really pushed. Generally they avoided them like the plague. A writ in 1327 against nine London victualling companies, including cooks, may partly explain the reason for this. It states that the companies were 'lax in their work' and were ordered to be punished. Later ordinances were issued against London pastelers (pastry cooks), who were found to be stuffing unwholesome rabbits, geese and even garbage (offal in this case) into their pasties. Apparently the cooks had been buying offal at the back doors of the better quality cookshops and wealthy households for putting in their pasties. John Welburgham, a cook in Bread Street sold pieces of conger eel that were 'rotten and stinking and unwholesome for man'. He was put in the pillory for an hour and his fish was burned under his nose; he was also made to return all the complainants' money.

Londoners had plenty to die from in the 14th century, even before they ate unwholesome hot pasties and ageing fish; butchers were often in trouble for selling bad meat. In 1319 the sworn warders of the city, who were appointed to supervize meat markets, condemned two carcasses of beef seized from 'William Sperlyng of West Hamme' for being 'putrid and poisonous'. Sperlyng was tried and pilloried with both carcasses burned in front of him.

At the same period, according to Reay Tannahill in *Food in History*, the butchers supplying the cooks, clung to their tradition of selling meat by the 'piece' rather than by weight and were ingenious in providing their customers with less meat for more money. This was not just a question of a sneaky section of a butcher's forearm resting on the weighing scales, as still happens occasionally. Among other tricks that the 14th century butchers often got away with, they padded out their veal and inflated stringy mutton by blowing air between the membranes, and they plumped out kidneys by stuffing them with 'rags and other foul things'.

Geoffrey Chaucer has plenty to say about public cookshop owners in *The Canterbury Tales* and little of it is kind. In *The Prologue*, the Cook, called Hodge of Ware, is introduced as a stereotype that readers and audiences alike would have enjoyed:

> And he could roast and seethe and boil and fry,
> Make good thick soup and bake a tasty pie.
> But what a pity – so it seemed to me,
> That he should have an ulcer on his knee.

And in the *Cook's Prologue*, Chaucer's tongue gets sharper still:

> Now tell on Roger, for the word's with you.
> You've stolen gravy out of many a stew,
> Many's the Jack of Dover you have sold
> That's been twice warmed up and twice left cold;
> Many a pilgrim's cursed you more than sparsely
> When suffering the effects of your stale parsley
> Which they had eaten with your stubble-fed goose;
> Your shop is one where many a fly is loose.

There was a common proverb in the 1540s: 'God sends meat, but the devil sends cooks.'

The working poor could snatch a meal – whatever its quality – in the middle of the day or, returning exhausted to a chilly room after markets closed, could pick up a meal that was ready to eat and required no clearing up. To accommodate these customers, the cookshops were open at night, although Henry IV's sons, Thomas and Edward when eating supper in an Eastcheap cookhouse became embroiled in an affray which led to a 9 p.m. curfew being imposed on cookshops and taverns. But not one that lasted. The consensus is that fast food in London flourished among those who could least afford it, but whose circumstances made it irresistible. The pattern today is slightly different in that being able to afford fast food is no longer so much the reason for buying it – the very rich and the very poor of London regularly buy takeaway food. It is more a case of convenience, saving time and trouble in shopping, cooking and clearing away.

The cookshops have remained a regular, and increasingly regulated, feature of London life, ever since the medieval period. In the 17th, 18th and 19th centuries, Londoners ate out as much if not more than they ate at home. The chop-houses were the McDonald's of Restoration and 18th-century London; the food was plentiful and adequate in quality, and cheap enough to attract a range of customers. Boswell reports how he relished a fat beefsteak in Dolly's steak-house in Paternoster Row. He liked the place because it was warm and comfortable and was pleased that his dinner of bread, beef and beer cost only a shilling, including a penny tip for the waiter. He tried many other London eateries of the kind: Chapman's Eating-house in Oxford Road, Clifton's Chophouse in Butcher Row by Temple, Harris's Eating-house in Covent Garden.

Those wishing to spend longer at the table would go to a tavern where they could dine with friends or meet mistresses or wenches recommended through the establishment. Alongside beef, they consumed lashings of dairy produce. Butter was heavily salted and bought by the barrel or gallon pot; it flooded the meat and vegetables much to the repugnance of French and other foreigners. Puddings were full of butter, eggs and cream or were converted into whipped syllabubs or mixed with pints of Rhenish wine to make 'thick creams' to suit the tastes of the day. These were often served as snacks between the main meals offered at the chop-houses or coffee-houses. Cheese was eaten in copious quantities. Ned Ward wrote of a Cheshire cheese introduced following a large meal that was 'of a groaning size', but he and his companions managed to 'devour more in three minutes than a million maggots could have done in three weeks'.

Everything in London had sugar in it, but above all the puddings. It was used in fruit tarts as well as for candying, preserving and conserving fruits. Sugar came cheaply thanks to the prospering slave trade, so that in the early 1700s it was costing no more than 6d a pound.

But these were the foodstuffs of the relatively wealthy who were often gluttonous in their intake and could afford to be. What of the poor in these later periods? Henry Mayhew, in his comprehensive study *London Labour and the London Poor*, pays particular attention to this group in the mid-19th century. The impression is of a great variety of food readily available from street-sellers and peddlers:

> Men and women and most especially boys purchase their meals day after day in the streets. The coffee-stall supplies a warm breakfast; shell-fish of many kinds tempt to a luncheon; hot-eels or pea-soup, flanked by a potato 'all hot' serve for a dinner; and many cakes and tarts, or nuts and oranges, with many varieties of pastry, confectionery, and fruit, woo to indulgence in a dessert; while for supper there is a sandwich, a meat-pudding or a 'trotter'.

Mayhew lists a variety of what he calls solids that were bought cheaply from the food stalls for a midday meal: pickled whelks; oysters; sheep's trotters; pea-soup; fried fish; ham sandwiches; hot green peas; kidney puddings; boiled meat puddings; beef, mutton, kidney and eel pies; baked potatoes. Among the pastries and confections were ingredients such as rhubarb, currant, gooseberry, cherry, apple, damson, cranberry tarts, mince pies, plum dough and plum cake, gingerbread nuts and heart-cakes, Chelsea buns, muffins and crumpets. Yet sweeter goodies included several kinds of rock, sticks, lozenges, candies and hard-bakes. There were medicinal confections of what Mayhew calls 'cough-dropes and horehound'.

In Greenwich Park you could buy the more luxurious street foods such as ices and strawberry cream at a 1d a glass. Vendors in the parks also sold milk, rice milk, peppermint water, curds and whey as well as tea, coffee, cocoa, ginger beer, lemonade and Persian sherbet. There were also some highly coloured beverages 'that have no name but are introduced to the public as "cooling drinks".'

Hot eels and pea soups were among the most popular takeaway foods of the London poor, who would flock to the stalls to buy this sustaining nourishment. Mayhew estimated that there were 500 sellers of these products alone, and the greatest number grouped in

Old Street and St Luke's. Hot eels consisted of five or seven pieces of fish in three-quarters of a cup of 'liquor' which was a thin soup thickened with flour and flavoured with chopped parsley and spices, sometimes with a little butter. The cost was generally 1/2d. One dealer in Clare Market did the biggest trade, selling 100 lbs of eels on most Saturdays. He and his son, dressed in Lenny Lind hats bound with blue ribbons, dispensed the hot eels while his daughter washed all the cups. The vendors mostly wore these types of hats, or broad brimmed 'wide-awake' hats with a white apron and sleeves.

Although Mayhew records plenty of street criers during this time, he notes that the hot-eel vendors were mostly silent. When questioning one as to the reason, the answer came: 'I likes better to touch up people's noses than their heyes or hears.'

Along with the pickled whelks eaten cold with vinegar and pepper, the tradition for fried fish was also well underway as a fast food of Victorian London. Plaice, sole, haddock, whiting, flounder and herring were dipped in a batter of flour and water and fried in oil. But even when the fish was fresh and the oil was good, the smell was rank, so that few wanted to lodge with the people who sold fried fish. Fried fish was sold in the alleys that run from Gray's Inn Lane to Leather Lane, and in similar places between Chancery and Fetter Lanes, and also in the courts running from Cowcross to Smithfield and from Turnmill Street and Ray Street, Clerkenwell. One of the costers of fried fish reported to Mayhew that the gin and drinking neighbourhoods were the best 'for people hasn't their smell so correct there'.

Baked potatoes became popular only in the 1840s. They were baked in ovens but served in cans with steam underneath to keep them hot. They were sold in all the main thoroughfares and street markets with butter and salt. Inevitably, the potatoes were most popular in the cold weather when they were sometimes bought to warm the hands as well as to provide a much-needed snack. Mayhew reports that the customers for potatoes were people of all classes, including gentlefolk who would slip them into their pockets to take home for supper.

Then of course there were the piemen, whose calls were among the most ancient heard daily on the streets of London; 'Penny pies 'ot – all 'ot' was shouted loud at every fair or holiday, or when the guards were being reviewed at Hyde Park and a crowd gathered, also at the Lord Mayor's Show, or the Opening of Parliament.

Bought mostly by boys – and occasionally disappointing the odd 'Simple Simon' – the meat pies were usually made by the piemen and their families and were heavily peppered to disguise the flavour of the meat. Gravy went with the pies and this was poured out of an old can into a hole made with the little finger on top of the meat pie crust; it was poured in until the crust rose. 'With this gravy a person in the line assured me, it was known for pies 4 days old to go off very freely and be pronounced excellent.'

A favourite pastime among the costermonger boys, 'some of whom aspire to the repute of being gourmands', was to 'toss the pieman'. A penny is tossed and the pieman always called, if he wins, he gets the penny and keeps the pie; if he loses he gives the pie free of charge. One pieman reported:

Gentleman 'out on the spree' at the late public-houses will frequently toss when they don't want the pies, and when they win they will amuse themselves by throwing the pies at one another, or at me. Sometimes I have taken as much as half-a-crown, and the people of whom I had the money has never eaten a pie. The boys has the greatest love of gambling, and they seldom, if ever, buys without tossing.

Mayhew had a keen eye for the problems of the poor of his day and seldom romanticized their situation. His report on the street food they often ate leads to the conclusion that a few pennies bought a lot of sustenance. And when there was food in the belly, Londoners' energy was quickly restored and there was always pleasure to be had.

BIBLIOGRAPHY

↶ BOOKS ↷

Ackroyd, Peter; *London The Biography*, London, Chatto & Windus, 2000

An Amateur Sportsman, *Sporting Anecdotes, Original and Select*, London, Thomas Hurst, 1804

Allen, Robert J.; *The Clubs of Augustan London*, Cambridge Mass., Harvard University Press, 1933

Allen, Stewart Lee; *The Devil's Cup*, Edinburgh, Canongate, 2000

Armitage, John; *Man at Play, Nine Centuries of Pleasure Making*, London, Frederick Warne & Co. Ltd., 1977

Arnold, Walter; *The Life and Death of the Sublime Society of Beefsteaks*, London, 1871

Bartlett, Vernon; *The Past of Pastimes*, London, Chatto & Windus, 1969

Berridge, Virginia; *Opium and The People*, London, Allen Lane, 1981

Blyth, Henry; *Hell and Hazard, or William Crockford versus the Gentlemen of England*, London, Weidenfeld and Nicolson, 1969

Bowen, Rowland; *Cricket, A History*, London, Eyre & Spottiswoode, 1970

Brailsford, Dennis; *Bareknuckles, A Social History of Prize-Fighting*, Cambridge, Lutterworth Press, 1988

Brailsford, Henry; *Sport and Society – Elizabeth to Anne*, London, Routledge and Kegan Paul, 1969

Brown, Peter B.; *In Praise of Hot Liquors. The Study of Chocolate, Coffeee and Tea-Drinking, 1600–1850*, exhibition catalogue, Fairfax House, York, York Civic Trust, 1995

Bullough, V.L.; *Sex, Society and History*, New York, Science History Publications, 1976

Burford, E.J.; *The Synfulle Citie*, London, Hale, 1990

Burford, E.J.; *The Orrible Synne*, London, Calder and Boyars, 1973

Carlin, Martha and Rosenthal, Joel T. (ed.); *Food and Eating in Medieval*

Europe, London and Rio Grande, The Hambledon Press, 1998

Chambers Encyclopaedia, A Dictionary of Universal Knowledge for the People, London, W. and R. Chambers, 1860-67

Chesney, Kellow; *The Victorian Underworld*, London, Temple Smith, 1970

Clark, Peter: *The English Alehouse. A Social History*, Longman, 1983

Davenport-Hines, Richard; *The Pursuit of Oblivion*, London, Weidenfeld and Nicholson, 2001

Dunning, Eric, and Sheard, Kenneth; *Barbarians, Gentlemen and Players – A Sociological Study of the Development of Rugby Football*, Oxford, Martin Robertson & Co., 1979

Emboden, W.; *Bizarre Plants: Magical, Monstrous, Mythical*, London, Studio Vista, 1974

Emboden, W.; *Narcotic Plants: Hallucinogens, Stimulants, Inebriants and Hypnotics*, London, Studio Vista

Gibbons, Ed; *All Bear and Skittles*, National Trust, 2001

Gifford, Edward S.; *The Charms of Love*; London, Faber and Faber, 1963

Gilbey, Walter; *Sport in Olden Time*, Liss, Hampshire, Spur Publications, 1975 (originally 1912)

Guttmann, Allan; *Women's Sport – A History*, New York, Columbia University Press, 1991

Hall, Peter; *Cities in Civilization*, London, Weidenfeld and Nicholson, 1998

Harner, M.J.; *The Role of Hallucinogenic Plants in European Witchcraft; Hallucinogens and Shamanism* (Harner, ed.), Oxford University Press, 1973

Harris, H.A.; *Sport in Britain, Its Origins and Development*, London, Stanley Paul, 1975

Harvey, A.D.; *Sex in Georgian England*, Phoenix Press, 2001

Haydon, Peter; *Beer and Britannia*, London, Sutton Publishing, 2001

Haynes, Alan; *Sex in Elizabethan England*, London, Sutton Publishing, 1997

Hibbert, Christopher; *The English, A Social History 1066-1945*, London, Paladin – Grafton Books, 1988

Hibbert, Christopher; *The Road to Tyburn*, London, Longmans, 1957

Hole, Christina; *English Sports and Pastimes*, London, Batsford, Ltd., 1949

Hutton, Ronald; *The Rise and Fall of Merry England*, Oxford University Press, 1996

Hyman, Timothy and Malbert, Roger; *Carnivalesque*, London, Hayward Gallery Publishing, 2001

Inglis, Brian; *The Forbidden Game*, London, Hodder and Stoughton, 1975

Jewell, Brian; *Sports and Games – History and Origins*, Speldhurst, Kent, Midas Books, 1977

Johns, Catherine; *Sex or Symbol*, Austin, Texas; University of Texas with British Museum Publications, 1982

Kerr-Cameron, David; *London's Pleasures From Restoration to Regency*, London, Sutton Publishing, 2001

Lichtenburg, Georg Christoph; *De Londres et Ses Environs*, Amsterdam, 1789

Mackenzie, Norman (ed.); *Secret Societies*, London, Aldus, 1968

Mackinder, Anthony and Blatherwick, Simon: *Bankside. Excavations at Benbow House, Southwark, London SE1*, Museum of London Archaeology Service

Mayhew, Henry, *London Labour and the London Poor*, London, Frank Cass & Co., 1967 (first edition 1851)

McIntosh, Peter; *Sport in Society*, London, West London Press, 1987

Mitchell, R.J. and Leys, M.D.R.; *A History of London Life*, London, Longman, Green and Co., 1958

Morley, Henry; *Memoirs of Bartholomew Fair*, London, 1859

Mote, Ashley; *The Glory Days of Cricket – The Extraordinary Story of Broadhalfpenny Down*, London, Robson Books, 1997

Mulcaster, Richard; *Positions*, 1581, ed. Quick, 1888

Parker, Derek; *Nell Gwynn*, London, Sutton Publishing Limited, 2000

Philip, Neil; *Working Girls*, London, Bloomsbury

Pickard, Liza, *Dr Johnson's London*, Weidenfeld & Nicolson, 2000

Porter, Roy and Teich, Miklaus; *Drugs and Narcotics in History*, Cambridge University Press, 1995

Pullar, Philippa; *Consuming Passions*, London, Hamish Hamilton, 1970

Radford, Peter; *The Celebrated Captain Barclay – Sport Money and Fame in Regency Britain*, London, Headline, 2001

Richards, Jeffrey; *Sex, Dissidence and Damnation. Minority Groups in the Middle Ages*, London and New York, Routledge, 1991

Robinson, John R.; *Old Q: A Memoir of William Douglas, Fourth Duke of Queensberry, Kt.*, London, Sampson Low, Marston and Co., 1895

Shearman, Montague; *Athletics and Football*, London, Longman, Green, and Co., 1887

Sheridan, Paul; *Penny Theatres of Victorian London*, London, Dennis Dobson, 1981

Sisman, Adam; *Boswell's Presumptuous Task*, London, Hamish Hamilton, 2000

Southworth, John; *Fools and Jesters at the English Court*, London, Sutton Publishing, 1998

Spencer, Colin; *Homosexuality, A History*, London, Fourth Estate, 1995

Sweet, Matthew; *Inventing the Victorians*, London, Faber and Faber Limited, 2001

Tannahill, Reay; *Food in History*, New York, Crown Publishers Inc., 1989

The Guinness Book of Traditional Pub Games

Tuer, Andrew W.; *Old London Street Cries*, London, Leadenhall Press, 1885

Uglow, Jenny; *Hogarth*, London, Faber and Faber, 1997

Underdown, David; *Start of Play – Cricket and Culture in Eighteenth Century England*, London, Allen Lane, The Penguin Press, 2000

Varey, Simon, *The Pleasures of the Table* in *Pleasure in the Eighteenth Century*, ed. Roy Porter and Marie Mulvey Roberts, London, Macmillan Press, 1996

Viney, Nigel and Grant, Neil; *An Illustrated History of Ball Games*, London, Heinemann, 1978

Visser, Margaret; *Rituals of Dinner*, London, Viking, 1992

Visser, Margaret; *The Way We Eat*, London, Penguin, 1997

Waller, Maureen; *1700, Scenes from London Life*, London, Hodder & Stoughton, 2000

Wilbraham, Anne; *The Englishman's Food*, London, Jonathan Cape, 1957

Wymer, Norman: *Sport in England; A History of Two Thousand Years of Games and Pastimes*, London, George G Harrop & Co. Ltd., 1949

✑ NEWSPAPERS AND JOURNALS ✎

The Craftsman, 13 September 1790

The Daily Post Boy, 16 August 1735

Jackson's Oxford Journal, 20 December 1787

Mist's Journal, 23 October 1725

The Penny London Morning Advertiser, 11 June 1744

The Penny London Morning Advertiser, 24 June 1748

The Postboy, March 1700

The Sporting Magazine, November 1792, p. 103

The English Chronicle, or Whitehall Evening Post, 10–13 March 1804

The St James's Chronicle, or British Evening Post, 8–10 March 1804

✍ INTERNET SOURCES ✍

The Questioning of John Rykener, A Male Cross-Dressing Prostitute,
www.fordham.edu/halsall/source/1395rykener.html
Roman Gladiatorial Combat http://depthome.brooklyn.cuny.edu/classics/gladiatr

INDEX